bridging art & science

Chris Wilkinson & Jim Eyre

Booth-Clibborn Editions

Essays x 08

essay 01

Bridging Art & Science
Chris Wilkinson

The title 'Bridging Art and Science' attempts to represent the philosophy behind the architecture of Wilkinson Eyre. As a practice we like to use the latest technology in our buildings and we draw inspiration from both art and science. We are keen to innovate and try to create something new with each project. A decade of work is illustrated in this book, with projects that range from buildings to bridges, from cultural to commercial projects, and from complex megastructures to small product designs. Each project is different and there isn't a clearly identifiable style but there is a distinctive design approach, which links all the work. It cannot easily be summarized in a few words but the following eight essays written by Jim Eyre and myself set out some of the thinking that has influenced the design.

The themes highlighted in the book recur throughout our work. Lightness, for instance, is a term much used in our design discussions and remains a prime objective in our architecture. Geometry is also vitally important to us, even though it is no longer a subject taught in schools of architecture. Through the use of sophisticated computer software, we are able to explore more complex geometries than ever before and with the use of current technology these designs can now be built. We are genuinely concerned with the movement of people through our buildings, and enjoy the dynamic perception of movement in geometry. At the same time, we find examples in nature and in the parallel technologies

of the aircraft, boat and car industries, which inspire us. The design of space is the very essence of architecture – and we are concerned with all aspects of spatial design. The concept of Universal Space is one that holds particular interest as a progression of the ideas proposed in my book *Supersheds*. The concept of a large roof enclosing a single volume of space, which can be used for a variety of purposes, is gaining momentum and our designs for Stratford Market Depot, Stratford Station and the Dyson Headquarters in Malmesbury are all examples of large roof enclosures.

We believe that building structures should be more responsive to the environment and their occupants. We design bridges that can open at the press of a button and we are looking to incorporate these systems in our buildings. Through our work with interactive science exhibits we are aware of the potential for buildings that are more active and responsive to their users. Sustainability is a key issue of our time and buildings should be more efficient and environmentally friendly. We look to incorporate both active and passive systems in our buildings where appropriate.

Quality is also a factor we strive for, which relates to attention to detail in design, and we have borrowed Mies van der Rohe's maxim, God is in the details, for one of our essays.

We are known for our bridge designs,

and Unabridged looks at the design of bridges and the input we have in terms of engineering. This leads into another relevant theme, that of Architecture or Engineering, in which we explore the boundaries and crossovers of these two interdependent disciplines.

In many ways the scope of Wilkinson Eyre Architects' work is different from other architects in that we design engineering structures as well as buildings. We have, for instance, been part of the team responsible for designing the hundred or so bridges on the new Channel Tunnel Rail Link from Dover to King's Cross in London. There were over 700 engineers involved in this project and our role was to help formulate design principles for a family of bridges and other visual elements for this important piece of infrastructure. This may seem an unusual area of expertise for an architectural practice, since we cannot calculate the stresses involved in bridges any more than we can with buildings. We do, however, have a good understanding of structural principles and a strong sense of aesthetics, which are invaluable to bridge design.

As our work is seen as technology-based, it is often assumed that we are more concerned with science than art, but this is not the case. We see ourselves more as artists than technicians and our primary concerns are with aesthetics not calculations. We like to use the latest technology but we are also passionate about what our

buildings look like and how they feel inside. Similarly, while we try to push the technological boundaries of bridge engineering we also want them to look good. Technology is for us only a means to an end.

Our buildings are functional but we strive for something more, something that gives depth and lifts the spirit. All good buildings have a spiritual quality, which affects one's emotions, but there is no simple formula for creating it. The process of architectural design is complex and difficult to define; it involves analytical decision-making combined with the application of technical expertise and creative innovation. It is in these creative aspects that architects look towards art for solutions but this is not an easy link to define because the artistic processes involved in design are quite different from those of fine art. Design involves a rational decision-making process where functions have to be fulfilled, risks eliminated and buildability ensured, whereas art demands high-risk factors and a freer, more intuitive process.

As both painter and architect, I am acutely aware of these differences. When I paint at the weekends I try to be free and lose the discipline of my architectural training but it is not easy. I decide on a starting point and see where it goes from there. Sometimes this leads to an almost complete painting in one session; but when I return to it, it almost invariably changes dramatically and this process continues

01

02

03

04

until I feel comfortable with the result. There are times when a decision has to be made but I try not to worry about the consequences and if it goes wrong, I quite enjoy having to retrieve the situation, for this often leads to something new and different. The implications of 'chance' seem to be important to the creative process in art but are seldom allowed for in design. Having been trained as an architect, I am still in favour of the rigorous design process of fulfilling functions but I now believe there should be more scope for intuitive input and at Wilkinson Eyre we try to accommodate this in our work.

Perhaps architecture can be a natural bridge between art and science. In the past the differences were less pronounced and the quintessential Renaissance man, Leonardo da Vinci, succeeded in being a master artist, scientist and architect.

The distinction between architecture and engineering is relatively new. When Brunelleschi, the architect and goldsmith, designed the great dome of Florence Cathedral in 1436 he also worked out the engineering and had to invent ways of constructing it as well. At the end of the seventeenth century Sir Christopher Wren was an eminent mathematician, Professor of Astronomy and President of the Royal Society at the same time as being the country's leading architect. Even in Victorian times, I.K. Brunel was able to engineer the Great Western Railway and design the station buildings as well.

Later, at the start of the Modern Movement, there was more of a bias towards the arts but the importance of innovation and technology was recognized. Le Corbusier, who painted in the mornings and designed buildings in the afternoons, succeeded in combining some of the fluidity and colour of his paintings with the latest technology in his buildings. More recently, the Spanish architect and engineer Santiago Calatrava has made a powerful impact on bridge design. Being trained in both disciplines perhaps allows him to break the rules with confidence. Certainly his designs are not necessarily the most obvious engineering solutions, but do make strong visual statements.

At Wilkinson Eyre Architects we seek a synergy between architecture and engineering and try to extol the best aspects of both disciplines. We like to take a broad look at each design problem with the design team, sort out the functional aspects first and then allow time for creative ideas to emerge which might shape the basis of a solution. There are always many possible options but soon one approach will stand out as offering the best way forward. This idea is then tested in design development with the production of sketches, working models and drawings of all kinds, including 3-D computer modelling. The structural and environmental concepts are developed at the same time. It is a team effort and through continuous design sessions the scheme is rigorously challenged in

01 *Bridge 1*, 1997 –
Chris Wilkinson / acrylic
on board.
02 Florence Cathedral, Italy,
1296-1462 –
Arnolfo di Cambio /
Dome added in 1436 by
Filippo Brunelleschi.
03 St Paul's Cathedral,
London UK, 1675-1710 –
Sir Christopher Wren
(1632-1723).
04 Chapelle Notre-Dame-du-
Haut, Ronchamp, France,
1950-55 – Le Corbusier
(1887-1965).
05 Diagram showing
relationship between art,
science, architecture and
time – Chris Wilkinson.
06 Sea Urchin
07 Nautilus Shell
08 Water spider's enclosure

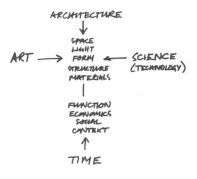

ARCHITECTURE

ART → SPACE
LIGHT
FORM ← SCIENCE
STRUCTURE (TECHNOLOGY)
MATERIALS

FUNCTION
ECONOMICS
SOCIAL
CONTEXT

↑

TIME

05

06

07

08

terms of its intellectual, visual and technical aspects. There is always an opportunity to change direction and we do whatever is necessary to reach the right solution within the deadline. Because much of our work is won in competitions, we have learned to progress from initial ideas to developed concepts in a very short time.

Good design comes from a combination of technical expertise, a high level of visual awareness and creative skills combined with confidence.

Science (technical) and art (creative) inform the five main visual elements of architecture: space, light, form, structure and materials. Other factors, such as context, social aspects, function, cost and programme may have more or less significance, depending on the kind of project. These all relate to time and are likely to change with time. They also relate to nature, which provides a source of inspiration for both art and science. It would seem likely that all known structures, geometries and proportions already exist in nature. They are clearly evident in plants, shells, landscapes and rock and bone structures, and if you look through an electron microscope you will discover a world of molecular structures that can open up an immense range of possibilities.

Space and light are two fundamental elements of architecture, which tend to work together and contribute to the quality of the interior environment. Most people are accustomed to regular

rectangular spaces of modest proportions and it is therefore always exciting to experience something different. In nature, spatial enclosures are often curvilinear, organic shapes and if you imagine shell structures large enough to inhabit, they would make dramatic architecture. Our design proposal for the Retail Warehouse in Merry Hill draws inspiration from the sea urchin and our Merry Hill Multiplex follows the spiral geometry of the nautilus shell. The transparent beauty of a water spider's air enclosure creates an interesting space and one can get an idea of what it might be like to inhabit from our Air Pavilion at Magna.

From art, we can admire the experimental installations by the Californian Space Light Artists. James Turrell, in particular, has produced spaces where the enclosing surfaces lose clarity. Solid elements become immaterial due to the way they are lit and the space becomes almost infinite without a picture plane, in much the same way as it might in a painting. The blue space of the Wellcome Wing at the Science Museum in London, designed by MacCormac Jamieson Prichard, explores some of these ideas and in many ways we found that it provides an ideal environment for computerized interactive exhibits and digital displays.

Richard Serra's planar steel sculptures explore and control space in a different yet new and exciting way, which relates to architecture. The space, defined by planes of thick steel plate, is reminiscent

01

03

of Mies van der Rohe's houses. These are modern spaces that allow free movement through from inside to out, which is something we have worked to achieve on a number of our projects, in particular the Four Seasons House, the Goldschmied House and more recently the Istanbul Science Centre, where the walls act as planes that define the space.

The control of light is also an important factor in the appreciation of space. Light from above, for instance from rooflights, is more powerful than from vertical planes and north-light glazing is more neutral than south-light glazing. Spaces that allow sunlight to penetrate the space feel more human and friendly, due to the warm colour of the light and movement of shadows, which animate the space and help with orientation. The rooflight at Park Hall Road, London, for example, draws inspiration from James Turrell's Meeting House installation and helps to create an expansive space in which the interior opens out to the sky. Clouds passing overhead seem to invade the space and when it rains, you are very much aware of the external elements.

At Explore at-Bristol the huge plane of glazing at the front of the building faces north. This not only prevents solar gain but also allows clearer views through the building and ensures that the light within the space is neutral and of even intensity. Where less light is required on the first floor, the glazing is restricted to a narrow band of clerestory glazing at each end, overlaid with a blue gel which

greatly reduces light levels within the space. The use of clerestory glazing here (and at the Dyson Headquarters in Malmesbury) also serves to separate the wall and ceiling planes, giving clarity to the construction.

Form is particularly important to sculptors concerned with the shaping of materials and how light falls on surfaces. Michelangelo took an idealized form of the body for his statue of David whilst modern sculptors often distort and simplify the body to great effect. Both are equally valid approaches and ultimately influence the space in which they are set.

Richard Deacon's work is more architectural, in that the forms enclose and engage with the surrounding space. His Let's not be stupid piece at Warwick University allows a twisted form of steel construction partially to escape from a pen-like enclosure, which seems to provide form and metaphor at the same time. The Spanish artist Eduardo Chillida also explores space and form in a way that relates to his training as an architect.

In architecture, form not only strongly influences the external visual appearance of a building but also affects the interior space; the two cannot be separated.

We are fortunate to be living in an age of advanced technology which allows us to design and construct much more sophisticated forms than ever before but

01 Wellcome Wing Galleries, Science Museum London UK, 2000 – Wilkinson Eyre Architects. (Building Design: MacCormac Jamieson Prichard.)
02 Goldschmied House, London UK, 1989 – Wilkinson Eyre Architects
03 Let's not be stupid, 1991 – Richard Deacon / stainless and painted mild steel / 545 x 1,380 x 450cm.
04 Park Hall Road Skylight, London UK, 1996 – Wilkinson Eyre Architects.

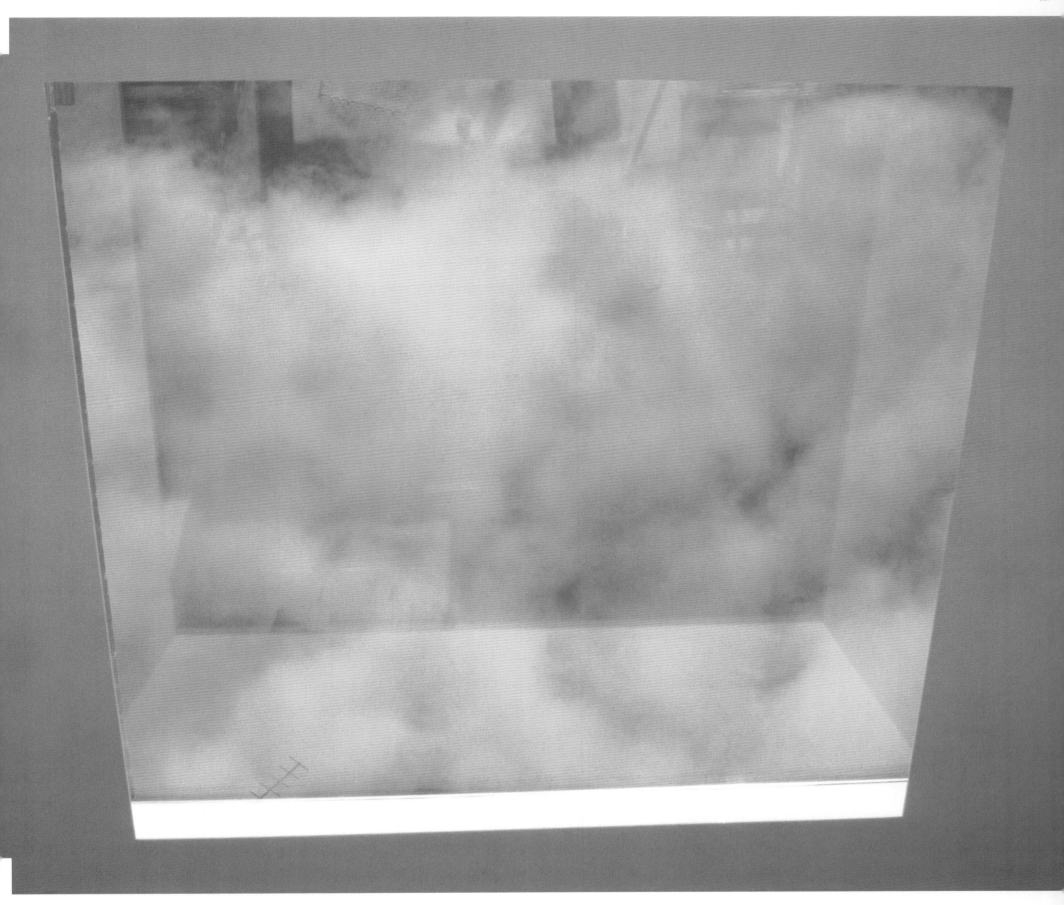

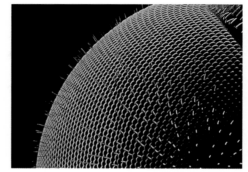

01

02

we cannot compete with nature which still provides the ultimate source of inspiration.

We are only now beginning to learn about the remarkable geometry and proportions that exist in our natural surroundings. It is fascinating to read in Ian Stewart's book *Nature's Numbers* how often spiral forms and the Fibonacci series (an infinite series of numbers in which each number is the sum of the previous two) occur. The magnified view of the fly's eye, for example, shows how a dome can be constructed of smaller elements in much the same way as a geodesic structure. The fluid form of sand dunes and wave patterns offers a rhythmic beauty, which surpasses most human constructions.

Similarly, there is much to learn about structural systems and how they work in nature. For in nature economy of means is invariably a priority: the shape of bone structures, for example, clearly follows the patterns of stresses applied to them, just as the skeleton works in conjunction with the tension members of muscles and tendons.

The remarkable structure of the beehive sets a precedent for lightweight honeycomb structures and parabolic curves occur consistently in plant forms, but even more basic is the geometric code of life itself in the wonderful form of the double helix. Crick and Watson's splendid first model of DNA resides in our Making the Modern World Gallery at London's Science Museum.

Embodied in our bridge and building designs is our extensive research into structures. For example, our 'tree structure' proposal for the Willis Faber Headquarters courtyard enclosure, which was worked out with the engineer Tony Hunt in 1984, would have been one of the first of its kind had it been built. It was unusual in the way it branched out like a tree, to cover a large area of support for the glazed roof above.

Then, more recently, the Challenge of Materials Bridge at the Science Museum drew inspiration from several different sources. In the initial dialogue with the engineer Bryn Bird, four images were produced which influenced the concept for the structure. These were a spider's web, a sculpture by the Australian artist Ken Unsworth called Stone Circles II, the first man-powered flight machine Gossamer Albatross and a glass sculpture by the artist Danny Lane. The completed structure utilized a deck of glass plates standing on edge, supported by an array of high-tensile steel cables so fine as to be almost invisible – like the spider's web.

Finally, the study of materials and the possibilities for their innovative use plays an important part in the development of our architecture. Understanding the qualities and performance of materials is essential to achieving the right design and specification. This is relatively easy with traditional building materials because there are so many precedents, but new materials provide more of a challenge and with it the

01 Magnified view of a
fly's eye.
02 DNA Model – Crick and
Watson / © Science
Museum London UK.
03 Drawing:
Ten Trinity Square
Courtyard Enclosure, City
of London, UK, 1986 –
Wilkinson Eyre Architects.

01

02

03

opportunity for innovation.

New products are developed to fulfil a need and although this may not be specifically for the building industry, there may be applications in our work so we keep an interest in parallel technologies. There are many opportunities for this transfer technology – the teflon coatings developed by NASA for the space industry, for example, are now widely used with fabric membranes to provide a long-life durable finish. Similarly, the 'shot-peening' process developed in the aircraft industry for creating smooth curves on metal sheeting, is now used for other applications. Following our own research, we specified its use for stainless-steel cladding at Stratford Station, where it has proved to be extremely durable and London Underground have adopted its use throughout the network.

Composite materials such as carbon fibre are also widely used in other industries, such as boat building and Formula 1 motor racing, but have been slow to take off in the building industry. With their great advantage of high strength to weight ratio, we see their obvious relevance to bridge building and we have been working on an experimental bridge project with DERA at Farnborough to progress these ideas. We have also used the material successfully on our Lockmeadow Footbridge at Maidstone – for the balustrade supports. This was originally instigated by a subcontractor working on our South Quay Footbridge, who suggested that he could match the price of stainless steel for balustrading in carbon fibre and give us any shape we wanted. He showed us a sample of the Lotus bicycle frame used by Chris Boardman to win the gold medal at the Olympic Games and we were hooked. It was then only a matter of time before a situation arose in which we could put the material into practice and the result is the spectacularly shaped balusters that support the stainless-steel wedge wire infill. We now have experience of this material and look forward to developing new uses for it in the future.

Materials science continues to advance and the new area of development is in the field of nanotechnology, where the molecular structure of materials is changed to suit the requirements. We know, for instance, that the molecular structure of carbon, when changed to a spherical geodesic form, becomes more fluid. This new carbon molecule C60 has been named a 'fullerine' or 'bucky ball' after Buckminster Fuller. With the progress of this kind of technology, it will not be long before we are able to specify the performance of the materials we want to use in construction instead of being restricted to the use of known materials.

Adriaan Beukers, in his book *Lightness*, says 'The most important thing to do when choosing a material for a certain function is to keep an open mind', but then this could be said to apply to most things in architecture and it is certainly

01 Glass balustrade detail by Danny Lane for V&A Museum Glass Gallery, London UK – Pringle Richards Sharratt Architects.
02 Suspended stone circle II, 1984 – Ken Unsworth / 103 river stones and wire / 1,100cm diameter / © Art Gallery of New South Wales, Sydney Australia
03 Gossamer Albatross
04 DERA Advanced Technology Bridge Project, Farnborough UK, 1999 – Wilkinson Eyre Architects.
05 Lotus Bicycle Frame

04

05

true in our office. At Wilkinson Eyre Architects we see ourselves as a creative design force, keen to take on new challenges and find exciting new solutions to old problems. Over the past decade we have moved into many new areas of design work and have been able to make a valuable contribution, which I hope can be seen in the portfolio section of this book. It wasn't until 1991 that we started to work on railway projects but now, several projects later, we are recognized specialists in that field. Similarly, it wasn't until 1994 that we designed our first bridge but we are now working on bridge design throughout the world. We very much enjoy designing museums, educational buildings and leisure facilities as well as industrial and commercial projects. We have successfully completed several commissions for product design, exhibition design, landscaping and masterplanning, all of which have been both challenging and enjoyable. There are no areas of design that we would not attempt, as long as the problem is interesting and the opportunity exists for a good design solution.

This book has been one of those challenges. We set out to publish our first book about the work of the practice in a different way to other architectural monographs, without knowing how this could be achieved. We were fortunate to meet Edward Booth-Clibborn who publishes great art books and persuaded him to produce it. His main demand was for something new and exciting, which also looks good. We

were lucky to meet the young graphic designer Joseph Burrin of BCD, whose raw talent has won through in our rigorous design sessions, aided by our own Helen Eger, who has worked tirelessly to keep us on schedule.

We have also been lucky enough to win exciting projects, to have been commissioned by enlightened clients, to work with great consultants and to have employed a wonderful team of dedicated designers who have helped us produce our architecture. Thank you and I hope you enjoy the book.

essay 02

Incredible Lightness of Being
Chris Wilkinson

01

02

Lightness is not a technical term and cannot be measured in a finite way. It can be neither quantified nor specified but is a qualitative ingredient of modern architecture which is gaining momentum – and it is a quality we at Wilkinson Eyre strive for.

The concept of 'lightness' concerns the physical weight and property of materials, but it relates as much to the visual appearance of structures, components and even spaces. It is a quality that comes from the form, composition and economical use of materials. It also relates closely to light and the way light is treated. Light in itself is a fundamental aspect of architecture, which probably reflects our innate instincts for survival, since we cannot exist without it. It follows therefore that buildings and structures which control light are pleasing to us.

Poets muse on the way light plays on water and there is something romantic about the reflections and the dancing movements that come from ripples on the surface. Water can have a powerful impact on architecture by transmitting light and reflecting it onto adjacent surfaces. The magical experience of Venice with its beautiful palazzi reflected in the canals on a sunny day has inspired architects of past and current generations to incorporate water into their designs. Reflecting pools can add lightness and interest. This led us to design the purple pool in front of the entrance to the Dyson Headquarters at Malmesbury and the long rectangular

pool at Explore at-Bristol, which reflects the arcade and the planetarium. Both succeed in enhancing the architecture with ever-changing light reflections.

Similar qualities come from the play of light on the surfaces of different materials and form is enhanced by the contrast of light and shade. Curved surfaces deal with light in an appealing way and a curved form will generally appear lighter than a corresponding square or rectangular form of the same volume. Projections and articulations pick up shadows and it is for this reason that traditional mouldings and decorative cornice details serve to enhance the appearance of heavy masonry buildings of the past.

Transparent and translucent materials also play with light in an interesting way. Glass is an abundant material in our lives but it still holds almost magical qualities for us. Its crystalline nature catches the light so that it sparkles like jewels. Glass buildings, however, can appear either light and transparent or solid and monumental depending on the lighting conditions at the time of day. Transparency by definition allows space and light through, and seems to offer the kind of freedom that people want. We like to be able to experience the comforts of the inside whilst still enjoying the delights of the outside. We need light from the sun and we like to see it moving round throughout the day, for it helps us to orientate ourselves and to define time. So it follows that buildings which offer this 'light freedom' can be described as

01 Venice Italy:
   view under Bridge of
   Sighs towards Riva Degli
   Schiavoni and San
   Giorgio Maggiore –
   Palladio (1508-80).
02 Villa Borghese Gardens,
   Rome Italy.
   Commissioned by
   Scipione Borghese
   Caffarelli in 1608 for
   Flaminio Ponzio.

Lightness is not a technical term and cannot be measured in a finite way. It can be neither quantified nor specified but is a qualitative ingredient of modern architecture which is gaining momentum – and it is a quality we at Wilkinson Eyre strive for.

01

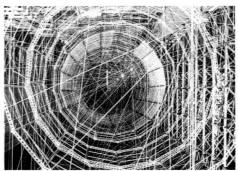

02

possessing lightness. Equally, materials, structures and building forms, which deal with light in a pleasing way, can be said to have 'lightness'.

Mies Van der Rohe's Barcelona Pavilion, constructed for the World Fair in 1929, was one of the early examples of the use of storey-height transparent walls to allow the free flow of space and light through from inside to out. This proposed a fundamentally different concept from traditional buildings, where the enclosing walls are solid with punctured openings. Here the walls and roof act as planes which define space without obstructing it, made possible by the steel-frame structure that allows the walls to be lightweight and non-loadbearing.

The combination of steel and glass in modern buildings has significantly lightened their apparent weight and the same qualities can be achieved as effectively in multi-storey towers as with single-storey examples. Even lighter-weight structures can now be achieved with the more recently developed composite fibres and membranes. The really lightweight, high-strength materials such as carbon fibre are still expensive to use in large quantities but membrane fabrics, such as teflon-coated fibreglass, make economic sense for tented structures.

Membrane structures perhaps offer the ultimate lightweight enclosure, the translucency of the fabric, the economy of materials and double curvature forms all adding to a sense of lightness. Recent developments with computer software have made form-finding much easier, so exciting new shapes are now possible and this is an area which we are interested in exploring further.

For inspiration we look at nature, where all the most beautiful plants and flowers possess a quality of delicacy and lightness. There is something inherently appealing about the form of a flower's petals or certain plant and tree forms. It may have something to do with their organic shapes, or it may relate to economy of material or clarity of function. Whatever it is, we feel comfortable with it. Nature is seldom clumsy and I can't think of any examples of heavy monumentalism, with the possible exception of rock formations. It is a pity, therefore, that many of our man-made structures are so heavy and monumental. They seem to draw inspiration from cave-like structures and at best they may be grand or defensive but usually they appear pretentious and self-conscious. I prefer the aboriginal concept of treading lightly on this earth and I believe that this becomes ever more achievable with modern technology.

To explain further the quality of lightness, we have only to look at images of a spider's web, the interior structure of an airship, or a Naum Gabo sculpture. The spider's web is principally light so that it can't easily be seen whilst the interior of the airship has to be lightweight to achieve lighter-than-air lift efficiency.

03

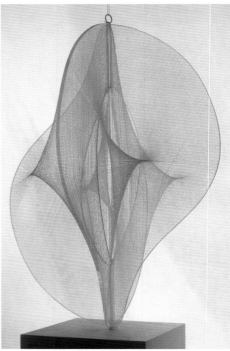

04

01 Barcelona Pavilion, Spain, 1928-29 – Ludwig Mies van der Rohe (1886-1969).
02 Interior of an Airship Structure
03 Spider's web
04 Linear Construction No 2, 1970-71 – Naum Gabo (1890-1977) / plastic and pylon filament / object 1149 x 835 x 835mm.
05 Challenge of Materials Gallery Footbridge, Science Museum London UK, 1997 – Wilkinson Eyre Architects.

01

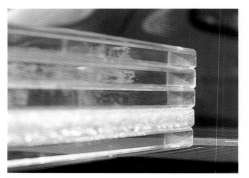

02

03

The Naum Gabo sculpture meanwhile, plays with light for visual effect.

Our recently completed bridge at the Science Museum in London is our attempt to explore all these aspects of lightness in a functional structure. With the engineer Bryn Bird, we set out to design a tensegrity structure of steel and glass, which would span the 16m across the atrium with the minimum amount of structural material. The deck is transparent with laminated glass planks laid on edge and these are supported by multiple cables of 1.5mm tensile steel, which are so fine that they are invisible unless they catch the light – like a spider's web.

In a similar way, the Air Pavilion in our Magna project also uses fine tension cables to support the transparent 'pillow fabric' enclosure. Here the design was worked out with the fabricator Vector and their engineers Atelier One. The cable solution was chosen in preference to a compression ring structure for reasons of economy, but the resultant design also possesses the quality of lightness we wanted within the dark interior space of the redundant Templeborough Steel Reprocessing Plant.

Tension structures invariably look lighter than compression structures and the elements of a structure which support tension forces are usually slimmer and lighter in weight. This is noticeable in bridges where long spans are required, and in particular with suspension

bridges, where the slenderness of the deck and the apparent thinness of the supporting cables are accentuated by the scale of the horizontal spans that they connect. For us, this point was emphasized in our competition design for a footbridge across the Seine at the Parc de Bercy in Paris. Working with the engineer Chris Wise, we were able to achieve a span of 200m with cables of only 180mm diameter, onto which the deck was seated. This minimal structure relied on a cable sag of 6m between supports and huge anchor bearings at each end taking loads of 9,000 tonnes from the cables. The incredible visual lightness of the structure is best seen in the working drawings [see p.205] and is compensated for only by the unseen substructure foundations.

Our footbridge at Bedford explores the concept of lightness in a different way – through form. Here the inspiration came from butterfly wings and, working with the engineer John Cutlack of Jan Bobrowski & Partners, we developed the concept for two inclined arched beams from which cables support a lightweight timber deck. The bridge over the River Ouse is sited in a park and the challenge was to create a piece of sculpture in the landscape. Whilst it may not be the most obvious engineering solution, it succeeds in terms of economy of material, visual delicacy and interest. The span is 30m and the total weight of the superstructure is only 18.5 tonnes.

In an entirely different way our Stratford Market Depot for the Jubilee Line

01 Glass deck, Challenge of Materials Gallery Footbridge, Science Museum London UK, 1997 – Wilkinson Eyre Architects.
02 Glass test sample, Challenge of Materials Gallery Footbridge, Science Museum London UK, 1997 – Wilkinson Eyre Architects.
03 Butterfly Bridge, Bedford UK, 1997 – Wilkinson Eyre Architects.
04 Computer visualisation: Air Pavilion, Magna, Rotherham UK, 2000 – Wilkinson Eyre Architects.

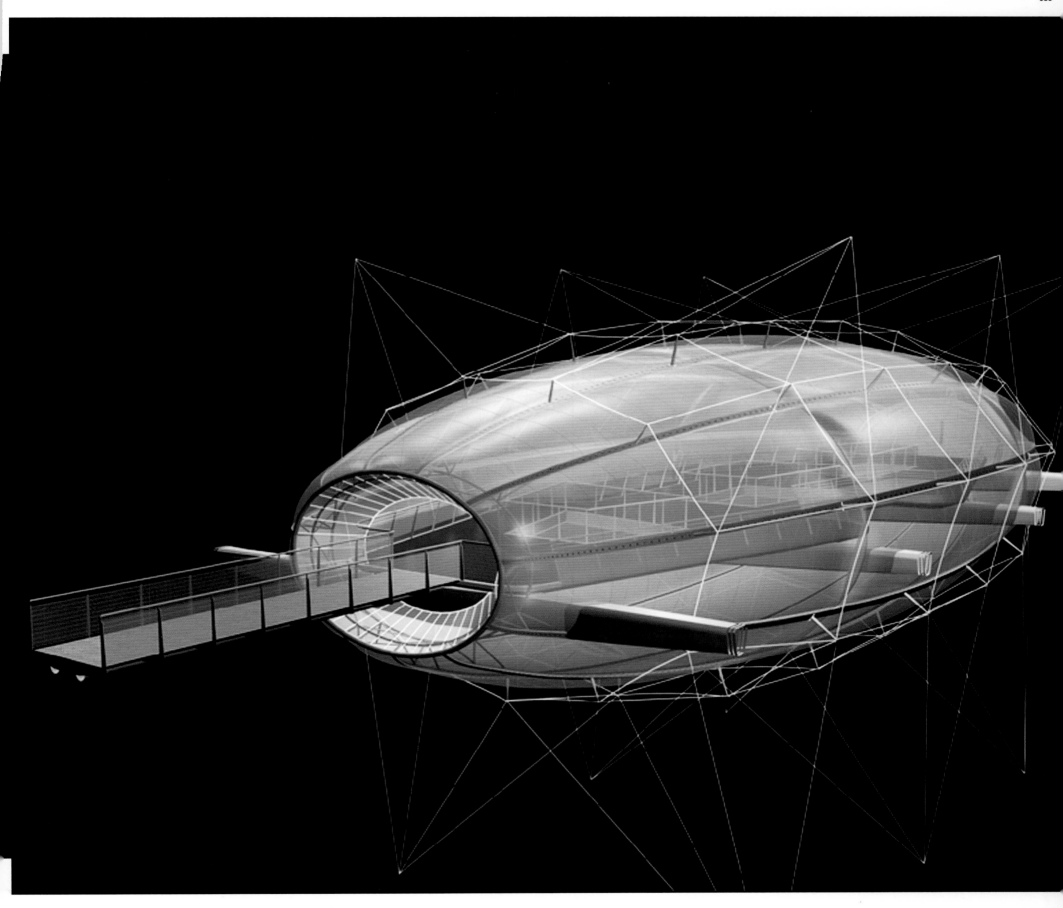

01   02

Extension achieves lightness through design, even though it requires a substantial structure to enclose the huge space, which measures 100 x 190m. Here the steelwork is fabricated out of circular sections with tapered ends and is clearly articulated from the building skin. The glazed end wall, which returns past the corner to give transparency, and the cantilevered floor structure, with the acuteness of the angle, both contribute to the feeling of lightness.

The detailing of the supporting windframe structure, together with the choice of materials for the south elevation, goes some way to achieving a delicacy and lightness similar to the Naum Gabo sculpture. Here the proprietary translucent fibreglass composite cladding, known as 'Kallwall', was used to provide daylight without solar gain and the effect of the 100m-long uninterrupted wall is rather like the traditional Japanese shogi. The supporting structure is composed of cellform beams, braced with yacht-rigging cables, which provide the visual lightness we required.

Many of these images serve to explain another aspect of our design vocabulary, which is the clear expression of structure and function. For us it isn't enough for the structure to work, it also has to look as though it works properly. At Wilkinson Eyre, we always try to separate the major elements, allowing them full expression, and we pay careful attention to the way they are joined together (see God is in

the Details, p. 94).

Lightness also plays a part in our design of the Dyson Headquarters Building. Here two vast industrial sheds, which house the design, administration, production and storage facilities, are separated by a small glazed pavilion, which forms the entrance to both buildings. The lightweight structure and crystalline transparency of its enclosure give it a lightness, which contrasts with the mass of the adjoining buildings. This is further emphasized by a fabric canopy in front, which floats above the reflecting pool that contains a light sculpture by the artist Diana Edmunds. This sculpture, which is based on the concept of long willowy reeds swaying in the breeze, conveys the very essence of lightness since it is composed of acrylic rods that have been abraded to refract the daylight and glow at night when lit with fibre optics.

Our design for Stratford Station incorporates structurally the concept of 'spatial lightness' through the transparency of the enclosing walls and the specially designed extruded aluminium ceiling surface, which reflects light downwards onto the floor. The mass of the steel-arched structural ribs is revealed and accentuated by the zone of wrap-around curved glazing at the base of the north side and this contrasts with the tension-supported suspended glass wall on the south side. A great deal of effort went into lending visual lightness to this steel truss, which spans 30m across the tracks, and the specially

01 Detail:
   Kalwall cladding
   of South Elevation,
   Stratford Market Depot,
   London UK, 1996 –
   Wilkinson Eyre Architects.
02 Japanese Shogi
03 Dyson Headquarters,
   Malmesbury UK, 1998 –
   Wilkinson Eyre Architects.

01

designed stainless-steel bracketry which supports the glazing. In this building all the components have been designed or chosen to create an internal environment which is light and uplifting for the user and which helps to make travelling more of a pleasure than a pain.

Colour is another factor which contributes to the experience of lightness. Of course, light colours help by simply reflecting the most light but the reflection of bright colours can have more exciting effects. I remember seeing a wonderful green reflection on the vaulted ceiling of a gallery at the Miró Foundation in Barcelona which was caused by the sun shining onto the grass lawn outside. The lawn was obscured from view by a solid wall, but the projecting soffit caught the reflections through a clerestory window – the effect was stunning.

We have used bright colour in the staircase enclosures at Explore at-Bristol for identity of circulation and the amount of colour pouring out of the space when you open the doors is a stimulating sight. It is an effect that we have also used in our façade design for the Multiplex Cinema at Merry Hill. Here the auditoria walls, which are painted in bright colours, can be seen through the enclosing building skin which incorporates six different levels of transparency ranging from clear to opaque. The amount of colour seen on the outside is dependent on the level of transparency, which adds visual interest and depth to an otherwise blank façade.

Adriaan Beukers and Ed van Hinte, professors from the Faculty of Aerospace Engineering at the University of Technology in Delft, in their recently published book *Lightness,* refer to 'the inevitable renaissance of minimum energy structures'. For them lightness is not just concerned with buildings, or aeroplanes, but with 'the structure of all things made and grown'. Their main message is 'the lighter the better', which follows on from Richard Buckminster Fuller's dictum of 'more with less'. But in architecture lightness is not only about weight but also appearance. Perhaps a better description is supplied by the poet Milan Kundera: 'the unbearable lightness of being'.

01 Stratford Regional Station, London UK, 1999 – Wilkinson Eyre Architects.
02 Model of translucent cladding, Merry Hill Multiplex, Rotherham UK 2000-1 – Wilkinson Eyre Architects.

essay 03

Responsive Structures
Chris Wilkinson

01

02

Buildings are usually thought of as being static constructions, but they don't have to be. We rate our cars by performance and when we order the latest model we expect it to incorporate the most up-to-date technical features. Car body designs are wind-tunnel tested to achieve the minimum drag co-efficient and the engines are constantly being developed to achieve higher performance and fuel efficiency. Internal features include electronic seat adjustment and on-board computers that can help you plan your route, tell you when the next service is required and how efficiently you are driving. Windows open with the press of a button and, with convertible models, the roof can be automatically folded away when the weather is fine.

Buildings should be designed to be more responsive to the environment and to interact with their occupants. All the features available in automotive design are available for buildings, too, and we should be looking to improve their performance. The building envelope could be more responsive and instead of relying on 'mass' for protection against the elements, it would make more sense to use a series of lightweight layers which deal with thermal performance, shading, wind deflection and even power generation. It is well known that wearing a number of thin layers of clothing conserves body temperature better than a single heavy coat.   Similarly, the fur on a cat provides the ultimate responsive

'enclosure'; the multiple thin fibres are able to compress or open out to vary the amount of insulation – to keep the skin at the required temperature without adding too much weight. Feathers work in the same way for birds and even the hairs on our own skin respond to temperature in a similarly active way.

The technology is now available to create more 'intelligent building envelopes'. It is theoretically possible not only to achieve zero heat loss/gain through the building skin, but also to collect heat from within the layers and use it to advantage. Curtain-walling has come a long way since the single glazed extruded aluminium systems of the 1950s, but it can be taken much further.

At a recent Architecture Conference at IIT in Chicago, Mike Davies described the experience of living in a responsive building of the future:

'Look up at a spectrum-washed envelope whose surface is a map of its instantaneous performance, stealing energy from the air with an iridescent shrug, rippling its photogrids as a cloud runs across the sun, a wall which, as the night chill falls, fluffs up its feathers and turning white on its north face and blue on the south, closes its eyes but not without remembering to pump a little glow down to the night porter, clear a view-patch for the lovers on the southside of level 22 and turn 12 per cent silver just before dawn.'

01 Centre Regional D'Art
   Contemporian,
   Montbéliard, Paris France.
   Day and night views show
   the effect of holographic
   film on Reglit glass.
02 Interior of Mercedes
   SLK Sportscar.
03 Computer Visualisation:
   North Gallery Glass Wall,
   Explore at-Bristol, 1999 –
   Wilkinson Eyre Architects.
04 Detail of responsive film:
   North Gallery Glass Wall,
   Explore at-Bristol, 1999 –
   Wilkinson Eyre Architects.
05 US Pavilion, Expo '67 –
   Richard Buckminster
   Fuller (1895-1983).

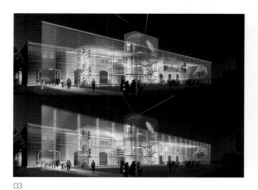

03

04

05

If this sounds too far fetched, it is worth noting that smart materials which can change colour and transparency already exist and computerized control systems are also available which can respond to time and environmental changes. So what used to be science fiction is now technically possible and could be incorporated in the next generation of buildings.

Arthur C. Clarke once observed that 'any sufficiently advanced technology is indistinguishable from magic.' It is therefore a kind of magic that we are trying to achieve with our 'active glass wall' at Explore at-Bristol. In an attempt to create a constantly changing façade to the street frontages, we have incorporated a number of intelligent glass systems combined with digital art and multiple light sources connected to a sophisticated control system.
The façade consists of a conventional outer skin of double-glazed units supported by 600mm-deep glazed fins, which are drilled to receive an inner layer of experimental glazing. This includes: electrophorretic glass, which changes from transparent to opaque and can be used for back projection; thermochromic films, which are heat-sensitive with a visible reaction to changes in temperature, so they show handprints when touched or could form the basis of thermic art; dichroic film, which refracts light like a prism to create a luminescent colour and works in reverse when seen from a different angle; and lenticular images, which

look like holographic forms adhered to the glass. The intention is to show how these 'intelligent glass' systems work and how they might be incorporated in buildings.

Our competition entry for the Royal College of Art extension and new studios experimented with glass in a different way, using areas of reflective fritting, dichroic film and panels of transparency as a pattern on translucent glass, giving interest and complexity to an otherwise plain glazed façade.

The thermal performance of a building is greatly improved if glazed openings are protected from direct sunlight in summer but this doesn't mean that permanent fixed structures are necessary the rest of the time. Shading devices can be folded away and extended outwards automatically when the sun comes out, or can be built into the glazing system. One of the earliest examples of this was the US Pavilion at Expo '67, in which segmental shading devices automatically opened up on the inside of the transparent geodesic dome when the sun came out. Unfortunately, the technology of the day was not quite up to the aspirations of the designer and there were mechanical problems which marred its performance, but the concept was extremely innovative and ahead of its time. Jean Nouvel progressed this idea further at the Arab Institute in Paris, with integral solar-activated camera-lens-

01

02

03

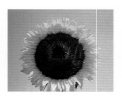

04

type screening to the glazing system.

Solar-cell-activated shading devices are no longer cutting-edge technology and are easy to specify. In fact, this technology generally seems to have been advancing so fast that it may have exceeded people's aspirations. But even though retractable roofs are commonplace, the Centre Court at Wimbledon is still subject to the mercy of the English weather. In many instances, it makes sense for buildings to be fully enclosed in winter but still have the capacity to open up in good weather, like the Mercedes SLK sportscar. You might think that this idea would be taken up by house builders dealing with tight sites but all too often they are still building conventional houses, which replicate past styles, rather than looking for innovative solutions.

In this aspect of architecture as with other aspects of life, there are many lessons to be learnt from nature. For example, the hibiscus flower opens during the day but closes up at night to preserve energy, and the sunflower tracks the sun throughout the day. It is always a joy to see a field full of sunflowers all facing in the same direction and it is not a matter of chance. In the same way, solar collectors can be designed to track the sun and now that photovoltaic cells are more efficient, it can make commercial sense to incorporate them into our building structures. The generation of

solar power is good for the environment because it saves on CO_2 emissions, the by-product of most other kinds of power. It seems particularly relevant to use photovoltaic shading devices because the dual-purpose role of providing shading and the collection of energy from the sun helps to justify the expenditure.

Sustainability is one of the main issues of our time. Lower-energy solutions can be found with natural ventilation systems, which save on installation and running costs. With the use of Computer Fluid Dynamic Programmes these systems can now be tested and perfected in the design stages. This doesn't mean that the architecture has to become earthy and low-tech. Our Stratford Station design for the Jubilee Line Extension, for example, uses the 'stack effect' through the structural void between the ceiling and the roof to ventilate the space above the high-level walkway. Here the sun on the outer roof surface and the tapering void space helps to draw air through; so you could call it solar-powered ventilation, with the result that there is no need for any mechanical ventilation plant or ductwork.

In an entirely different way, buildings can also interact with the people using them. We are all familiar with the interactive exhibits, used extensively in museums, which have been designed to interest the users, but why shouldn't the building also play its part?

01 Arab Institute, Paris
   France, 1987-88 –
   Jean Nouvel (b.1945).
02 Mercedes SLK Sportscar
03 Hibiscus Flower
04 Sunflower
05 Glazing detail:
   Royal College of Art
   Competition for Extension
   and New Studios, 2000 –
   Wilkinson Eyre Architects.

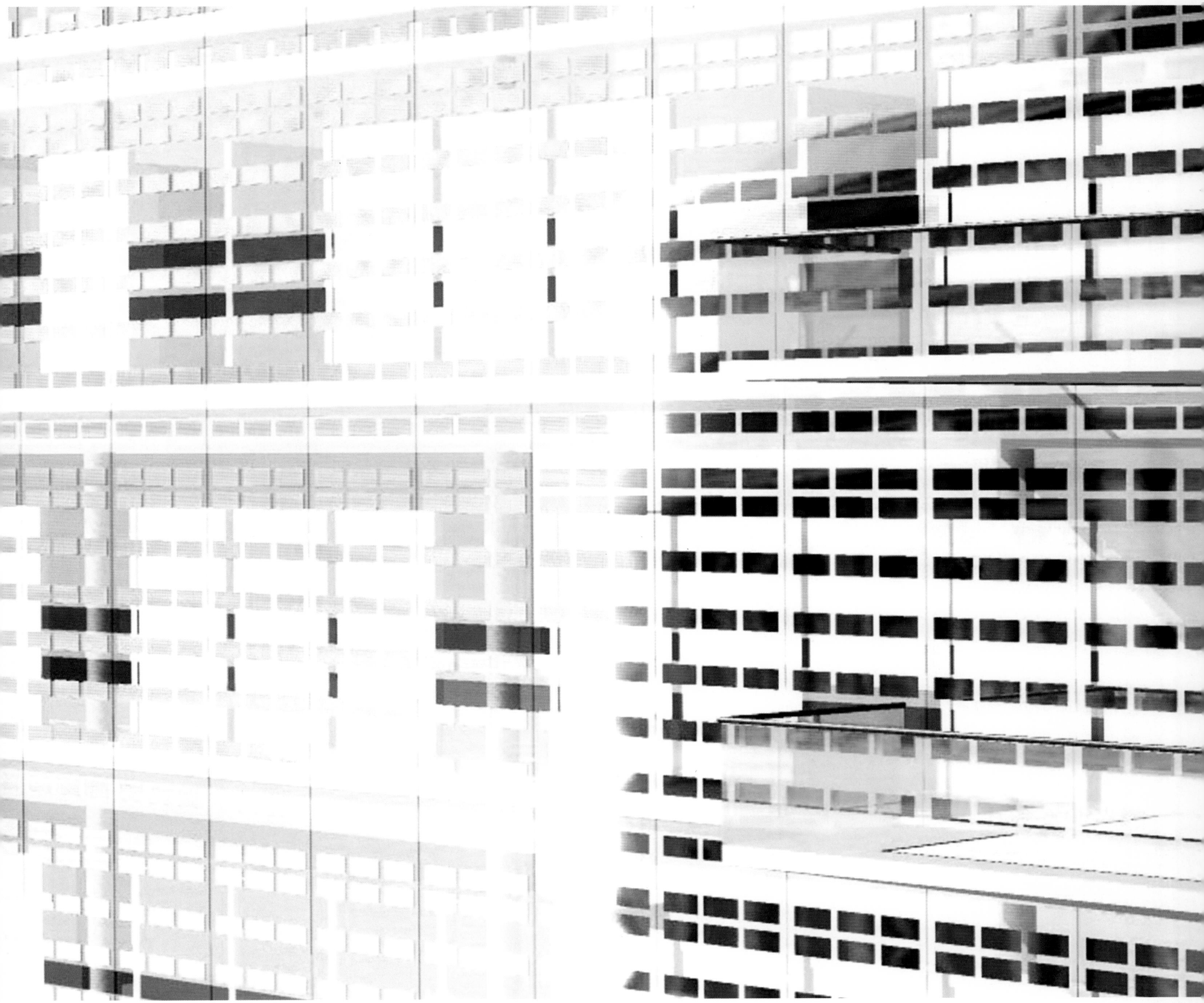

In science centres it is particularly relevant that the building communicates with its occupants and this is an area we have been experimenting with further. At the Challenge of Materials Gallery in London's Science Museum, we collaborated with the sound and light artist Ron Geesin to create an active bridge which spans the atrium and responds to the load variations of people walking across it. The glass deck is supported by a tension structure of fine steel cables and these are strung onto a crescent-shaped stainless-steel plate, which is fixed back to the main building structure through load cells. Each cable and load cell is wired up to a computer that plays sounds which vary according to the superimposed loads. Further sounds are overlaid, triggered by sensors placed under the glass planks of the bridge deck, so that music is produced as you walk on it. The bridge not only looks like a huge stringed instrument but sounds like one. In fact, the cables are tensioned with piano keys and make a deep humming sound when amplified or can be plucked like a harp.

This responsive approach has been progressed in the fit-out design of the new Wellcome Wing at the Science Museum, where interactives have been incorporated into the signage, seating and even the dining tables.

Building structures can also be more responsive and dynamic. At the press launch of our first bridge, completed at Canary Wharf in 1994, there were about 30 people standing on the bridge when, to their surprise, it started to move. The 90m-long, cable-stayed southern half of the bridge is fitted to a slew-bearing pivot mechanism, which enables it to rotate – and we had rather mischievously set it in motion to show how it worked. No one was too alarmed because the slow, controlled movement seemed completely natural. In many ways people are used to technology and have faith in what can be achieved, but sadly the number of innovative projects constructed are still rare.

However, we at Wilkinson Eyre are keen on innovation and fired with the experience gained on the rotating South Quay Bridge, we went on to develop the horizontal pivot bridge at Gateshead in which the entire 700-tonne steel-arched structure is mounted on two hydraulic pivot mechanisms, which enable it to open like an eyelid in less than 3 minutes at the press of a button in order to allow ships through. There are many examples of opening bridges and this is by no means the largest, but there are very few examples of this kind of structure being incorporated into buildings. It is only recently that a growing number of sports stadia have incorporated opening roof systems, but for climates such as ours this must surely become the norm.

There are many other opportunities for kinetic building structures and it is heartening to see the results of Chuck Hoberman's research into what he calls 'unfolding structures'. This young

01 Challenge of Materials Gallery Footbridge, Science Museum London UK, 1997 – Wilkinson Eyre Architects.

01

American engineer/sculptor, who invented the popular Hoberman Sphere Toy (a collapsible skeletal ball made of brightly coloured plastic), has been working on the design of building structures which expand from a small kit of parts into an enclosing form. Hoberman has taken the engineering discipline of deployable structures to a new level with his expanding geodesic and iris dome structures and we are looking to collaborate with him on building structures in the future.

Engineers involved with the design of buildings are usually terrified of creating structural mechanisms; yet this would seem to be an area ripe for future advances. It now seems feasible to accommodate in buildings load-shifting mechanisms that respond to applied forces, like muscles in our bodies, and help reduce the weight of structure. In fact, the human body provides an excellent example for architectural structures. Donald E. Ingber, in his article 'The Architecture of Life' (*Scientific American*, January 1998) compares the human body to a tensegrity structure:

'The principles of tensegrity apply at essentially every detectable size scale in the body. At the macroscopic level the 206 bones that constitute our skeleton are pulled up against the force of gravity and stabilized in a vertical form by the pull of tensile muscles, tendons and ligaments. In other words, in the complex tensegrity structure inside every one of us, bones are the

compression struts and muscles, tendons and ligaments are the tension-bearing members. At the other end of the scale, proteins and other key molecules in the body also stabilize themselves through the principles of tensegrity.'

He defines tensegrity as 'an architectural system in which structures stabilize themselves by balancing the counteracting forces of compression and tension' and compares cell composition to Kenneth Snelson sculptures and to Buckminster Fuller geodesic domes.

As architects, we are attracted to tensegrity structures for their visual lightness and their efficiency. They offer the maximum strength for a given amount of material, which keeps the member sizes slender and light. This is particularly relevant to bridges, where long spans can be achieved with slender suspension structures, such as our Metsovitikos Bridge in northern Greece. Cable structures have movement and life, which adds to their appeal. When a bridge structure moves in response to your weight as you cross it, you know that it has been designed for efficiency. A certain amount of movement in structures is generally a good thing, so long as it is controlled within defined limits.

In racing yachts, where the sail structures are designed for performance and the materials are pushed to the limits, rigs are actively tuned,

01 Hoberman Sphere Toy
02 Racing Yacht mast and sail structure.
03 Computer Visualisation: Camera Arm designed for London Underground Limited, 1997 – Wilkinson Eyre Architects.

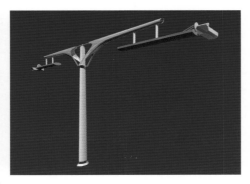

02   03

manipulating tensions and deflections to optimize performance. No one would suggest that bridges and building structures should be pushed that far, but dead loads should be kept to the minimum. More use could be made of dynamic dampening. For some time now, hydraulic load dampers have been used on the top of skyscrapers in the United States to reduce the effects of windload on the structure and thereby save on the weight and cost of the building structure. It is a principle which could be applied to more situations in the interest of improved efficiency and performance.

In a modest way, dynamic dampening was used on a small project of ours to reduce deflections on our camera arm structures at the heritage Northern Line Stations for London Underground. We wanted the structure to be light and elegant but the client's performance requirement for minimum movement deflections for the cameras, mounted at the end of the structural arm, called for a stiff bulky structure. Bryn Bird, our structural engineer on the project, solved the problem by using a sprung mass damper to soak up vibrations. It was something of a relief, when the prototype was tested, to find that this inventive solution succeeded in dampening the structural movement and vibration to within the permitted tolerances. They are now installed at more than 20 stations on the line.

Architecture is steeped in history but it has always been inextricably linked with technology. Today we have the opportunity to explore completely new fields and we must look to creating more efficient and more intelligent buildings, which respond more actively to the environment and attend to the needs of the user. We should welcome innovation so that we can enjoy increased sustainability and a new genre of responsive structures.

essay 04

Movement & Geometry
Jim Eyre

01
02

Buildings, by their very nature, tend to be static, a condition hitherto reinforced by their architecture. The built environment is dominated by ordered rectilinear forms, in clear contrast to the array of diverse shapes that occur in nature. In a sense, the rigour of the orthogonal is alien in the world and subverts the natural order. A strand of contemporary architecture is gradually emerging from this tyranny of form. Based on geometry that goes beyond that of rectilinear relationships, it exploits the visual dynamism of forms that evoke movement. Nothing excites me more in architecture than this unleashing of a potential that engages the mind in the experience of built form on terms that react to consciousness and the very sensations that prove we are alive. Next in line to a sense of consciousness is the sense of movement.

Order comes from geometry but we can be liberated from that of the box by those geometries that arise everywhere in nature – related to curves, angles and patterns. Neither does rectilinear architecture need to be devoid of movement; rather, the transition from point to line to plane to volume must be more informed than to lead one every time to a box-like form. Visual movement in buildings is shaped by geometry, and whether it is through a sequence of interrelated planes defining spaces, or via the line of a curve, the architect has available the vocabulary to express it. While I enjoy the contrasts in form arising from mankind's imprint on nature, I think there is something extra to

be found in an architecture that concerns itself with movement. We live in an age of high mobility – brought about principally by the development of transport and communications. Beside the static condition of buildings the rest of the built environment revolves around a proliferation of various means of enabling movement. In this sense we are, compared to previous eras, hyper-mobile and, as constant movement has become increasingly possible, so the appetite for change has enlarged.

Technology has facilitated physical movement but I am more concerned here with how apparent movement is experienced in the mind; after all, buildings do not really move very much at all. The links with capturing a sense of movement are most obvious in infrastructure design – an area in which Wilkinson Eyre is very much involved.

It is possible to see, by looking at the art of the period, that even at the beginning of the era of powered movement perceptions of space were beginning to change. In his famous *Rain Steam and Speed* J.M.W. Turner captured the blur of movement that characterizes high-speed transportation. The new technology of movement emerges in an instant, and heads off towards the modern landscape of embankments, cuttings, bridges and tunnels that support the ultralinearity of high-speed travel over land.

The agitations of the Futurists during the early 1900s drew attention to issues of

01 Stealth Bomber
02 *Rain, Steam, and Speed –
The Great Western
Railway*, before 1844 –
Joseph Mallord William
Turner (1775-1851) / oil on
canvas / 90.8 x 121.9cm /
© National Gallery.

Visual movement in buildings is shaped by geometry, and whether it is through a sequence of interrelated planes defining spaces, or via the line of a curve, the architect has available the vocabulary to express it.

01

02

speed, mechanization, violence and movement in the new world of triumphant technology. Attempts were made to represent physical movement within the confines of the two-dimensional picture plane at a time when not even film – let alone television – had been invented. In architecture, as opposed to infrastructure design, one struggles to identify movement as the powerful guiding force or influence, except, perhaps, for limited periods and as isolated incidents. In the work of Borromini and other Baroque architects, for example, there is an almost riotous sense of movement and Gothic ecclesiastical architecture possesses a strong sense of (upward) movement.

The battle between the Classical and Gothic traditions is almost a thousand years old, but in the context of a discussion about movement and geometry, it is still a conflict worth a moment's reflection. The spirit of Classical architecture evokes a rather static view of the world. A set-piece view of a building in a landscape symbolizes the idyllic existence of a measured art, which transcends and even improves on nature. The language of Gothic in architecture offers an equally potent but different spirit; yet it is, in fact, just as measured and rooted in a carefully calculated geometrical system of proportions.

The Classical and Gothic traditions seem, then, to be fundamentally at odds with each other not only on an obvious level in terms of image, but also in

the way they connect with their surroundings. The Classical somehow engages horizontally with the land or townscape whereas the predominant sense of movement in the Gothic is one of verticality. There is a further distinction between the two: on the one hand, the development of Classicism is very arts-based, whereas, on the other hand, it is possible to argue that the achievements of the Gothic were technologically enabled.

I think of the architecture created by Wilkinson Eyre as straddling this divide: inspired by a strong sense of movement, our buildings are shaped through the deployment of geometry. Like so much of twentieth-century modernist architecture, our work is often characterized by essentially Classical preoccupations about how space works and how a structure inhabits a setting. At the same time we are keen to push technology to its limits, achieving lighter, longer-spanning structures for a given amount of material. This interest in progressing technology is essentially derived from a desire to be inventive about ways of doing things; the urge to be creative, following in the footsteps of Le Corbusier and his 'L'Esprit Nouveau', is both powerful and inevitable. For us it is imperative to innovate.

In Wilkinson Eyre's buildings the manifestation of both movement and geometry is the result of many considerations, but it is interesting to consider first the cognitive process of design. Forming ideas follows – at least

01 San Carlo alle Quattro
Fontane, Rome Italy,
1634-41 – Francesco
Borromini (1599-1667).
02 *Landscape with Aeneas
at Delos*, 1672 – Claude
(1604/5?-1682) / oil on
canvas / 99.7x134cm /
© National Gallery.
03 Gothic Arch,
Glastonbury Abbey UK.
04 Movement Diagram:
Anglia Polytechnic
University competition
scheme, 2000 –
Wilkinson Eyre Architects.

03

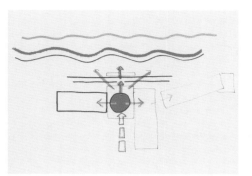

04

in part – a structured pattern which is evolved through training and experience; the other part is intuitive, a function of how the mind works, and in this regard I can speak only for myself. Firstly, then, considering the structured pattern: it starts with an analysis of the brief and the formulation in the mind of what is being asked. On an objective level, this involves the accumulation from all the various sources of all the hard information about the project – through site visits and conversations with, or briefings by, the client. From this it is possible rigorously to define the main options for laying out the principal spaces. Already a sequence of simplistic diagrams can be constructed that, though simplistic, contain coded information not only about the basic geometry of the spaces that would arise but also about how people will move through them. Immediately, directional issues come into play: the vistas or the 'lines of force', or just basic patterns of anticipated movement. At Wilkinson Eyre this is known as 'establishing the diagram'. In order for the project to be successful the essence of a clear diagram must be safeguarded.

The intuitive part of the process involves reading between the lines. As you are looking at how to join up or arrange sequences of spaces, the story about the building or structure is unfolding in your mind. Intuition comes into play many times as possibilities emerge about how to arrange things. This can be a fast or painfully slow process depending on the complexity of the

proposition. It is possible to see in the mind's eye the character and shape of a series of three-dimensional spaces and this may include a mental image of (amongst other things) light and dark surfaces, texture, mass and voids. These curious and seemingly haphazard workings of the mind involve journeys of the imagination through architectural space. And as ideas form in the mind, more and more aspects are worked at in order to inform the notional concept, and these can be surprisingly detailed. Order comes out of this apparent chaos, however, as the various elements are organized by the sense of movement. This may literally be a vision of how people will move around the building or may take account of more psychological aspects – the visualization of the lines of force, the axiality of some particular arrangement, or the mere feeling of being pulled along or guided by the spaces or the structure.

In attempting to describe process and expose the designer's vision, I am assuming a leap of faith; I have to believe that the way others experience built form can connect with the same ideas and sensations. The objective is that everyone can sense this movement and relate to its governing geometry.

In nature there are very few materials that are fully inert; all materials are gradually trying to return to their natural state. A building, therefore, is inevitably trying to fight this erosion; thus, like a person, it has a life and ages with time. The inevitable linear geometry of time is at work. The economics of design life and the selection of materials will influence how long this battle against time will last. Inextricably linked to both movement and geometry, however, is another aspect of life: the growth of living forms – both flora and fauna – exhibits patterns and structural arrangements evolved over time which enable growth and provide the strength to defy the forces acting on them. While man-made structures and growth patterns often share a governing geometry, in nature – conversely – growth merely provides one form of movement, and there are also myriad patterns of growth for us to wonder over. Many of the more interesting to enjoy analogous representation in built forms comprise elements that repeat over and over again – the spiral growth of a shell, for instance. Here a familiar geometry becomes symbolic for us of our growth in knowledge and the passage of time, and can be inspirational in terms of the built form.

Spirals can hold a considerable fascination. They have been extensively explored in architecture and the arts over the years, from the capital scroll of the Ionic column, to Dürer's spiral, made up of a series of arcs. This latter is really only an approximation of a spiral, but nevertheless can work as prescribing the form of the Golden Section or following the golden ratio. An early two-dimensional spiral is that of Archimedes, which represents an object moving out from the centre of a disc in a single direction at a uniform speed while the disc rotates at a constant speed. More sophisticated is the equiangular spiral, studied in the seventeenth century by Descartes, Torricelli and Bernoulli. Here, any tangent on the spiral always subtends the same angle to a line back to the origin, wherever one looks at the spiral. Moving around the spiral through any given angle of rotation about the origin, the same proportions are always maintained, a property which can be seen in cross section through the Nautilus shell, where clearly the programmed growth is repetitive. Bernoulli was fascinated by the extraordinary properties of this spiral; his tombstone was even inscribed with the relevant curve and the words 'Eadem mutata resurgo' ('Though changed I rise unchanged'). Spirals do have a certain mystical quality. Perhaps there is an appeal for us in the orbitting movement drawing ever closer to the centre.

I believe that the pleasing visual quality of these special curves or proportions is derived from their innate order. The fluidity of curves is important and this sense of movement is enhanced by a seamless transition in the geometry that sets them out. When a profile is printed out on paper in the Wilkinson Eyre office I encourage people to look along the curves, for only when you look from one end and get a foreshortened view does the subtlety of the geometry reveal itself. The purer forms tend to work best.

As a firm, we make extensive use of the parabola – and particularly in bridge design – for it possesses some neat

01 Ionic Column
02 Golden Ratio and
   Dürer's Spiral
03 Equiangular Spiral
04 Nautilus Shell

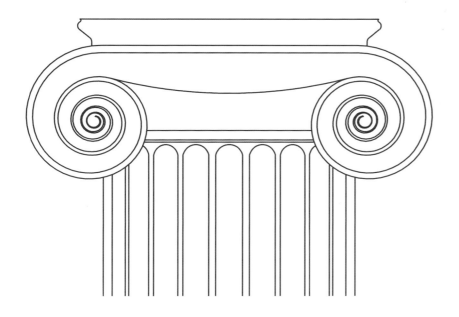

01

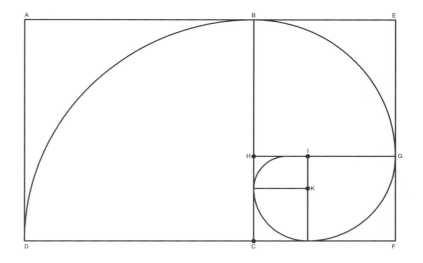

02

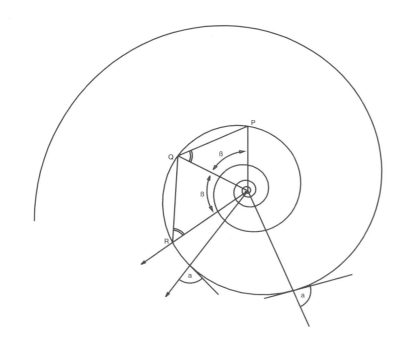

03

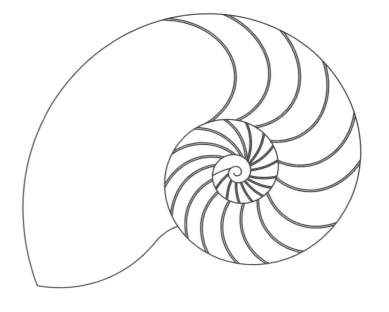

04

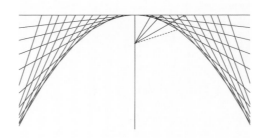
01

02

03

geometrical properties that make it easier to use than a circle. Not only is the parabola used to establish the vertical alignment of bridge decks; our arches tend to be parabolic curves, too, though why an arch looks better when it follows such a profile rather than a semi-circle is an interesting question. The competition for the Hulme Bridge project provided Wilkinson Eyre with real hands-on proof; our design started life as a semi-circular form but was latterly changed to a parabola. (In retrospect, this was probably due to inexperience, for this was the firm's first design for an arched structure and I am sure that the comparison was a familiar one among bridge engineers.) The reason why the parabola works better is partly because it resembles much more closely the path of natural forces – with minimum bending in the arch member. In short, the parabola resembles more closely the purest structural shape. It also has a sense of direction, whereas a circular form is directionless, and it has a specific central axis. The question becomes, then, one about perception and the legibility of a structure, and again this involves movement – both the flow of force and the projection of the form in a particular direction.

Wilkinson Eyre makes use of curved forms; such forms imply a sense of visual movement. The eye is drawn to move around curves, and it, in turn, can draw the mind to want to follow the curve. South Quay footbridge is a good example: the visitor is visually drawn along the bridge by the combined forces of the S-shaped plan, the varying-width deck – which gives an exaggerated perspective – and the perforated metal screen. Moreover, the fact that the structure is leaning at an unusual angle and the arrays of cables radiate and splay both in plan and in three dimensions further reinforces this visual dynamism. The effect on the user suggests a kind of movement which could be described as 'psycho-kinetic'; directionality is important at South Quay and there is a feeling of being virtually drawn along by the form. Equally, South Quay is what could be described as a 'fast' space; it evokes a feeling of speed. Inherent in the whole structural form, alongside the literal movement of its function as an opening swing bridge, there is a feeling of an arrested movement (you can just feel those forces galloping around the structure and the masses counterbalancing each other).

In bridge design, it is generally the physical movement that is the most problematic. When a man-made structure mimics a life form by actually moving, it can get rather cumbersome. To capture the gracefulness of natural movement in an opening bridge is a serious challenge and I look forward to seeing the operation of the 'opening eye' at Gateshead, where the whole structure is mobilized. Designers of opening bridges seldom achieve the holy grail: the best example to date is the footbridge to the inner harbour at Duisburg, designed by Schlaich Bergermann – a suspension bridge

01 Parabola Curve
02 Convertible Footbridge over the Inner Harbour, Duisburg, Germany, 1999 – Schlaich Bergermann and Partners.
03 Villa Emo, Fanzolo di Vedelago, Italy, 1559-65 – Andrea Palladio (1508-80).
04 Hulme Arch, Manchester UK, 1997 – Wilkinson Eyre Architects.

made to deform itself in an almost elastic way to rise up and create an opening.

Sinuous curves are not the only inspiring and powerful forms. I will never forget a visit to the Palladio's Villa Emo where the building is anchored into the landscape by the incredibly powerful interaction of two long vistas and a ramped change in level. Straight lines govern the composition here, and locate the portico entrance to the otherwise quite modest villa. This was a source of inspiration during the development of our design for the Four Seasons house, where there was a square walled garden with openings in the wall midway along each side giving onto the surrounding countryside. The axiality here depended on 'lines of force' inherent in the site or brought into the composition – very different from the reading of structure and the 'flow of forces'. Lines of force exist in the mind as well as in the spaces or landscape that we create, contributing to a sense of spirituality; they are the result of how spaces or objects in space relate to each other to create a greater power. Although these spaces or objects may be static, a movement is implied which prescribes a geometry. Moreover, the spaces and objects which possess the power to generate lines of force often have a strong presence themselves – usually traceable to their own geometry.

Despite a self-confessed interest in geometry – and that of movement –

I would resist the application of proportion systems as a formulaic way of designing a building. It just does not work. What use is a Golden Section to an architect if he or she can neither recognize one nor draw one freehand without aid? Besides, there is another curious aspect of geometrical form that I find intriguing and that is the visual tension that can be achieved through the approximation of pure shapes. Thus, something which is just out of square can be very lively and will contribute, more than the dead-pan rigour of precision, to an overall feeling of movement.

An architect should not only look in the mind when considering perceptions of movement in the static reality of built forms because there are other factors that can bring buildings to life. The way spaces are inhabited by people, whether singly or in crowds, is obviously crucial, but architecture would be virtually nothing if it were not for light, ever changing. Here the notion of how mood can be affected by external conditions becomes an important consideration. Depending on the surfaces on which it lands, the sun can brighten up a space and can bring both the interior and exterior of any building to life, its constantly changing nature throughout the day prompting changing perceptions of the structure. The play of light on form is a powerful animating agent, brought about by orientation, careful modelling and the skilful disposition of the transparent or

translucent elements of a building. Moreover, the transparency that during the day made the outside look bright, with light seeping or flooding into the building, at night is reversed, allowing buildings to radiate light.

Today it is difficult to stand still; uncertainties exist everywhere and technology is shrinking the world. Aware of this, architecture attempts to serve a demand for excitement and interest, and there is a confidence about an architecture which not only asserts itself by appealing to man's appreciation of movement but which also explores new geometries and forms made feasible only through computer technology. Architects can become masters – rather than servants – of this new technology, and can enjoy – on a conscious level – the strength of new forms specifically shaped to bring buildings to life. Buildings too are more liberated by what can be conceived, realized and manufactured economically while at the same time becoming ever more responsive to our senses.

01 Drawing:
Four Seasons House,
Design Proposal 1989 –
Wilkinson Eyre Architects

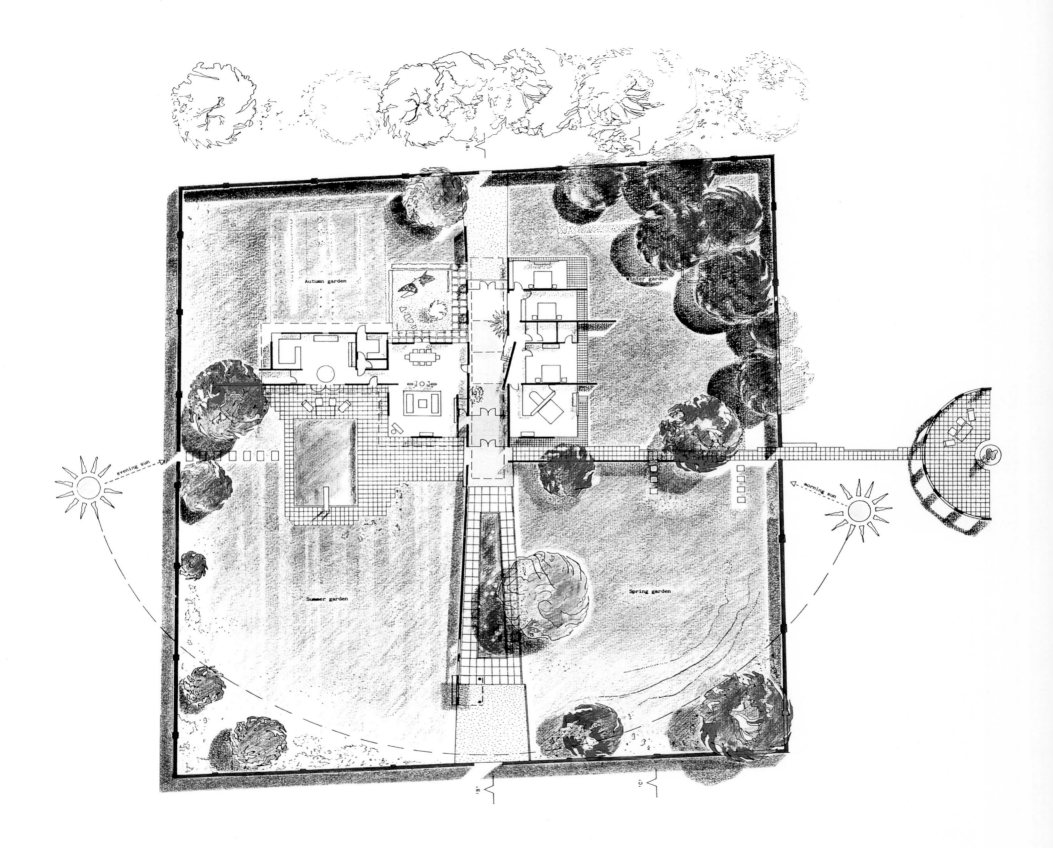

essay 05

Architecture or Engineering?
Jim Eyre

01

02

If the architect just chooses the colour of the paint and the engineer taps out a few numbers on a calculator, who actually does the work?

Until recently the domains of the civil engineer and the architect had rarely coincided but increasingly, nowadays, infrastructure and bridge projects have required a cooperation between the two professions. No civil project team today is complete without an architect on board, and there is a growing recognition of the architect's contribution, particularly in a project's early stages, when concepts are in development.

Engineering as a separate, 'stand-alone' discipline began to break away from architecture/building at the end of the eighteenth century, once the Industrial Revolution had got up some steam. This must have been an incredibly exciting time for anyone interested in design, for as a whole technology for infrastructure and transportation started to emerge, there arose with it a demand for new buildings and structure types. An architect at that time would probably have spent most of his time designing private houses or perhaps religious buildings, and a sideways look then, at all the developing new technology, might have seemed rather seductive. In contrast, the architect's diet today is so interesting and varied, that to consider changing disciplines is almost unthinkable.

The early 'engineers' came from other professions: Telford from architecture, Capt. Brown (designer of the beautiful Union Bridge over the River Tweed) from the Navy, Finley in Pennsylvania from the judiciary. These people are not only linked by their spirit of invention and a willingness to innovate; they also share an understanding of the importance of aesthetics. Telford's interest in the appearance of his work is documented and his structures are admired the world over for their clarity and beauty, the quality of their engineering and remarkable durability. On the other hand, with his Scottish Presbyterian background, Finley eschewed aesthetics as being somehow a surplus 'add-on'. He little realized at the time, of course, that he was initiating a whole new aesthetic in the process.

In a sense, the very essence of the misunderstanding between civil engineers and architects is revealed in terms of their diverging attitudes to aesthetics. Historically, aesthetics was generally viewed as an 'add-on': the so-called engineering structures that we admire today (principally stations and bridges) were often subjected to aesthetic add-ons merely to make them acceptable for society. Such additions were usually undertaken by architects. Even when Brunel was designing these 'front-of-house' buildings, however, he abandoned the clarity of thinking that characterized his spanning structures for the sake of good manners.

The early engineering pioneers in Britain and America made progress through

01 Isambard Kingdom
   Brunel (1806-59).
02 Paddington Station,
   1852-4, London UK –
   Isambard Kingdom
   Brunel (1806-59).

If the architect just chooses
the colour of the paint and the
engineer taps out a few numbers
on a calculator, who actually
does the work?

01

experiment. They found out what worked by examination and testing and then built it, using intuition and intelligence to progress the technology. The ability to analyse structures properly came much later. The elitist educational system in France produced generations of engineers who believed in the primacy of a theoretical approach to design – and that rooted in mathematical analysis. The science was undoubtedly advanced but there were some expensive failures: Navier's 1826 Pont des Invalides in Paris, for example. According to the great German engineer of our time, Jorg Schlaich, structural engineering really only began to be meaningful as the ability to analyse structures properly was consolidated. Cottancin's stunning Galerie des Machines in Paris (1889) best exemplifies what can be achieved with this new capability. Here the world of engineering is literally turned on its head. All the thick bits of the structure are up in the sky, while the thin bits are near the ground; the structure has learnt to 'float'. Surely this was a defining moment in architectural history.

The world of engineering thrived during the nineteenth and early twentieth centuries, creating many fine monuments. Indeed, the mid- to late nineteenth century was widely recognized as the 'Age of the Engineer'. These people had almost taken on the status of gods.

What I call the utilitarian nightmare only really began in the 1930s; before this

there was always at least an attempt to produce structures characterized by grace and beauty. In the Reichsautobahn structures of the 1930s banality rears its ugly head, along with dullness and repetition.

Engineering's drive to improve efficiency used to go hand in hand with a desire to develop ways of using as little material as possible (for the sake of lightness), which helped to keep costs down when iron was involved. In the twentieth century, however, engineering began to pursue cost savings at the expense of appearance. Issues of value were forgotten while production methods dictated ever more simplistic forms. This resulted in dull structures that did not even reflect generic structural behaviour. It might be argued that the pared-down aesthetic of the Modern Movement led people to believe that such basic forms were all that they needed. Moreover, uglier and uglier structures continued to be justified by the fact that they made better use of public resources. There seems to have been little – if any – regard for the environment.

It is unfortunate that the civil engineering discipline permits a working ethic which can disregard the one part of the design process that cannot be empirically measured. For this abandonment – by some – of aesthetic values not only degrades a structure's appearance, and its contribution to urban design, it also has negative implications in terms of a structure's real environmental impact, its sense of

01 Galerie des Machines
Paris France, 1889 –
Cottancin & Dutert.

Some people maintain that the essential difference between engineers and architects is that engineers are concerned with controlling forces while architects control spaces.

01

place and its connection with humanity.

Clearly, this creates an opportunity for architects, as these concerns are central to our thinking. Some people maintain that the essential difference between engineers and architects is that engineers are concerned with controlling forces while architects control spaces. Others separate the two professions differently: engineers, they suggest, are responsible for the safety of people through the strength of structures, while architects function in the realm of social wellbeing – the former always a scientific job, the latter always arts-connected.

Having had the chance to talk on several occasions to Roland Paoletti (Architect in charge of the Jubilee Line Project) about the roles of engineer and architect, and in the light of his experience working with the great Pier Luigi Nervi – who understood that good engineering needed to be beautiful – it seems that today, in fact, architects are 'controlling the forces' too, by having a significant input into structural form. Certainly, the architects working on the Jubilee Line stations had a major influence in terms of their general arrangement as well as their appearance. It is curious that the architects' work on these stations is sometimes described as the 'finishes' – as if someone else had already engineered the solutions before the architects came along and chose a few finishes. Obviously the realms and roles of the two disciplines is a very grey area.

Paoletti pointed out, however, that a civil engineer can 'conceptualize design, quantify, arrange, let and administer the contract and calculate', and surely this is the only essential difference: the architect's inability to undertake the calculations and analysis. Nothing else is the exclusive responsibility of either one or the other.

Moreover, I take great comfort from the fact that none of the many engineers with whom I have worked, who can talk about design and generate ideas, has ever brought out a calculator. Instead they have relied on an intuition informed by knowledge and experience.

Architecture is a process requiring a series of aesthetic choices, each heavily informed by other (sometimes multiple) factors – light, spatial, programmatic, social, structural, climate- or at least weather-related, environmental, technological or economic. Nevertheless, the part of the creative process that generates the relationship between all the components of a building, or the spaces between them, and the way the whole sits with its surroundings, need not be ignored by engineers. And, by the same token, the architect should not ignore the means by which enclosures are achieved. To make architecture out of a structure is not a soft option; the decision to do so, however, is the biggest single factor in asking whether architecture has become engineering.

The engineering profession seems

01 Italian Airforce Hangar,
   Orvieto Italy, 1939-41 –
   Pier Luigi Nervi
   (1891-1979).
02 Proposal for tripoidal
   footbridge, Rivers Ribble
   and Calder UK, 2000 –
   Wilkinson Eyre Architects.

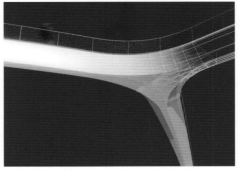

02

suspicious of any of its own that dares to step outside the safe science of the discipline into the nebulous world of the arts. Calatrava, for instance, is not admired by as many engineers as architects. Unfortunately, it is also possible to detect a mistrust, in some camps, of the architect who uses the expression of structure to define space, as if this is somehow not pursuing a serious theoretical agenda.

At Wilkinson Eyre there is an unashamed interest in structures; engineering and structural form are considered a wonderful resource, there to be exploited. At the same time there is a recognition that to use and exploit that resource requires knowledge. I believe that, through talking with engineers, we have developed an intuitive understanding of what will and will not work and there is an appreciation of contrasting lightness/mass and the efficiency of materials. In this way there is little scope for time-wasting – no room for inelegant structures that mock notions of clarity, purity and our understanding of the legibility of structures. Long gone are the days when the fully planned-out architectural proposal was just passed – with no discussion – to the engineer in order for the structure to be built. How could anyone have been so lazy?

The other great resource in the contemporary architect's armoury is computer technology. Suddenly there is available the capacity to draw and navigate a course around shapes with incredible ease; in the past, we could barely have even drawn the shapes. This is as liberating for the architect as was the invention of the flat roof in the early days of the Modern Movement for the future of the plan.

In the dawn of the new technology the pioneer spirit of Telford, Brown et al. is re-emerging. And just as architects can find new ways of doing things, engineers can analyse them more quickly and, with beautiful symmetry, the same technology facilitates new – and more economic – manufacturing methods. What an opportunity to make technology (only the means of doing work, after all) subservient to art.

The new architecture is a dynamic one, full of movement. The new architect has at his/her fingertips the means and resources to push all those involved to their limits – within the framework of a team that, as a whole and individually, has an increasing knowledge of the common goal.

'Is it architecture or engineering?' The answer is 'Yes.'

essay 06

Unabridged
Jim Eyre

Since the invention of the railways, methods of transport have edged ever nearer to the Roman ideal of travel in a straight line. Depending on your view, mankind has either consistently triumphed over nature or violated it – with railroads in the nineteenth century, motorways since the war, and more recently with the ultralinearity of high-speed rail travel. As the line gets straighter, more cuttings, embankments, tunnels and bridges arise. Bridges occur as incidents in transportation that overcome natural topography, while cuttings and embankments are more insidious, more damaging to the landscape, beating nature into submission.

The sheer number of structures involved in crossing an impassable natural obstacle means that the bridge becomes more a utilitarian artefact than something exceptional. Perhaps the prevalence of banality that has arisen as a result is symptomatic of the second half of the twentieth century. Dullness and repetition first appeared in the 1930s, however, in the Reichsautobahn structures, despite the heroicization of its programme – the emblematic Mang Falls, for instance, was used in a stamp design and became subject to 'bridge tourism'.

The history of bridge design can be traced from fords and primitive bridge forms, developing both in complexity and span alongside technological and material progress. With the Industrial Revolution bridge design underwent

radical change but it is interesting to note how new developments at that stage still represented old forms. Abraham Darby's 30m cast-iron span at Coalbrookdale was designed to resemble an arched stone bridge.

The opposite of the compressive arch is the suspension bridge, with its tensile catenaries. There were pedestrian suspension bridges in sixth-century China – and rope bridges in Tibet even before that – but it was not until 1800 that a Pennsylvania judge, James Finley, built a suspension bridge for vehicles at Jacob's Creek; he patented a design for bridges in 1810. Although Thomas Telford is usually credited with building the first major suspension structure, the first long-span suspension bridge for vehicles was, in fact, designed by Captain Samuel Brown: the Union Bridge over the River Tweed at Horncliffe, dating from 1820. Still standing today, its 91m span is characterized by an incredible lightness and the deck is completely unstiffened.

The development of wrought iron provided new scope as regards tensile strength and in the early nineteenth century ingenuity was directed at making efficient use of this precious material. Telford's 1825 bridge over the Menai Straits used wrought-iron suspension chains. The railways required greater load capacity; however, new techniques were developed that provided the solution. The benefits of rolled and riveted steel can be seen in Stephenson's Britannia Tubular Bridge

02

03

04

05

06

07

08

01

02

03

(1846–50). Engineers of vision pushed the boundaries of knowledge in structural analysis even further – sometimes with success, as in the daring long-span arches in Eiffel's 1878 Douro Bridge (with a span of 140m), and sometimes, as with Thomas Bouch's Tay Bridge in 1879, with failure. The iron bridge as a form in the 'Age of the Engineer' culminates in the Forth Bridge (1881–89), its spans a breathtaking 521m. Here the bridge becomes a defining monument of the Industrial Revolution and a destination in its own right. Critical reaction to the bridge illustrates the essential dichotomy between design philosophy and appreciation. While William Morris wrote: 'There never will be an architecture of iron, every improvement in machinery being uglier and uglier until they reach the supremest specimen of ugliness – the Forth Bridge', Alfred Waterhouse admired it, and saw it as creating its own style. The debate about the validity of so much of twentieth-century modern art and architectural endeavour was already looming.

Developments continued apace in the twentieth century: Maillart produced the first box bridges and Freyssinet increased the capabilities of reinforced concrete with prestressing techniques. Then there were long-span suspension bridges, such as the 2,220m Humber Bridge – made slender by its aerodynamic design and its high-strength cables. The poet Philip Larkin, who lived in Hull, described it as

'swallow-fall and one plane line'. Most recently there has been the development of cable-stayed bridges which use the principles of incremental balanced cantilever construction – seen before in the railway bridge over the Firth of Forth.

The history of bridges is deceptive, however – as so much of history is deceptive – because it catalogues the triumphant and the exceptional. Since 1945 too many engineers have begun to worship the false god of economy. In the past loved ones were sacrificed or actually even built in to bridges to placate the river gods; recently the aim seems to be to achieve a design at absolutely minimal cost while issues of value to the environment are entirely forgotten. Cost is quantifiable and value is subjective.

Nevertheless, throughout this period there is a well-documented and discernible thread of excellence in bridge design – with architects having no more than a peripheral role: Christian Menn's Ganter Bridge, for example, is perhaps the defining bridge monument of the twentieth century – an absolute triumph of man over natural topography. It contains all the ingredients: concrete, a combination of tensile and compressive elements, curvature, visual movement, elegance and proportion, economy and efficiency, all in a spectacular mountain setting and without an architect in sight.

Since the 1980s architect/engineers

01 Forth Bridge, Queensbury, Lothian, UK, 1882-90 – Sir Benjamin Baker (1840- 1907) / Sir John Fowler (1817-1898).
02 Humber Bridge, Kingston-upon-Hull UK, 1972-81 – Freeman Fox & Partners.
03 Ganter Bridge, Valais Switzerland, 1976-80 – Christian Menn (b.1927).

(and there are only a few) such as Santiago Calatrava have promoted bridges as urban sculpture, acquiring for them the status of civic icons (his Alamillo Bridge of 1987–92, built for Expo '92 Seville, for example). The architectonic possibilities are fully explored and structural expression overcomes the dogma of minimizing material at all costs. The practice of adding weight for the sake of appearance is, in strict engineering terms, anathema and for this Calatrava makes himself unpopular in certain engineering quarters. Indeed, when conscious decisions are made to deviate from purist solutions, they should be made after careful consideration of the step's worth – and mindful of this alleged sin. I believe that there are value judgements to be made, and the designer should be given sufficient latitude to determine the disposition of mass for any given form. The real sin is making a structure ungainly simply because it is cheaper to design it that way, and justifying it on the basis that an ill-fitting component makes it cheap to build.

In the 1990s a number of architects were quick to see the latent potential in bridge design in the United Kingdom. Architects with an interest in structure, materials and the tectonic rather than exclusively the narrative could readily and successfully adapt, working on a collaborative basis with engineers who possessed the innovative vision but who recognized the conceptual skills on offer.

The common and insidious misconception held particularly by many civil engineers is that architects just come along and 'prettify' a structure once the engineer has determined the form and details. Certainly, nothing could be further from the truth on the bridge projects with which Wilkinson Eyre has been involved. If a bridge turns out 'pretty', it is felt that the client's money has been wasted, with no consideration given to any genuine civic, urban value that may have been contributed by architectural and sculptural intervention. This nonsensical view has its roots in ignorance; and it is ignorance which equally informs the sense of bewilderment that anyone other than an architect can make a contribution to buildings. (The reality, of course, is that there are as few innovative engineers as there are creative architects.)

There are numerous books on bridges and it is possible to sense a common theme in even the most erudite that, broadly speaking, the architect has been a disruptive influence, essentially undermining the confidence of the designers. The feeling, really, is that there is hardly a place for the architect in 'structural art'.

The architect's role, however, has always been to attempt to civilize what at the time would have been perceived as brutal structures. With hindsight, of course, it is possible to see that many of these bridges were either not brutal at all or else that the raw power of their

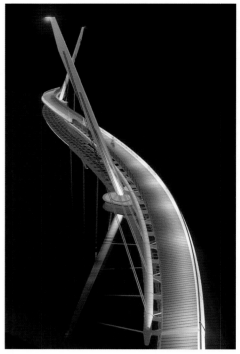

01

construction (on such a large scale) merely transcended normal perceptions of beauty and aesthetics. This argument can still hold true today, for some structures are so big and ugly that they are – perversely – beautiful. This beauty, however, comes from a different set of parameters; and the fact that there is progressively less and less for the architect to do, as the bridge gets bigger, is proof of that.

It is, however, the architect's contribution now that I find interesting. The era of twentieth-century functionalist design, ranging between the extremes of the reductionist 'no design' approach to more expressionistic styles, has, in fact, been most instructive. Architects now not only know how to use all the elements of construction, they tend also to adopt a broader palette when making architecture – including form, space and the subjective in their designs.

Wilkinson Eyre's architectural approach grew out of the rigour of 1970s' modernism, with an obvious interest in context, utility, structure, construction, form, proportion and lightness. Arguably this way of thinking is much more relevant to bridge design than the rather divergent agendas of previous generations' architects. And just as the architecture is more engineered, so the bridges are more 'architected'. Wilkinson Eyre, by working collaboratively with engineers, manages to fill a gap in their armoury, and brings more to the design as well. It is through just this type of collaboration and

standard-raising that cultural vision and civil engineering will associate again.

It seems worth stressing that when Wilkinson Eyre is involved in a bridge project, more often than not the raw concept comes from that quarter. To do this requires not only a degree of ingenuity, which architects generally possess, but also some knowledge – albeit modest – of general engineering principles. Some sort of intuitive understanding of what feels as if it might work is also essential – not just the bridge's capacity to stand up but whether it will be intelligible as a structure in its own right, with a legible flow of forces and a spatial sequence that seems rooted in its context.

It is only through the altruism of clients who recognize that infrastructure can make civic gestures that the firm has had the opportunity to express their concern for architectural space and the potential to modulate the urban fabric using as a vehicle that most symbolic of engineering structures: the bridge. One such client is the London Docklands Development Corporation who, in the mid-1990s, nearing the end of its remit, embarked upon a series of competitions – for bridge designs – and enlisted architect/engineer teams.

Wilkinson Eyre was fortunate to participate in the 1994 competition to design an opening bridge at South Quay near Canary Wharf – and to win the commission. The rather complex requisites of the brief, including a

01 Computer Visualisation:
   South Quay Footbridge,
   London UK, 1997 –
   Wilkinson Eyre Architects.
02 Oresund Bridge,
   Denmark, 1999 –
   Ove Arup & Partners.
03 Butterfly Bridge,
   Bedford UK, 1997 –
   Wilkinson Eyre Architects.

02

03

navigable opening span and the potential for shortening and relocation to a different alignment in the future, were turned to advantage and addressed in a single constructional idea. Employing the diagonal and a swinging configuration, the bridge takes the form of an 's'-shaped deck with canted masts and stay cables, its curvilinearity acting in contrast to the austere urban grain of its context. Perceived movement across the bridge is accelerated by the psycho-kinetic form. Despite the proximity of Canary Wharf Tower, which stands as a regional visual landmark, Wilkinson Eyre's bridge at South Quay carves out its own place, modulating the urban fabric on a more humane level.

This was a happy introduction to the genre of the bridge. It was followed by further competition wins in Manchester, Bedford, Maidstone and – perhaps most significantly – by a commission to span the Tyne [between Gateshead and Newcastle] – a river defined by its bridges.

An enduring quality of many bridges is their sense of arrested movement. What can imply more movement than the graduated curves of an arch or a suspension catenary? The form of the structure is obviously important in this regard but the sense that all the various elements are juxtaposed in a dynamic counterpoise – where balance is only just maintained, somewhere close to the limits – is crucial too. The new architecture is also concerned with the careful composition of surfaces and

lines which can bring a gracefulness to the bridge structure.

At the barest minimum a bridge engages with the space defined by the area of its deck. While the bridge's relationship with the sky above is indeterminate, the space below the structure is easily defined; the two spaces are not always related, however. I regard the space above and below the bridge as being continuations of the landscape in both directions and in my mind the spaces over and below the bridge are also connected. When there is a structure above deck level these interconnected spaces are easier to read, and there are overt visual clues to the bridge's spanning capacity for all to see. When the structure of the bridge reaches out beyond the conventional confines of the vertical plane that define the edges of the deck the bridge moves into a new dimension. Suddenly a dynamism has evolved and the architect gets a real gut feeling that the structure is engaging with its surroundings, and the space above the deck opens out. Geometrical devices, such as the twisting of a plane of cables into the third dimension, can enhance the feeling of movement in space. In open landscape such structures can become at one with nature, while in an urban context the excitement of the forms is potentially magnetic and other-worldly.

As ubiquitous as the bridge itself is the symbolism of the bridge. Today 'architecture' is used as often to describe the construction of a political

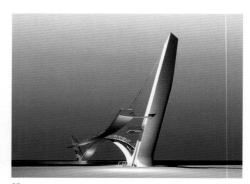

01

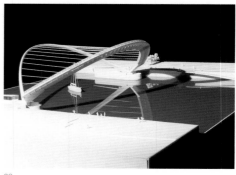

02

03

agreement or a piece of software design as it is to discuss the built environment. In the same way, 'bridge' metaphorically spans any divide. More than the word, however, the power of the bridge as a symbol of regeneration has few peers.

In a machine age interwoven with information technology and media power, bridge structures stand as potent symbols of how mankind has tamed nature. Images of bridges appear constantly in advertising – usually for cars or cigarettes. Deployed as powerful symbols of technological triumphs, they also represent an acceptable face of modernity, their daring structures provide good, dramatic, attractive imagery. The subtext: 'If you can fly in the face of nature with such daring structures you can fly in the face of nature by smoking or driving too fast.'

The power of a well-designed bridge lies not just in its symbolic strength but also in the quality of its imagery. The scale of the image, presented in settings that make it highly visible, using structures that contrast sharply with all the other usual constructions in the environment, ensures that the bridge as a typology is pregnant with possibility. Beautifully designed and well rooted in its setting, a structure can provoke more than pure admiration; a bridge can become an icon. The Golden Gate Bridge is the definitive icon for San Francisco just as the opera house – harbour bridge image stands for Sydney.

'Landmark' is a word increasingly used

by those who commission buildings and bridges; it reflects their aspirations for the project. The word means different things to different people, however: for some a landmark has iconic status, while literally, a landmark is something big that stands out from its surroundings, and on another level it is no more than qualitative recognition. While I realize it is an obvious watering-down of the word, I would like to promote the latter usage because – obviously – not every new structure can be a landmark statement.

Art differentiates itself from science by being in essence unmeasurable: as Louis Kahn pointed out, a great building must begin with the unmeasurable, must go through measurable means when it is being designed and built, but must, in the end, be unmeasurable. While a bridge cannot be sculpture in the purest sense because of its inherent functionality, which is measurable, and because it is an engineering structure, it can nevertheless possess extraordinary sculptural qualities, drawing it closer to art than science.

Innovation is an imperative. I believe, however, that technological advance is less often the result of direct scientific discovery than part of a creative process – thinking out new ways of doing things. Working in bridge design, however, this effort – and the identification of any achievement – is always very focused, because one is operating in a language which essentially has only three basic forms: the truss or beam, the arch and

01 Golden Gate Bridge, 1933-37, San Francisco, California USA – Joseph Strauss (1870-1938) / Irving Morrow (1884-?) / Blair Birdsall (1907-97).
02 Computer Visualisation: Lyckoben Bridge, Stockholm Sweden, 1997 – Wilkinson Eyre Architects.
03 Model: Gateshead Millennium Bridge, 1997-2001 – Wilkinson Eyre Architects.
04 Computer Visualisation: Passerelle Bercy-Tolbiac Paris France, 1999 – Wilkinson Eyre Architects.
05 Hulme Arch, Manchester UK, 1997 – Wilkinson Eyre Architects.

04

05

the suspension or cable stay. All bridge proposals are variations on a theme working within these parameters of basic type.

Opening bridges provide the opportunity to create an entirely integrated design – one that actually speaks of its method of opening. The act of opening is something to celebrate. The structure is transformed as the bridge opens: this can either be a surprise and a revelation, or a clear expression explicit in the structural form. Our bridge over the River Tyne for Gateshead Metropolitan Borough Council belongs to the former category; the whole bridge is mobilized in an unexpected manner to change like the opening of an eyelid. The static is imbued with a sense of movement and then real movement becomes a spectacle.

The contrasts that can be experienced in architecture, whether they be contrasts of form, weight, texture, space or setting, are hugely enjoyable. And everyone's perspective on every structure built is influenced by comparison and contrast, within and without: there is no such thing as a truly stand-alone building. By their very nature, bridges are relatively unusual structures so the contextual contrast is emphatic. And the inherent contrast created by the apparent lightness of bridges is well established and much enjoyed. Historically, however, it was the introduction of iron in the Industrial Revolution that fostered an altogether new design aesthetic though,

initially at least, it was combined with contrasting masonry elements. Interestingly, it is with these great compressive elements that architects have in the past been involved, as if it were too risky to delegate to the engineers. Since then technological progress has marched on ceaselessly, creating ever lighter structures and pushing further and further into engineering territory. I sense now that there might be room for bridge structures which contain both light and heavy elements, the contrast between them accentuating the quality of each as it does in architecture.

'Form follows function' is an old mantra widely known beyond the limits of the design profession: it is a paradox, however, that in structural terms the reverse is also true. The structural function of a form follows the determined geometry of that form. The form is in the hands of the designer; he/she effectively selects a geometry which sets the framework for controlling the forces and the forces flow where they need to. Material is then added to or taken away from a given form or geometry – to respond to the flow of forces. The geometry used with bridges is always clear cut but the sophistication of the spaces created by those bridges are dependent on quite subtle interventions, none of them scientific in any sense – except in the ways they have been worked out.

Just like an aeroplane's wings, which must deflect or else their stiffness would

01

cause them to fail in the face of shock loads, buildings – and bridges too – must never be without elasticity. This, in a sense, can be construed as a passive form of responsivity. Technological progress and analytical capacity are now so advanced that architects can design structures that are responsive in an interactive way with loads or encounters with other forces. Wilkinson Eyre explored the expressive potential of an interactive bridge structure at the Science Museum in London; light, sound and graphic imagery were activated by changing loads. The firm is now looking forward to designing adaptive structures that can respond to loads, environment or even location.

Intuitive thinking is of paramount importance in the creative process; knowledge and intellect are important because they can put us further in touch with how and why we feel we like something or believe it is right for what we are trying to achieve. The most powerful positive sensation that a structure – or bridge, in particular – can provoke is a sense of wonder. This combines admiration with a 'wow factor' – usually having caught sight of something outside the normal range of experience. Although, in the art world, immediacy is not always regarded as an attribute, in the world of engineering structures that exhibit a clarity of thought and execution have a very direct appeal. The daring and defiant bridges that span long distances or that seem to challenge our sense of the possible are a constant source of great wonder.

01 Challenge of Materials
   Gallery Footbridge,
   Science Museum,
   London UK, 1997 –
   Wilkinson Eyre Architects.
02 Metsovitikos Bridge,
   Greece, 1997-2001 –
   Wilkinson Eyre Architects

essay 07

Universal Space
Chris Wilkinson

01

02

03

Architects and astronauts share a preoccupation with the exploration of space, but for architects it is limited to the design of contained space. To envisage and design spaces is a fundamental part of our job and convention has made it easy for us by limiting the size and shape of rooms to what people can readily understand. Most buildings are made up of essentially rectangular spaces with modest headroom related to human proportions. In Japan this was regularized by a traditional formula for domestic spaces, which was derived from the size of the tatami mat and the way in which it was laid on the floor in various layout patterns. In post war Britain space standards for housing were clearly defined in the Parker Morris Standards. In both instances, innovation was discouraged and difficult to achieve. Yet throughout history there has been recognition of a need for spaces which are more exciting and uplifting.

The ancient Egyptians, Greeks and Romans all constructed spaces of grand proportions which were designed to inspire the people who used them. These were spaces for the gods and had to be beyond domestic human scale. A millennium later the great Gothic cathedrals provided the kind of awe-inspiring spaces that would make us feel humble in the sight of God. Since that time, the generators of grand spaces have changed from religion to industry, transportation, leisure and more recently retail. The need for huge enclosed spaces has been rapidly

increasing as the technology for providing them becomes more accessible.

The term 'universal space' was first proposed by Mies van der Rohe to describe a kind of long-span single-volume flexible enclosure. In order to explain the concept, he used an interior photograph of the Glenn Martin Aircraft Assembly Building, designed by Albert Kahn in 1937, as a backdrop for a montage onto which he superimposed a number of free standing planes to represent walls and ceilings that could be moved to suit changing requirements. It's a wonderfully descriptive image with which to identify the kind of space that can house a wide variety of uses, ranging from industrial to transport, sports and leisure activities. Moreover, the big single-volume enclosure is the ultimate flexible space, which can be modelled or adapted to suit almost any user requirement.

Richard Buckminster Fuller was also preoccupied with this concept, which fitted in well with his philosophy for achieving 'more with less'. With the development of the innovative geodesic dome structures, he succeeded in enclosing large-volume column-free spaces with minimum weight and materials. He took this idea even further with a project in the 1950s for a tensegrity dome 2 miles in diameter over Manhattan and although nothing of this size has yet been constructed, it is now technically possible. More recently, Richard Rogers's Millennium Dome at

01 Montage: Mies van der Rohe (1886-1969) Glenn Martin Aircraft Assembly Building, USA, 1937 – Albert Kahn (1869-1942).
02 Tensegrity Dome over Manhattan, 1950 – Richard Buckminster Fuller (1895-1983).
03 IBM Greenford UK, 1974-80 – Foster & Partners.
04 Crystal Palace, London UK, 1851 – Joseph Paxton (1801-65).
05 Galerie des Machines Paris France, 1889 – Cottancin & Dutert.
06 Paddington Station, 1852-4, London UK – Isambard Kingdom Brunel (1806-59).
07 St Pancras Station, London UK, 1864-68 – WH Barlow (1812-1902) and RM Ordish.

04

05

07

06

Greenwich goes some way to exploring the potential for this kind of large roof enclosure with its huge fabric roof covering an area of approximately 80,000m².

My own interest in the concept of universal space was born in the mid 1970s when I was working for Foster Associates on the design of industrial buildings, which we called 'sheds', for clients who required big, flexible and extendable spaces. It became clear that for these clients, who were mostly involved in the assembly of electronic components, the kind of space required for the production areas was much the same as for the offices. The need was for a flexible space with wide column spacing, which could be 'tuned' to suit their specific requirements.

Whilst working on the design for the huge IBM London Distribution Centre at Greenford in 1974, I started to research its roots in earlier industrial architecture and I soon found parallels with transportation, exhibition and leisure buildings which all generated the same requirement for long-span large-volume spaces. The research was eventually published as *Supersheds* (Butterworth Architecture, 1991).

The term supersheds can be applied to the buildings which enclose universal space and can be defined as 'buildings enclosing a large single volume of space with relatively long spans and without major subdivision'. The introduction starts 'There is a kind of

architecture which is not formal, decorated or mannered, but which derives its aesthetic from a clear expression of its purpose and component parts, where the demands of function and economy have led to simplicity of form and construction, but where the basic requirements of enclosure and structure are extended by design to create buildings of quality.'

It is a category of building which has largely been excluded from the mainstream of architectural classification and left to the province of engineering. It is here, however, that the skills of architecture and engineering converge. The development of these buildings has closely followed technological progress and began in the early nineteenth century with the advent of the railways and the Great Exhibitions, which generated the need for long-span enclosures at a time when the technology of cast-iron structures was sufficiently advanced to be able to provide them.

In Britain the 1850s saw the construction of two fine buildings which exemplified the spirit of the new age of architectural engineering: the Crystal Palace by Joseph Paxton and Paddington Station by IK Brunel. Both of lightweight construction, these vast universal spaces were functional, economical and expressed simplicity of form and clarity of structure.

Further technological progress in the latter half of the nineteenth century saw

01

02

04

the development of vaulted structures that could span ever larger spaces. Barlow and Ordish's train shed at St Pancras Station in 1868 spans 74m, while Cottancin and Dutert produced the first significant three-pinned arch structure for the Galerie des Machines at the Paris Exhibition in 1889 with the incredible span of 114m. The development of airships at the turn of the twentieth century prompted the next major technical advances. Huge-volume enclosures were required to house the airships and this sparked off the search for new lightweight materials and structures. Also, for the first time, aerodynamics became an important factor. In order to reduce turbulence for docking and launching airships, streamlined hangar designs were developed in wind tunnels, producing such innovative designs as the Sunnyvale Naval Airbase in California.

Later developments, related to aeroplane technology and the emergence in 1970 of the Jumbo Jet with its 60m wingspan, created the need for a new generation of long-span large-volume buildings. The largest of them was the Boeing Assembly Plant at Everett, near Seattle, which is the world's largest building by volumetric capacity with five bays 488 x 35m high and clear spans of 35m. Visitors enter this huge building through a below-ground tunnel and emerge from a lift in one of the central cores to experience an awe-inspiring space, where it is possible to assemble twelve Jumbo Jets at one

time and still have room to manoeuvre. The requirements of industry have constantly changed with the development of new manufacturing techniques and the buildings which house the processes have evolved to meet these requirements. The most significant development this century has been the introduction of the production line assembly, which originated primarily in the United States for the automobile industry and created the brief for the single-storey, rooflit, wide-span industrial shed that we know so well. Considerable progress was made in the design of this form of industrial shed by Albert Kahn who, in his lifetime, built more than 2,000 factories characterized by strong functional forms with clear expression of purpose, structure and materials. In Europe there are relatively few examples of good industrial architecture from that time, although the Bauhaus did make a considerable impact and leading figures such as Behrens, Gropius, Mendelsohn and Mies van der Rohe all worked on the design of industrial buildings. At the Werkbund Exhibition in Cologne in 1914 the Machine Hall was designed as a 'model factory' and its pitched portal frame has almost become an industry standard.

Another milestone for change was derived from the World War II blackout armament factories in the United States, where the need for air conditioning generated a constraint on the overall building volume for reasons of economy. This led to the flat-roofed,

03

01 Steel hangar, US Naval Airbase, Sunnyvale, California USA, 1933.
02 Boeing 747 Assembly Plant, Everett, Seattle, USA, 1968 – Austin Company of Cleveland, Ohio USA.
03 Machine Hall at the Werkbund Exhibition, 1914, Cologne Germany
04 Renault Distribution Centre, Swindon UK, 1980-82 – Foster & Partners.
05 INMOS Microprocessor Factory, Newport, South Wales UK, 1980-82 – Richard Rogers & Partners.
06 Stratford Market Depot, London UK, 1996 – Wilkinson Eyre Architects.
07 Stratford Regional Station, London UK, 1999 – Wilkinson Eyre Architects.
08 Dyson Headquarters, Malmesbury UK, 1999 – Wilkinson Eyre Architects.

05

06

08

07

rectangular-grid 'cool boxes' designed at first by the Chicago practices, such as SOM and CF Murphy, and later popular in Britain in the 1960s and 1970s. It was the turn of British architects to popularize industrial architecture in the 1980s with exciting new structures such as the Renault Distribution Centre by Foster Associates and the Inmos Microprocessor Factory by Richard Rogers & Partners. These designs involved a close collaboration between architects and engineers, a process which seems to occur more naturally in London than elsewhere and, in particular, in the offices of Foster and Rogers where I was working at the time.

So it was with this background knowledge and interest in the architectural engineering of long-span large-volume spaces that I set up in practice in 1983 and was joined by Jim Eyre in 1986. It was not until 1991, however, that we were offered the chance to compete for the design of a big shed - the Stratford Market Depot train maintenance facility for the new Jubilee Line Extension. It was our first major commission: a huge single-volume building measuring 100 x 190m, on which we worked with the engineers Hyder Consulting Ltd. The site constraints and track layout led to a parallelogram-shaped building layout, which in turn generated the form of diagrid roof structure. Since clear spans were not required, it proved more economical to have intermediate columns at 18 x 42m centres, which branch out like trees to connect to three

node positions on the shallow-vaulted space structure above. This unusual hybrid structure works well and with the excellent daylighting provides an exciting and functional space for train maintenance. It could just as well be used for other purposes. It is a universal space.

Following the success of the Depot, we were asked by London Underground Ltd in 1994 to take part in the competition for the design of the new Stratford Station, to be the terminus for the Jubilee Line Extension and an interchange with four other lines. We won the commission, and here again, the incredibly complex design brief was translated into a clear diagram with a single column-free space. The asymmetric form of the structure moves away from the simple box to a dramatic and exciting space, which suits the specific requirements of function and context.

A year later in 1995, the brief for the design of the headquarters building for Dyson Appliances Ltd in Malmesbury, Wiltshire, required a more conventional kind of space for the design, research, testing, manufacture, assembly, storage and distribution of their vacuum cleaners. The phenomenal success of the innovative bagless vacuum cleaners, invented by James Dyson, led to the need for fast, flexible, economical and extendable space. He also wanted the building to express the identity of the company and its products. The resulting structure, which was designed with the

01

02

engineer Tony Hunt, uses standard universal steel sections rolled to a curve for the roof on a 10 x 20m grid, 7.5m high, with long-span profiled-steel decking that provides lateral bracing. The same structure provides the spatial enclosure for all the different activities housed within the building and allows for the inclusion of a mezzanine floor level where required. Parts of the building are highly serviced and these run on purpose-designed ladder beams suspended from the structure with flexibility to add more as required. The cladding varies from low-cost profiled-steel sheeting in the storage and production areas to a sophisticated glazed curtain walling system in the office areas, but there is flexibility to accept many alternative cladding options. It has already proved to be an extremely adaptable building and will no doubt continue to undergo changes throughout its life, a universal space limited only by its column grid and its height.

Universal space implies a kind of 'loose-fit flexibility', which is not specific to a single user, and there are many examples of redundant industrial structures being transformed with considerable success for an entirely different use. Wilkinson Eyre, for example, has been involved in converting both a Grade II-listed GWR train shed in Bristol into a Science Centre and the redundant Templeborough Steel Reprocessing Works at Rotherham into a new Millennium Visitor Attraction.

The somewhat clumsy Henebique concrete structure of the Bristol train shed has adapted surprisingly well to the highly serviced requirements of the new Science Centre and adds a note of historical reference to the advanced technology contents. The large-volume area, with relatively long spans between columns, provides flexible exhibition space which combines well with the bright new spaces constructed alongside. The new reads clearly alongside the old, and a fresh identity is created.

At Magna in Rotherham, the vast cathedral-like structure of the redundant steelworks provides a dramatic dark space, 350m long and over 7 storeys high. The powerful steel structure is enhanced by a patina of surface rust and the rough steel cladding bears the scars of extreme heat from the furnaces and the cauldrons of molten steel, which were transported through the space by overhead cranes. Too dark for modern manufacturing processes, the space nevertheless provides an exciting backdrop for the new Millennium-funded visitor attraction, which has 'steel' as its major theme. Our design places four separate pavilions within the space, accessed by bridges and walkways suspended from the existing structure. Each pavilion in different and takes one of the four elements as its theme: earth, water, air and fire, which all play a part in the steel-making process. The new interventions represent current technology and provide a dramatic contrast to the industrial archaeology of

01 Magna, Rotherham UK 2001 – Wilkinson Eyre Architects.
02 Explore at-Bristol, 1999 – Wilkinson Eyre Architects.
03 The Andromeda Galaxy.

03

the recent past of heavy industry. A long-span, single-volume space, with flexibility for adaptation and change of use, the essence of the original space has been retained for visitors to appreciate.

In summary, there is a general requirement for large flexible spaces to house all kinds of activities, but there is also a fundamental need within us to experience space of a higher order. Perhaps we have a psychological desire to see man-made space on the same scale as nature in order to assert our place in the universe. Most of us are moved by the views of a panoramic landscape, or by the sight of a clear, starlit night sky, and we experience a similar feeling when we enter one of the great Gothic cathedrals. The scale and proportions of the space trigger the feeling of spiritual reverence. Similarly, the parish church fulfils the same requirements and the spires and roofs of these important buildings, which stand out above the surroundings, punctuate both rural and urban landscapes.

Fewer people go to church regularly nowadays but perhaps other forms of building can provide this need for spiritually uplifting space. Perhaps it is now the turn of the huge regional shopping malls or the massive sports stadia – in which case let us all try to raise the quality of their architecture so that these buildings not only fulfil a practical function but also a spiritual need.

essay 08

God is in the Details
Jim Eyre

Like most architects, I have a great reverence for Mies van der Rohe. When I think of him, his exquisitely detailed and extraordinarily elegant buildings come immediately to mind. He is also known for two famous sayings. The first – 'Less is more' – is now so much part of common parlance that perhaps few people know where or when it originated. These three small words have been the focus of great debate ever since; they have even received the dubious accolade of a mocking misquotation – 'Less is a bore.' Perhaps they have become an easy target because the phrase is so widely recognized; yet their simplicity is profound, and they summarize an entire architectural manifesto. Mies's second famous dictum is that 'God is in the details.' This latter reveals the absolute nature of Mies's architecture, which displays such clarity that our perception of his buildings is elevated to an almost spiritual experience. There is also a strong hint that working out details requires great application – something akin to religious fervour. It is always worth remembering these two sayings when things are getting a little complicated, particularly with regard to detailing on buildings. It is often worth going back and reminding yourself what it is that the details should speak of. A concise expression is usually more enduring.

At Wilkinson Eyre we recognize the importance of good detailing. An ingenious concept is not enough on its own. Indeed, in my view, however striking the concept, it will stand or fall on the quality of its detailing. Considered alongside the Miesian approach, which values clarity and simplicity, a very careful and studied look at this aspect becomes even more crucial. Our architecture, which I see as being broadly founded on the Miesian tradition, would be very unforgiving to clumsy details or poor workmanship. In order to be considered complete designers, architects need to be interested in how to make things, how all the different components function together. We express ourselves by working out the configuration of the various components and it is anathema to hand over control of this element to anyone else. It is our responsibility as architects to try to retain control wherever possible in order to safeguard good design and avoid unnecessary compromise – with its inevitable loss of quality.

At Wilkinson Eyre we promote an architecture which concerns itself (amongst many other things) with the surfaces, edges and lines of structural form. This means that the junctions between components require special care. It was Charles Eames who said 'When two materials come together, brother, watch out', and however fantastic the technological developments that have have taken place since then, the statement still holds true. It doesn't get any easier.

Today detailing has become a rather more complex issue than it was in Mies's

01 Detail drawing:
Isometric of wall and structure, South Gable, Stratford Market Depot, London UK. 1996 – Wilkinson Eyre Architects.

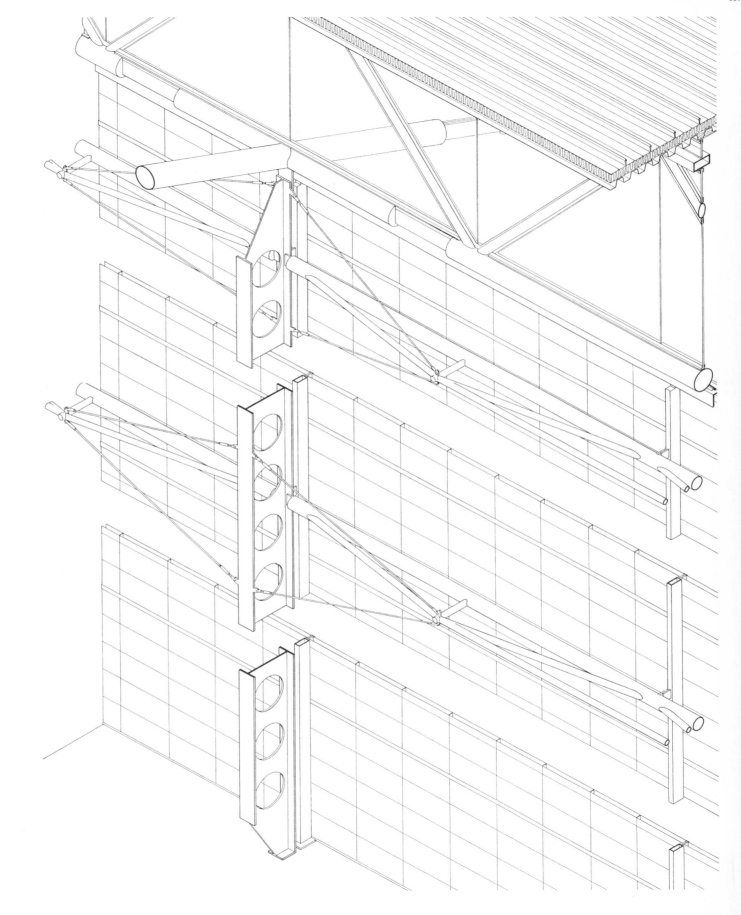

01

02

03

time. Some of the pioneering modern buildings were unfortunately prone to problems of durability and there can be little doubt that in the spirit of progress certain fundamental principles to do with weathering, moisture and thermal behaviour were overlooked (though I believe this tended to afflict lesser buildings). Now the issue of sustainability means that our concerns are more focused on energy usage, pollution and the renewability of materials. A building's thermal performance is becoming increasingly important as a more holistic approach to energy usage and broader environmental issues moves centre stage. Unfortunately, this means that some of the more beautifully simple details of yesteryear need more attention in the contemporary context. We have to work even harder in order to express what we want to in a building's architecture while at the same time making it perform and being economical with the use of precious materials.

I think it is interesting that often, while buildings are said to have been 'designed', the details are deemed to have been 'worked out'. It may seem a curious use of language because similar skills are needed for both; with detailing, however, the technical requirements mean there is less room for pure creative thought. The implication is somehow that the design of the building possesses a set of details and the architect is charged with finding out what they are. Obviously, as an argument, this line of thought is

idiosyncratic; nevertheless, there is some truth in the notion that there is a 'right' set of details that go with any given concept. To develop these details and go through the process of designing them successfully requires an ability to think in three dimensions about the assembly of a range of components and the various junctions between them. In a sense, at this stage the architect is undertaking a form of 'planning' akin to laying out a series of spaces, but working with and laying out a series of solid components of a different scale. There is something of the jigsaw about the process, the pieces being a mix of standard products and, where none exists, purpose-designed components. And at the same time there are all the other considerations – like keeping the weather out, preventing corrosion and constructing something durable.

The ultimate luxury would be to work out all the key details of a building in three dimensions using physical models, for only in this way can the physical appearance and the relationship between the various elements be fully explored. There are some architectural practices that are able to do this, and in particular I have great admiration for the work of Renzo Piano; he is unequalled in this respect. At Wilkinson Eyre details are formulated by being sketched out repeatedly on paper; we rely on vision and imagination and experience to predict what the end result will look like.

The most easily overlooked aspect of building design is that of tolerances. It is

01 Detail:
Rib base casting,
Stratford Regional Station,
London UK, 1999 –
Wilkinson Eyre Architects.
02 Detail:
Wind truss,
Stratford Regional Station,
London UK, 1999 –
Wilkinson Eyre Architects.
03 Detail:
Column head,
Stratford Market Depot,
London UK, 1997 –
Wilkinson Eyre Architects.
04 Detail:
Canopy support,
Dyson Headquarters,
Malmesbury UK, 1999 –
Wilkinson Eyre Architects.
05 Detail:
Front truss glazing,
Stratford Regional Station,
London UK, 1999 –
Wilkinson Eyre Architects.
06 Detail:
Diagrid roof structure,
Stratford Market Depot,
London UK, 1997 –
Wilkinson Eyre Architects
07 Detail:
Cable connections to
mast, South Quay
Footbridge, London UK,
1997 – Wilkinson Eyre
Architects.

04

05

06

07

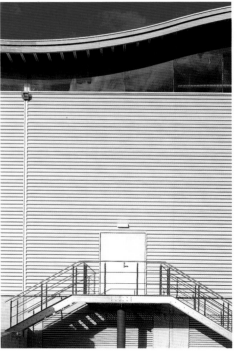

01

such an important consideration although, unless something goes wrong, it is not usually apparent in the finished work. Every component of a building is manufactured to a designated set of dimensions, whether on- or off-site, and each one can vary a certain amount. Such tolerances are set by what a human being can reasonably achieve, or by what is economically viable in a mechanical manufacturing process. The accuracy with which components can be placed into the works on site at installation varies too, depending both on the care taken by the person responsible for the placing and also on the positional accuracy of the component which it adjoins. The architectural detail drawing is thus a snapshot of where a series of components is ideally intended to be in space; in reality, each piece defines a space around itself within which it could actually end up. Naturally, an understanding of this moving three-dimensional jigsaw requires some special skills, both spatial and technical.

Dealing with tolerances seriously challenges the young architect in particular because he/she has been brought up in a technological age in which computers foster an illusion of accuracy. The temptation to believe in fractions of a millimetre is as alluring as the Sirens were to Aeneas. In fact, computers have had a hugely liberating effect in Wilkinson Eyre's offices and in our whole approach to design; they have encouraged freedom of thought and allow us to represent quite complex

forms possessing geometries that previously would have been preventatively difficult to draw. However, the precision that the computer offers is very seductive and being divorced from the reality of a building site can create serious problems. There is no better way to overcome these problems than spending time actually on a building site or at a manufacturing plant. Architects in our office are encouraged to gain hands-on experience wherever possible, following the detail right through from the original drawing – seeing how these representations are translated into reality on site.

Linked with the issue of accuracy of detailing and what is achievable on site is the real problem of diminishing craft skills. The number and availability of skilled site operatives in the various trades is definitely in decline, a shift that goes hand in hand with the drive, now becoming a necessity, towards off-site manufacture. The fabrication of building components is usually better undertaken in factory conditions by specialists. As a consequence new opportunities are opening up for the architect because the machines of manufacture, controlled by computers, are making it increasingly possible to make one-off components. At the same time the increasing specialization means that architects need to have a good understanding of what can be achieved, before defining the architectural intent as a series of profiles on drawings. To retain control one has to explore fully what is possible even if, ultimately, the

01 Detail:
Cladding and eaves,
Dyson Headquarters,
Malmesbury UK, 1999 –
Wilkinson Eyre Architects

The temptation to believe
in fractions of a millimetre is as
alluring as the Sirens were to
Aeneas.

fabricator is to produce the specialist design.

At Wilkinson Eyre we have been fortunate to be involved in a wide range of building and structure types. Some of these have involved large-scale and very public spaces which, because they are unheated, are not tied by the challenges of having to insulate everything. In these structures we have been able to enjoy a certain bold freedom in our treatment of detailing, a freedom that allows material connections to be made in a simple, sculptural way, displaying the properties of the respective materials and using them expressively. Stratford Station is the obvious example but many of the wide range of bridge projects we have undertaken display the same characteristics. Other buildings have demanded different approaches: the self-build aspect of the Princes Club Ski-Tow Pavilion imposed constraints on our design, for example, as did the economic considerations of large-scale industrial cladding in play at Dyson Headquarters and at Stratford Market Depot.

In all our projects the firm endeavours to achieve a consistency in the detailing. Nothing is left to chance. Every aspect of the building must be worked out and predicted. The very nature of the architecture relies on a disciplined approach. Though it is difficult to generalize, we look carefully at surfaces, thicknesses, modulation, contrasts in mass and lightness, simple framing and uncomplicated junctions between

materials. For us, 'Less' is more work. My admiration for Mies van der Rohe's work extends particularly to his economy of means. The intentions are always clear and, by considering very carefully what appears at the surfaces of construction, he emphasizes planar qualities, or lightness, or proportions. The profiles of his details are masterly in the way that the play of light and shade works to accentuate the qualities of the architecture. In this respect – in our approach to architecture – I believe that Wilkinson Eyre shares strong spiritual ties with Mies. Our concerns about proportions, planes, lines and expressing lightness are concerns that preoccupied Mies, though our overall conceptual approach to architecture embraces a greater vocabulary of form. Whether God has been anywhere near our details, only time will tell.

01 Detail:
Tensegrity supported
glazing, Stratford
Regional Station,
London UK, 1999 –
Wilkinson Eyre Architects

Portfolio
Sections x 05 / Projects x 27

01

Transport & Industrial

Stratford Market Depot

The Jubilee Line Extension is the most ambitious and exciting architectural scheme in Britain for decades and should shatter the popular image of commuting.
Naomi Stungo –
Observer / 21 / March / 99

Stratford Market Depot was one of the first buildings to be completed on the Jubilee Line Extension. It represents a pivotal point in the history of the practice, being its first major new-build project. The commission was awarded as a result of a design competition, which was won by Wilkinson Eyre in 1991, and construction was completed in 1996.

Both the Jubilee Line project and Wilkinson Eyre's involvement were widely publicized through early computer-generated images.

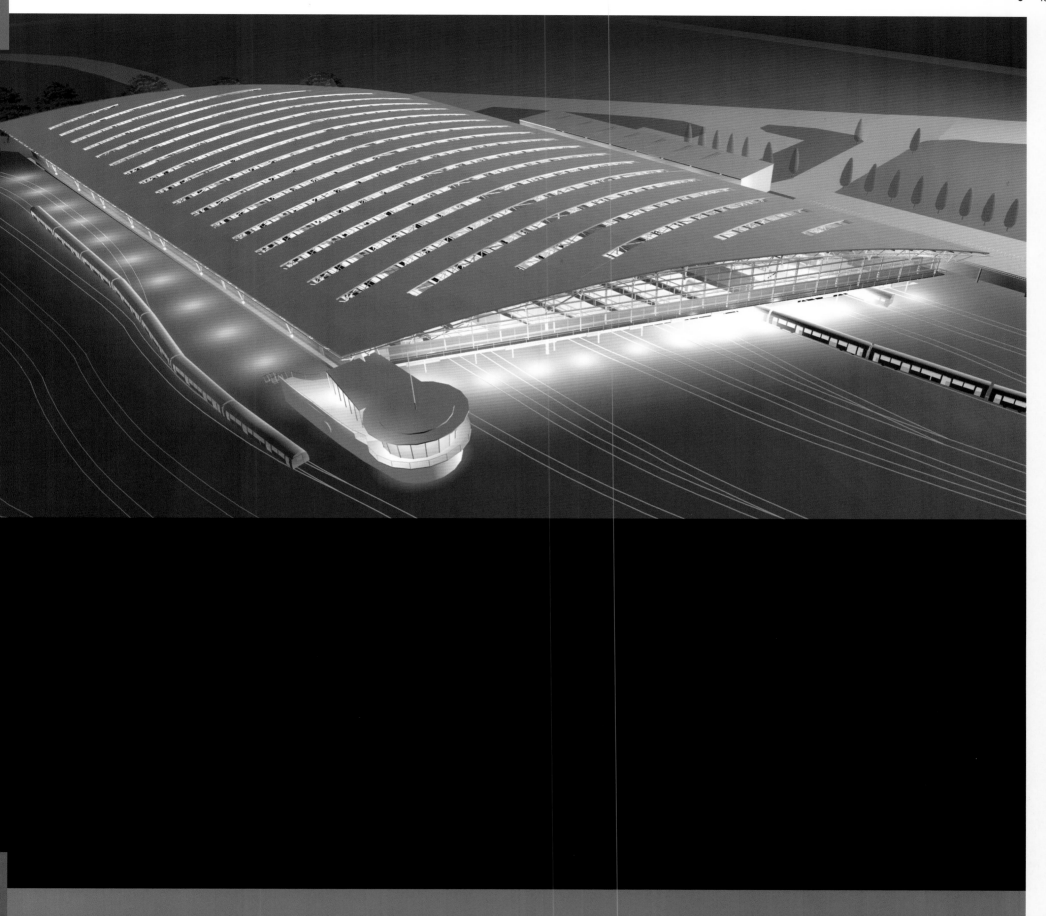

It will be a pleasure
to use while having all
the dignity of a modern
cathedral.
Colin Amery –
Financial Times /
27 / November / 97

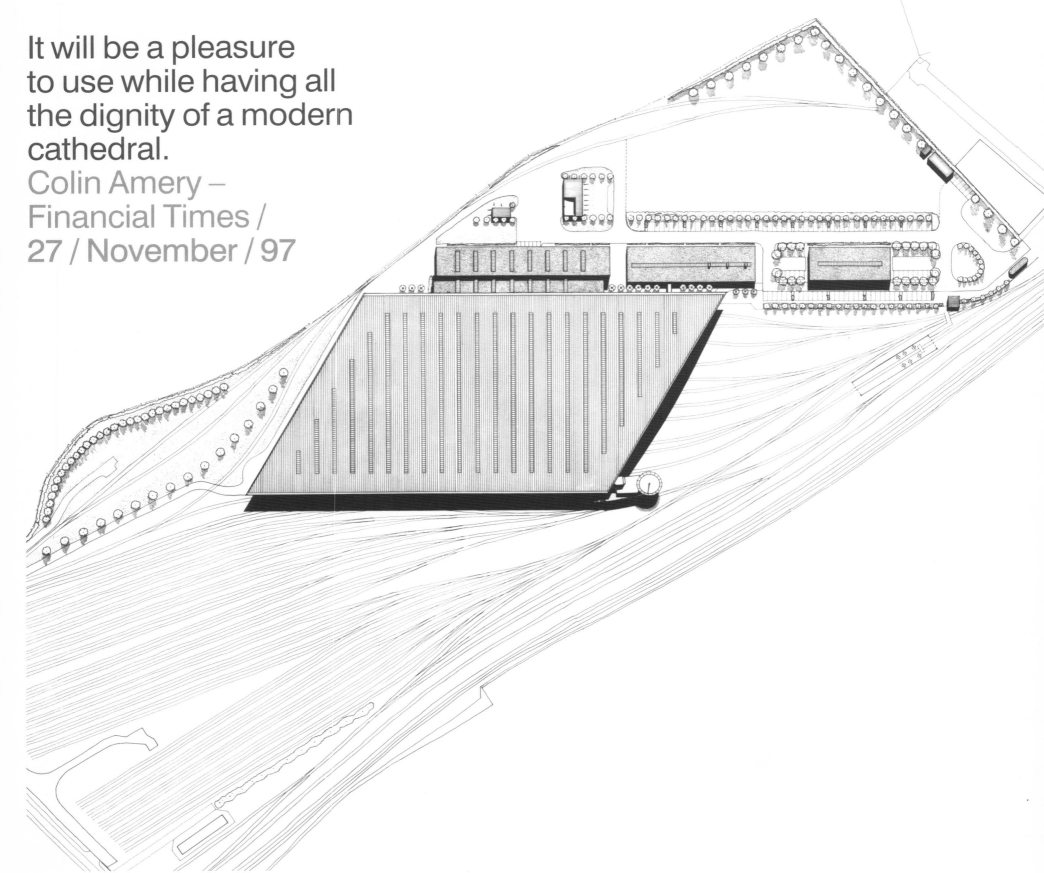

01◁ The design brief called for a depot for the new Jubilee Line Extension – to include maintenance and stabling facilities and associated ancillary buildings. High-quality design in keeping with the general ethos of the project was advocated in the commission.

A coherent approach to the layout of the site (11 hectares) was essential, given the different spatial characteristics of the varying accommodation. A 'supershed' was the ideal solution as the main train shed – an industrial building of considered design, providing flexible, durable space that would be enjoyable to work in.

The main train shed is the structural and visual focus of the complex, positioned to avoid the archaeological remains of Stratford Abbey at the far end of the site.

Safety requirements, which dictate that trains must enter the main shed on straight tracks, determined the track layout, which in turn determined the building's distinctive parallelogram shape – 100 metres wide by 190 metres long.

02◁ A line of subsidiary structures is arranged adjacent to the main shed. These align with the entrance and comprise (from the entrance): a traction substation, an office and amenity building, and workshops and stores. The Control Building is located on the blunt corner of the major shed.

03▷ The main shed contains 11 train 'roads', separated into bays by partial-height fire screens. There are three main bays to which the main spurs also relate: Heavy Lifting Shop (three roads), General Maintenance (five roads) and Cleaning (three roads). The last bay is further subdivided: two roads have platform access while one road is used for under-car cleaning.

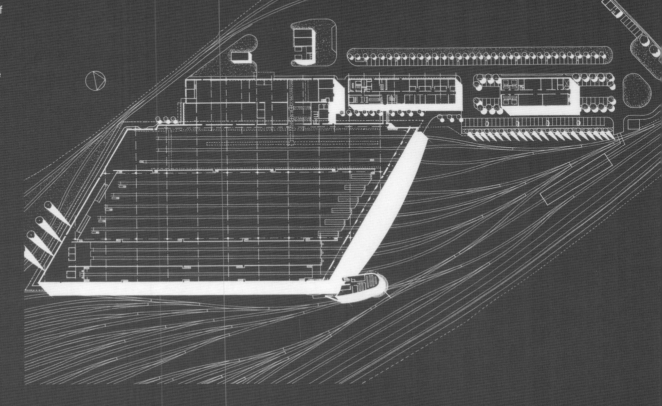

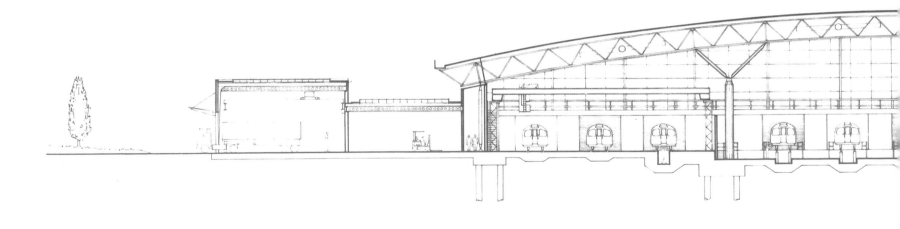

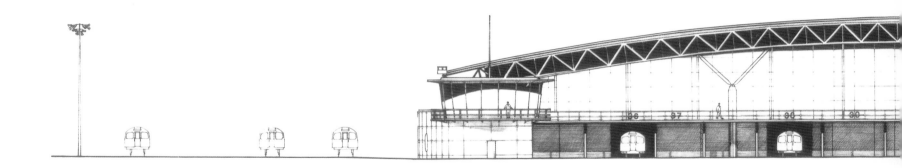

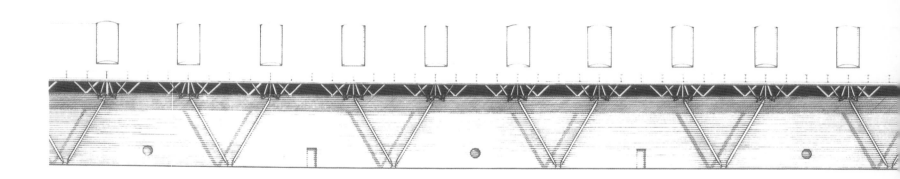

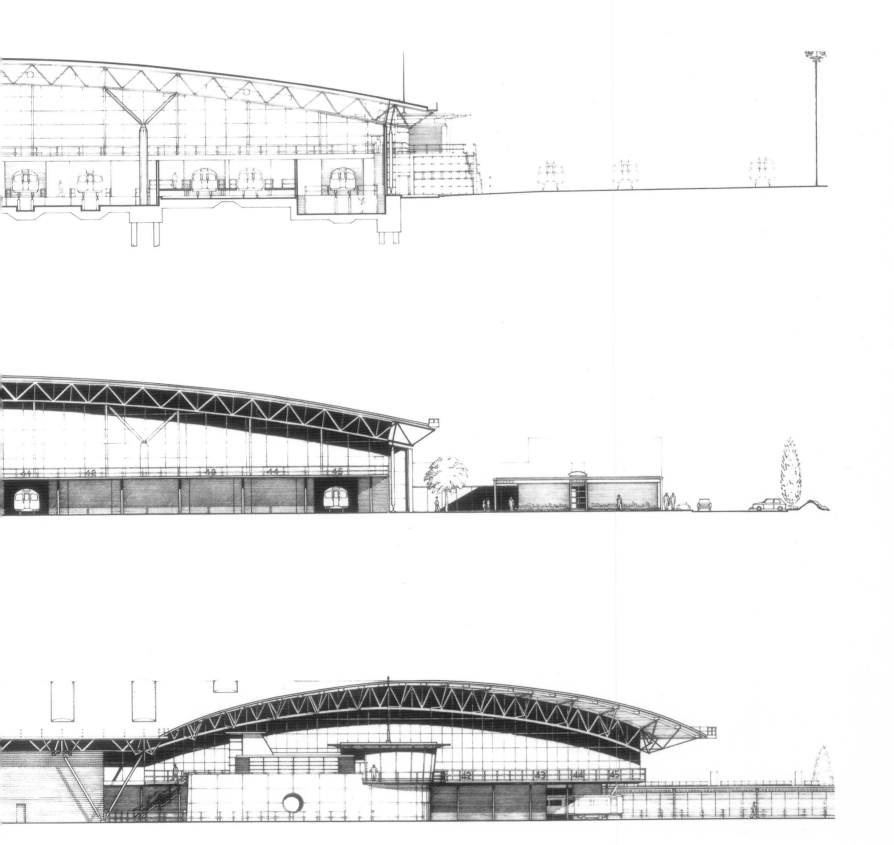

It is beautifully simple and architecturally exciting, with its single-span aluminium roof cut by diagonal slit windows like a giant slice of hi-tech apple pie. Train sheds have never been this glamorous.
Wallpaper* / Sept - Oct / 98

04▷The main shed required an economical long-span structure with plenty of good daylight and 8 metres of clear headroom above the tracks. The parallelogram shape suggested the use of a diagrid rather than a conventional orthogonal grid, and this generated the concept for a space-frame roof. The sides of the diamond-shaped bays are made up of trusses each 9 metres long x 2.4 metres deep. The lines of trusses are at 60 degrees to each other.

05◁Internally the space frame is supported by tree-like columns spreading the loads from the roof out onto the supports in bays of 18 x 40 metres.

06▷Longitudinal bracing on the side edges is provided by V-shaped columns.

07◁On the top the truss connections are plated at the node; at the bottom, to maintain clean lines and reduce complexity, they are plated away from the node.

08◁The structure was erected first, followed by the roof deck and finishes, in order to provide a dry area to cast the concrete floor slabs below.

09◁The roof of the main shed is clad with a self-finished aluminium standing-seam system; its gentle curve eliminates the need for internal gutters. Strips of roof lights are provided at intervals to offer good natural light and penetrations are restricted to these zones.

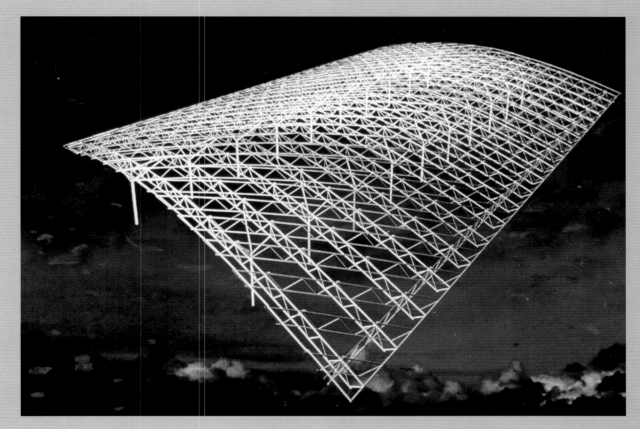

07

08

09

10 ▽ The principal space can house up to
11 trains. In some instances elevated on rails,
they are dwarfed by the scale of the shed but
the prevailing atmosphere of the working
environment is comfortable, calm, and well lit.

Bathed in daylight, and painted a very serendipitously chosen shade of green that somehow homogenizes every last strut, this beautiful roof is both as awesome as a cathedral, and as secret as a Pharoah's tomb.
Martin Pawley –
Architects' Journal / 14 - 21 / August / 97

Providing a particularly glamorous setting for resting trains, this bold and revolutionary depot 'takes glass into fluid curves without any ugly corseting'.
Nonie Niesewand – Independent / 3 / October / 98

11◁Both gable ends of the main shed emit light. The north elevation is fully glazed, providing excellent clear light for working conditions.

12◁The side elevations are similarly structured with cell-form posts and cable-restrained wind trusses.

13◁The south end is Kalwall-cladded to eliminate direct sunlight and reduce glare.

14▷The Kalwall cladding absorbs and diffuses light by day but glows when lit from within at night.

15 ◁ The composition at the junction between the gable end and side walls wraps around to express the principal elements of each elevation.

16 △ The overhanging roof articulates the separation from the walls and the space frame is expressed externally, with the diagonal arrangement referred to again in the 'V'-shaped columns.

17 ◁ Clerestory glazing both admits light around the perimeter and assists in reducing the bulk of the building by allowing the roof to 'float'.

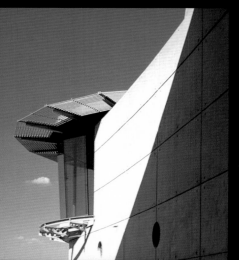

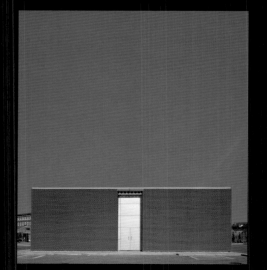

Location:	London UK
Commission date:	1991
Buildings completion date:	April 1996
Main building area:	19,000m²
Client:	London Underground Limited
Structural engineer:	Hyder Consulting Limited
Services engineer:	Hurley Palmer Partnership
Environmental concept design:	Loren Butt
Quantity surveyor:	Hyder Consulting Limited
Main contractor:	John Laing Limited
Awards:	Civic Trust Award	1998
	Financial Times Architecture at Work Award	1997
	RIBA Commercial Architecture Award	1997
	The Stirling Prize Shortlist	1997
	RIBA Regional Award	1997
	Structural Steelwork Design Award	1997
	British Construction Industry Building Award	1997

18▷Approaching trains are overseen from the Control Building to the east of the north elevation. An adjacent walkway over the train road entrance doors offers safe access to the shed across its entire width and links the Control Suite with the other support buildings.

19◁The Control Building is curvilinear in plan in order to fit between nearby train tracks. Construction is in white concrete cast in-situ, with panel joints expressed. The form of the Control Building acts as a counterpoint to the larger-scale main shed.

20▷The control room in the Control Building offers a clear view of all train movement.

21◁The office and amenity building is arranged with spaces off a central top-lit corridor.

22◁The abstract form of the traction substation, which provides power to the nearby section of the Jubilee Line, contrasts with that of the inhabited areas of the depot complex. The louvre cladding allows for ventilation.

Stratford Regional Station

Seamless, fluid, seemingly weightless, this beautiful, bold station built for London Underground Limited and the Stratford Development Partnership gives the area a new identity.
Independent / 11 / June / 99

Wilkinson Eyre won their second commission for the Jubilee Line Extension Project in August 1994: the comprehensive redevelopment of Stratford Railway Station. Roland Paoletti, JLE's chief architect, commissioned architects working in a contemporary idiom to design nine of the new stations, aiming to achieve a striking identity for the new line. Stratford Station is not only a terminus; it is also one of the few stations above ground.

The challenge for Wilkinson Eyre – after the Stratford Depot project – was to develop railway architecture in the heart of the public domain.

The new surface-level station concourse replaces the existing passageways and brings the Jubilee Line into Stratford. By addressing the town, a new public transport interchange achieves civic status.

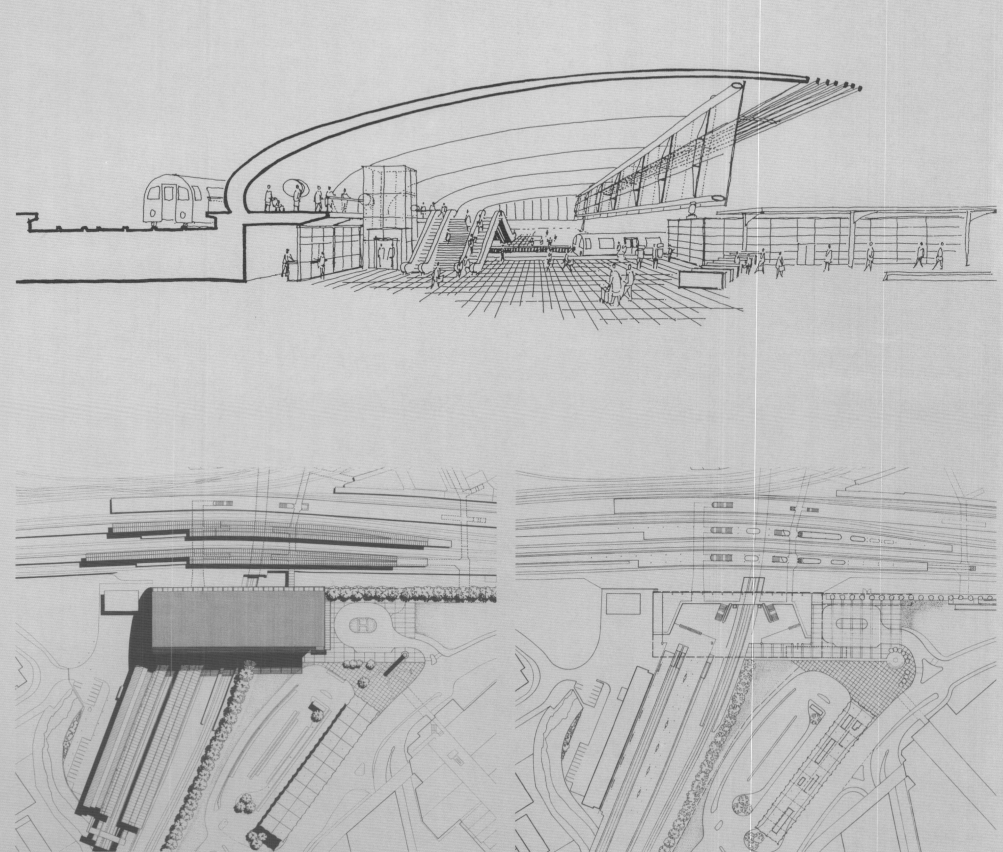

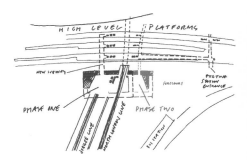

01 ◁ The concept evolved around the decision to develop a roof structure and concourse with a public face that looks outwards rather than inwards, while endeavouring to resolve at the same time a circulation puzzle and so ease interchange between several rail services.

02 ▷ A series of rail lines and platforms already existed, running east-west at about 5 metres above ground level, while the North London Line passes north-south through the middle of the station at ground level and separates the new Jubilee Line platforms from the street entrance.

The primary components of the project were therefore firstly, an interchange concourse on two levels traversing the North London Line and secondly, a new jacked-box subway under the existing high-level platforms to facilitate direct interchange with the Jubilee Line.

03 ◁ The complex circulation requirements are resolved within a single-volume space.

04 △ In addition to the interchange complexities, the project design also had to accommodate construction in two phases: the first to allow for the Jubilee Line and a second to provide a ticket hall with direct street access, replacing the previous obscure and convoluted arrangements. Although the design did take phasing into account, the construction of the whole station was ultimately carried out in a single phase, as funding for the entire project became available prior to the commencement of work on site in April 1996.

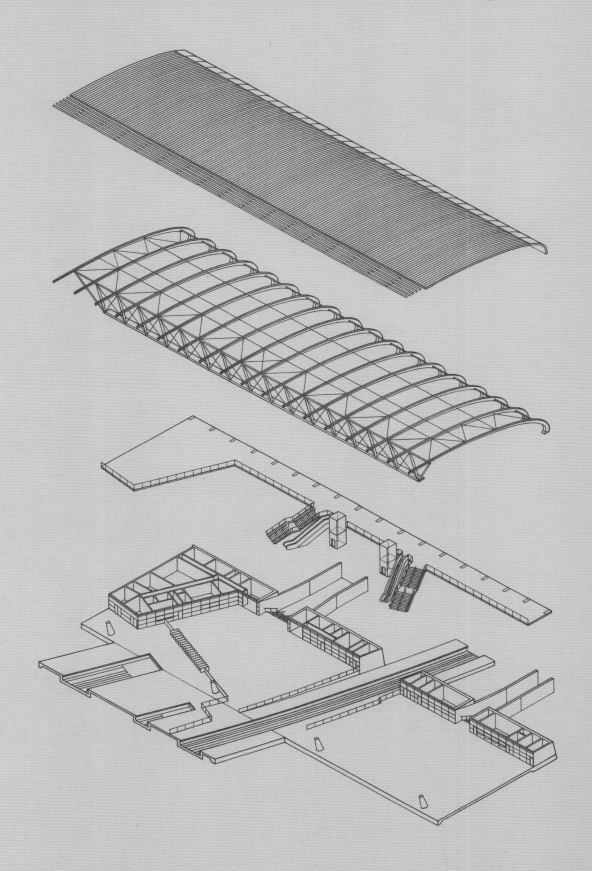

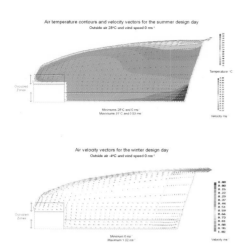

Air temperature contours and velocity vectors for the summer design day
Outside air 28°C and wind speed 0 ms⁻¹

Air velocity vectors for the winter design day
Outside air -4°C and wind speed 0 ms⁻¹

05 ▽ The form of the building is expressed as a curved roof springing from an upper-level walkway, geometrically defined as a sector of an ellipse in section.

06 ◁ The apparently simple form of the building serves a number of separate purposes:
– it shows a dramatic public face to the town;
– being south-facing, the shaded glazing produces good-quality light;
– it provides a passive ventilation system: the whole of the roof void is used as a thermal flue drawing air across the concourse (verified by computer fluid-dynamics analysis) ;
– the uninterrupted roof soffit acts as a reflector for artificial light, bouncing it back to illuminate the floor;
– it provides an acoustic ceiling.

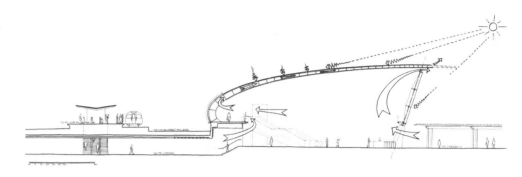

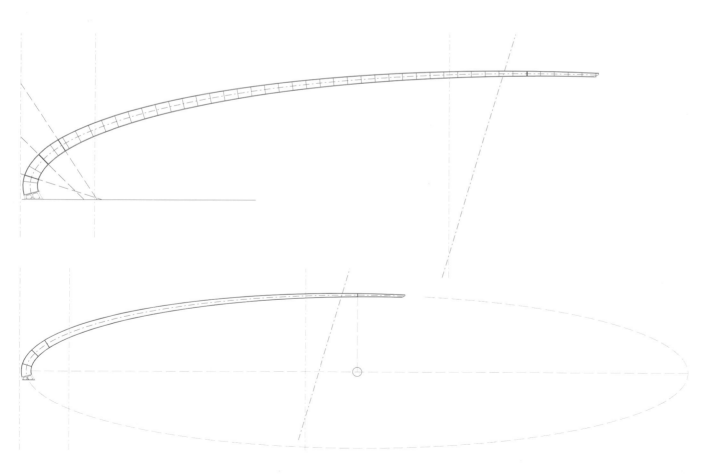

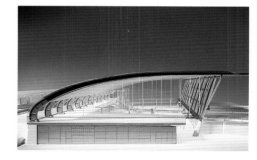

It all seems so simple at first sight. But to create the clarity of the space, and allow its very complex interconnections, to make a silk purse out of a sow's ear of a site, and to relate structure and climate control in such a satisfactory way shows architectural and engineering skills of a very high order.
Peter Davey –
Architectural Review / May / 99

07 △ On the north side of the building a curved facade faces a zone reserved for the CrossRail Project; behind it are the existing Central Line platforms. Fritting to the glass provides shade for commuters crossing the North London Line via the high-level walkway inside.

08 ▷ Plated-steel ribs, seen here under construction, reach out from the high-level walkway to support and shape the concourse roof. Each rib has a cast base which is bolted down using high-strength macalloy bars.

Wilkinson Eyre has designed an engineering tour de force using steel as expressively as Gustave Eiffel. The huge oversailing roof is supported on sickle-shaped steel beams that shoot out to form a canopy on the other side.
Marcus Binney –
The Times / 2 / March / 99

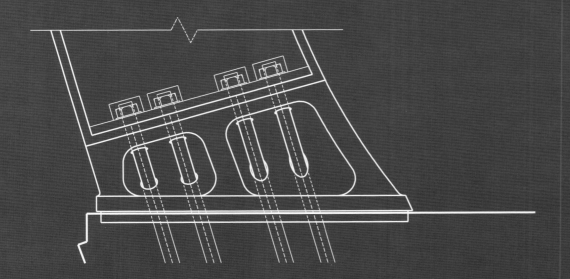

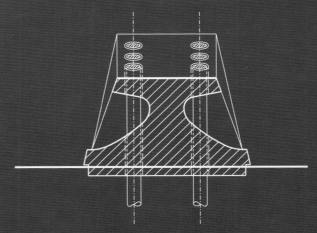

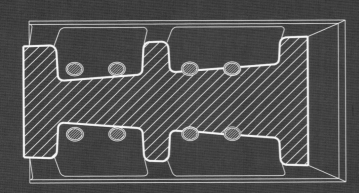

The form maximizes natural lighting and provides an uplifting environment more akin to sea ports than underground stations.
Nicola Turner – World Architecture / June / 99

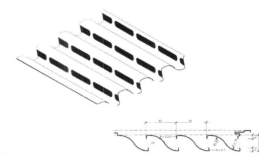

09◁ The concourse ceiling is lined with a purpose-made ribbed aluminium extrusion that has also been perforated in order to be acoustically absorbent. The profile is designed to reflect artificial light down onto the concourse floor.

10▷ The uplighting of the ceiling, which is free from suspended fittings or equipment, lends an ethereal quality to the space, both internally and externally.

11△ The front truss (south elevation) of the building is inclined at 11 degrees to the vertical, which introduces a visual dynamic to the space as well as effecting reflections. The truss, which is 8 metres deep, spans three bays, each measuring 30 metres. One bay spans the end of the Jubilee Line platforms, a second bay spans the North London Line, and the third defines the entrance.

12◁ Glazing is supported by cable trusses and bolted connections through the glass. A filigree of very fine members acts as a counterpoint to the smooth and uninterrupted curvature and form of the concourse's soffit.

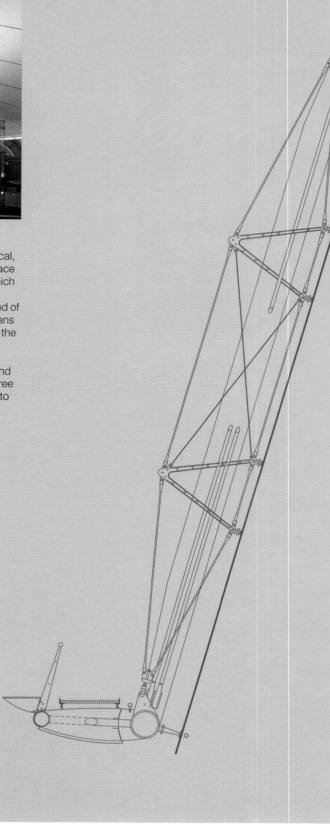

13 ▽ The front elevation is shaded externally at a high level by projecting louvres, which form a continuation of the roofline.

14 ▷ The bottom edge of the glazing includes a beam which acts as a maintenance walkway, giving access to cleaning rails, uplighters for the concourse soffit, and station equipment.

13

14

15 △ Details of the interfaces between glass facades, steelwork and concrete support columns are carefully considered.

16 ◁ Junctions between the members in the front truss assembly are made with precision castings (seen under construction here).

17 ◁ Internally the concourse resembles closely the computer-generated images produced at the start of the project.

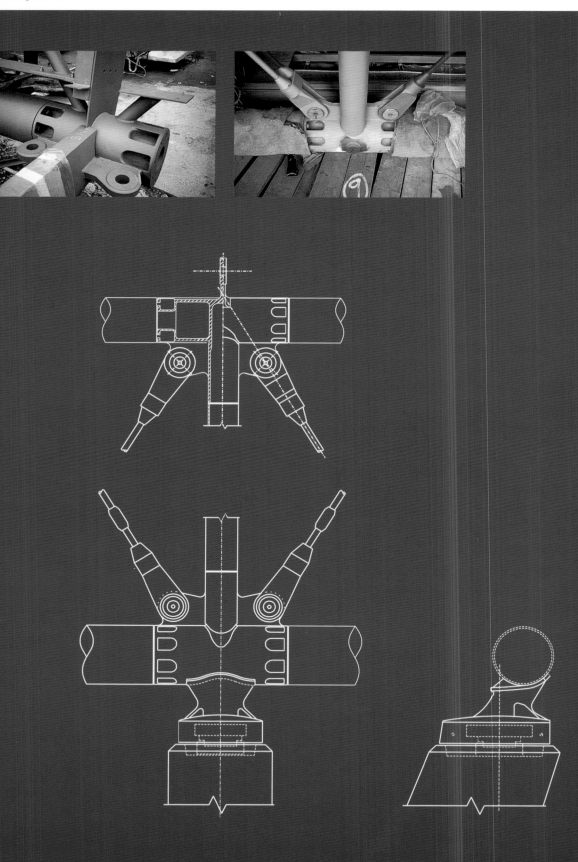

15

16

Inside the station, awesome heights and a sense of spaciousness make it almost cathedral-like, without dwarfing the commuters.
Independent / 11 / June / 99

18◁The station forecourt forms a plaza which links the bus station and vehicle set-down areas with the commercial centre of Stratford.

19▷The entrance to the station is at the eastern end under a low-level canopy which incorporates station signage.

20▷At night the station glows in the townscape, providing a bright, welcoming aspect.

Location:	London UK
Commission date:	1994
Completion date:	May 1999
Building area:	4,000m²
Client:	London Underground Limited,
	Stratford Development Partnership Limited,
	London Borough of Newham
Structural / Services /	
Highways & Traffic engineer /	
Landscape consultant:	Hyder Consulting Limited
Environmental concept design:	Loren Butt
Civil engineer:	Ove Arup & Partners
Quantity surveyor:	Franklin & Andrews
Awards:	Civic Trust Award 2000
	Civic Trust Special Award for Urban Design
	(in association with the Jubilee Line Extension) 2000
	Structural Special Award 2000
	RIBA Civic and Community Architecture Award 1999
	The Stirling Prize Shortlist 1999
	RIBA Regional Award 1999
	Aluminium Imagination Architectural
	Award for Extruded Aluminium 1999
	Design Council Millennium 'Product' Award 1999
	Structural Steelwork Design Award Commendation 1999
	Concrete Society Award Commendation 1999
	British Construction Industry Award Commendation 1999

This extraordinary form-meets-function building not only sets exemplary standards in public architecture but it is a highly visible landmark within the local environment. The mere sight of this extraordinary building puts a spring into the step and sends out a message of hope to those living within, or passing through, this 'borough with a future'.
Roland Paoletti –
Client / London Underground Limited

CrossRail Liverpool Street

01△ The Liverpool Street Arcade Ticket Hall was designed by Wilkinson Eyre for the CrossRail Project in 1992-93. The proposals for the station, which straddles the existing Metropolitan and Circle Line platforms, were fully designed ready for tender and construction.

The proposals included a 9,290-square-metre air-rights development which received planning consent in April 1994.

02◁ The floor space at ground-floor level is almost entirely occupied by a dual-entry ticket hall.

03▷ Escalators lead up to a reception area at first-floor level, and the office floors above comprise regular, rectilinear spaces, accessed by a sky lobby.

04△Immediately below ground level the site is extremely tightly constrained by platforms and tracks, and below that by the Central Line, CrossRail and Post Office railway tunnels.

A section was developed which, by using an arrangement of raking columns, obviated the need for a transfer structure.

05△A 'crash' slab separates the operational areas from the development above. This is strengthened and supported by an arrangement of pre-cast concrete struts and beams, forming a sculpted skeletal framework for the ceiling soffit of the ticket hall.

06△The raking structure is expressed externally on the western elevation to mark the entrance to the public areas. A trochoidal tower of conference rooms within the sky lobby marks the corner between Liverpool Street and Old Broad Street.

Location:	London UK
Commission date:	1992
Building area:	13,000m²
Client:	London Underground Limited & London Transport Property
Structural engineer:	W.A. Fairhurst Partners
Services engineer:	MPBL and Mott McDonald
Quantity surveyor:	Currie and Brown

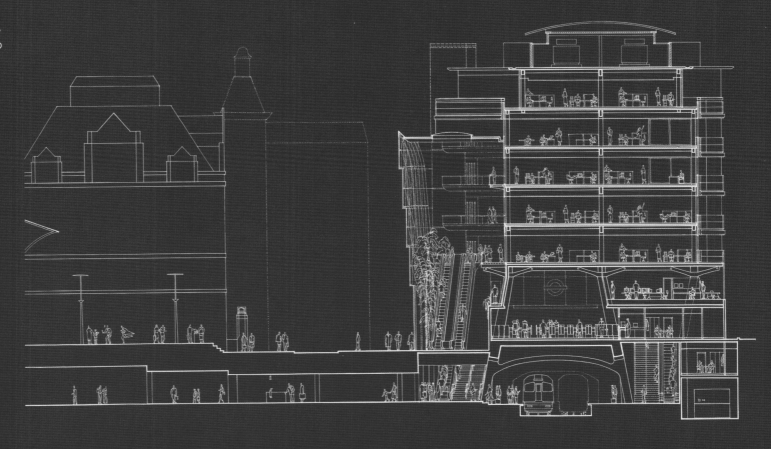

05

04

06

Dyson Headquarters

The new factory is a lithe structure, shot through with a sense of energy and movement.
Jonathan Glancey –
Guardian / 26 / October / 98

It was in 1994 that engineer Tony Hunt introduced Wilkinson Eyre to James Dyson. Following a limited competition the practice was asked to prepare designs for a new factory in Chippenham. Sales of the bagless vacuum cleaner exploded in the mid-1990s so that by the time planning permission had been granted, the scale of the original scheme – covering some 6,000 square metres – was already too small.

In 1995 a replacement site was found in Malmesbury: the Linolite factory, with a plot alongside. Wilkinson Eyre was asked to design a master plan for its development.

01▷The factory needed to embrace an extensive range of uses: research and development, including facilities for the rigorous testing of the vacuum cleaners; manufacturing and distribution; offices for management functions; and, of course, storage. The design needed to optimize the site's existing accommodation, while developing flexibility for future expansion.

The master plan for the site allows for the existing building to be expanded by 2,500 square metres with a new development alongside of 25,000 square metres – to be constructed in phases.

A glass pavilion placed between the two buildings not only provides the main entrance to both but also acts as a focal point for the site. The area behind has been landscaped to provide a series of recreational courtyards. A car-parking area is located at the front, amongst trees; a ring road serves the truck-loading bays at the back.

02▽The buildings are planned with design studios and offices on the north side – on two levels behind a fully glazed facade. The production, assembly, storage and distribution functions are housed behind them to the south.

Phasing was planned in footprints of 5,000 square metres, but because of demands on space, the whole development was completed by the same contractor on a rolling programme over two years.

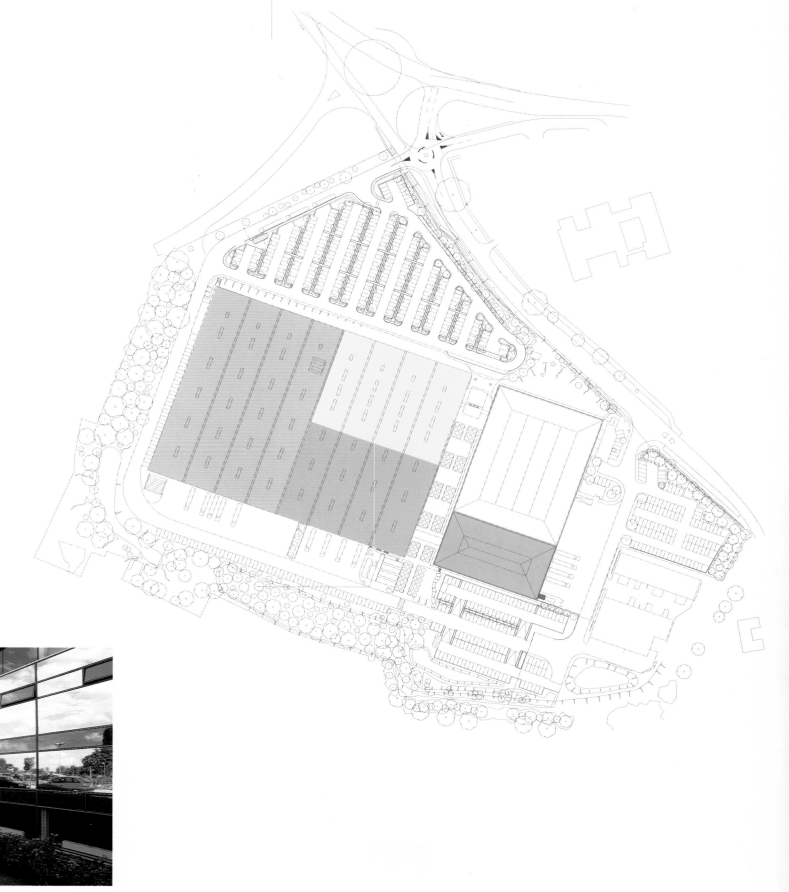

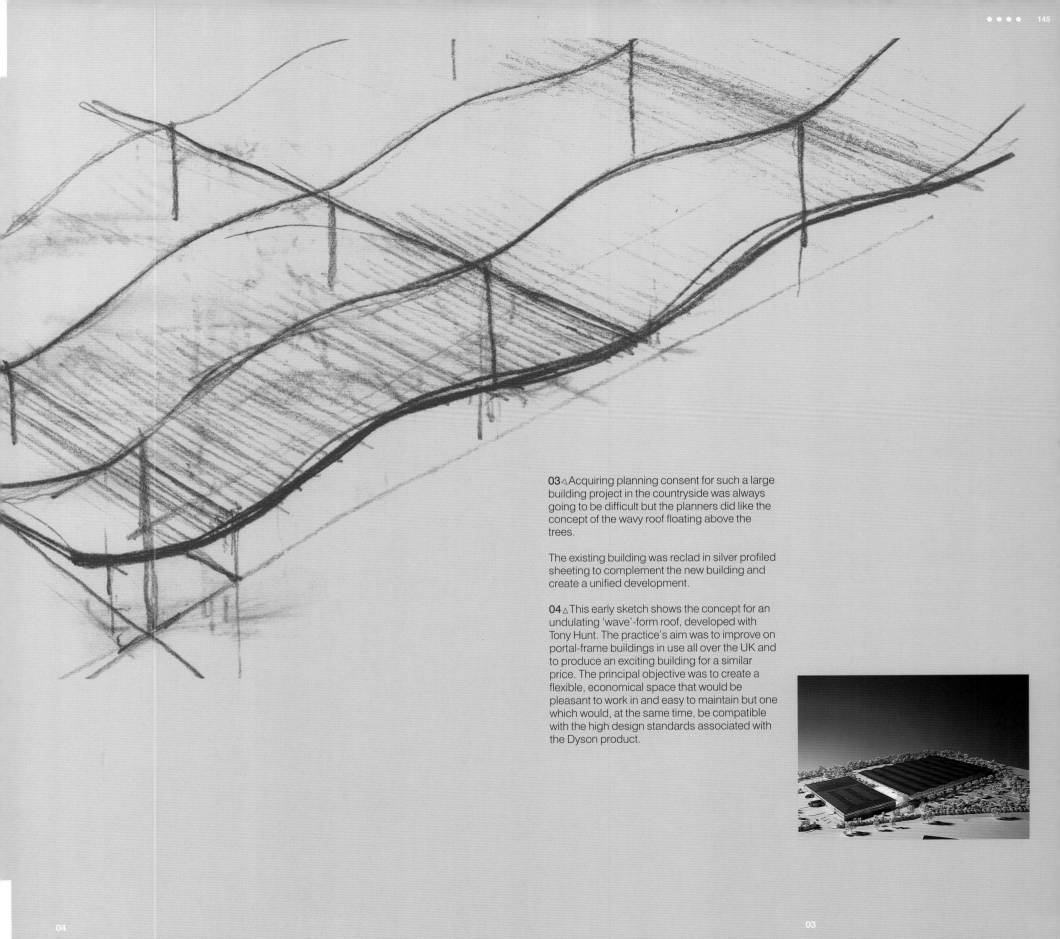

03△ Acquiring planning consent for such a large building project in the countryside was always going to be difficult but the planners did like the concept of the wavy roof floating above the trees.

The existing building was reclad in silver profiled sheeting to complement the new building and create a unified development.

04△ This early sketch shows the concept for an undulating 'wave'-form roof, developed with Tony Hunt. The practice's aim was to improve on portal-frame buildings in use all over the UK and to produce an exciting building for a similar price. The principal objective was to create a flexible, economical space that would be pleasant to work in and easy to maintain but one which would, at the same time, be compatible with the high design standards associated with the Dyson product.

05▷The architecture is derived from a clear expression of the structure and a limited palette of construction materials. The elevations are designed as repetitions of a standard module that relates to the 10 x 20-metre structural grid. On the north elevation, a curtain walling system of extruded aluminium is faced with silicone-jointed, frameless double-glazed panels on a 3.3-metre module with opening lights at eye level. The other elevations comprise 10-metre bays of horizontally mounted, sinusoidal, profiled-steel sheeting, with a silver PVF2 finish up to the clerestory glazing line, which separates it from the wavy roof plane.

06▷The design concept is based on structural simplicity, underpinned by flexibility for change and ease of expansion.

07▷The cut-away isometric diagram shows details of the main elements of construction: the curtain walling, profiled sheeting, clerestory glazing, roof structure at the eaves and the decking.

08◁The site's countryside location in Malmesbury and the fragile relationship between the industrial building type and its rural surroundings required sensitive treatment. Badgers, great-crested newts, slowworms and wild orchids all shared the site and careful management was essential to ensure that the delicate natural balance was not disturbed.

09◁The structural frame of the main building was designed to facilitate swift, economic construction. Standard universal beams were rolled to the required radius and reversed to create the wavy form. The total weight of structural steel, including columns and bracing, amounts to 25 kilograms per square metre – considerably less than a conventional structure.

10◁Long-span decking sheets maintained the speed and simplicity of construction. Spans of 10 metres between frames are bridged by steel decking (200 millimetres deep), providing a diaphragm action within the plane of the roof.

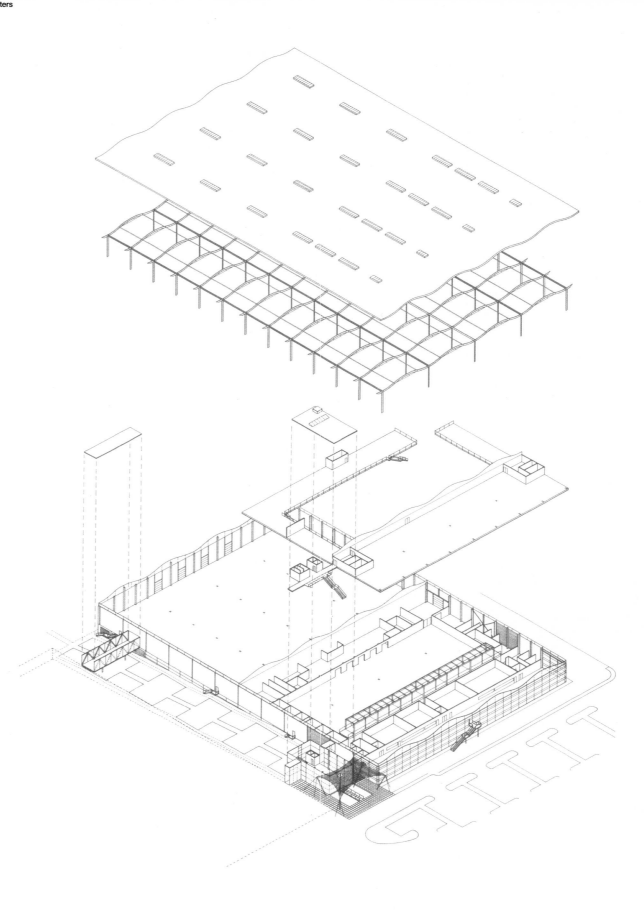

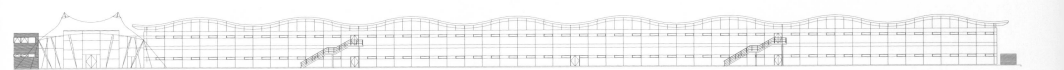

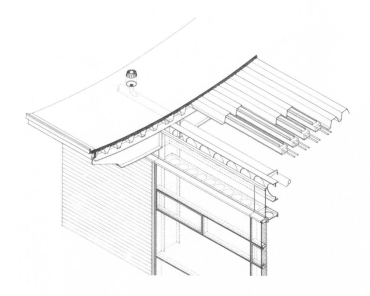

It wasn't a matter of imposing a concept, but of addressing a series of problems and understanding the needs of the users. We wanted to produce a complex of buildings which would hang together.
Chris Wilkinson

05   07   08   09   10

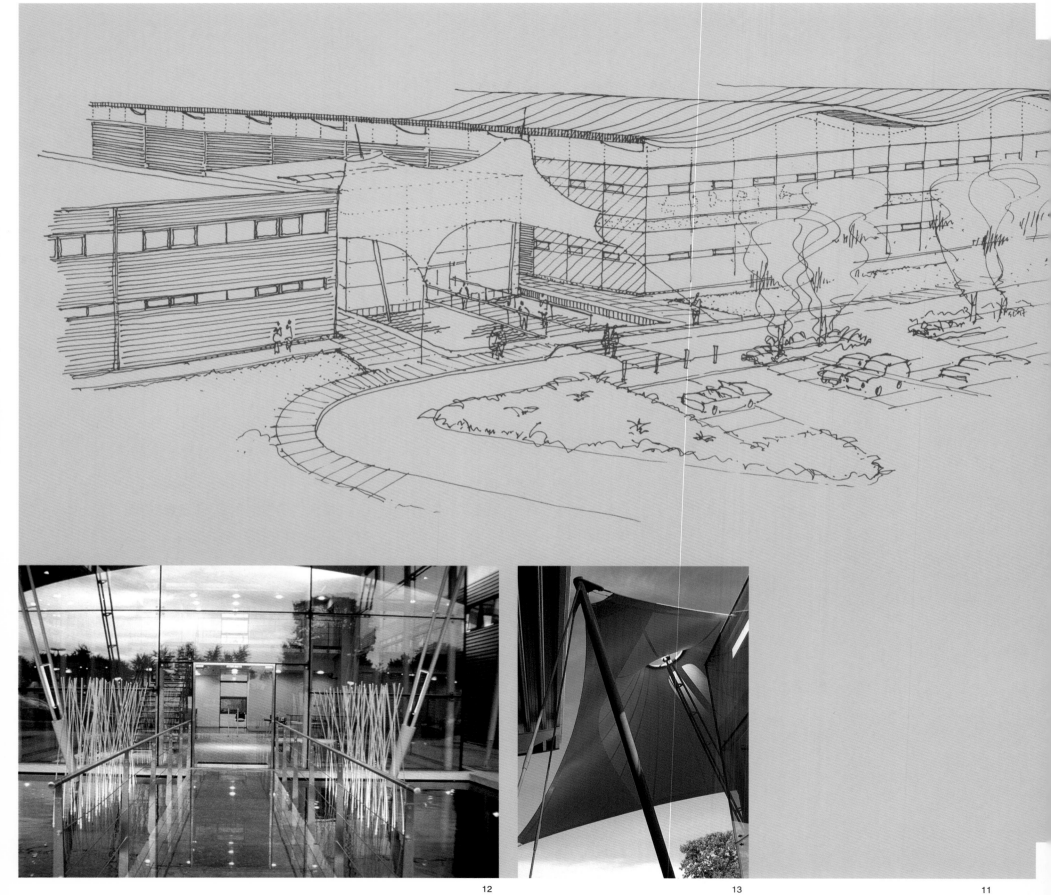

11 ▷ The entrance provides both a visual and a physical link between the new and existing buildings. A crystalline transparent double cube, it contrasts with the adjoining big sheds and draws in approaching visitors.

12 ◁ Leading to the entrance, a glass and stainless-steel bridge crosses a purple pool with beds of 'light reeds' on either side that sway in the wind.

The 'light reeds' sculpture by Diana Edmunds is composed of acrylic rods bedded in granite and lit by fibre optics.

13 ◁ The details of the raking steel masts have been designed to appear light and elegant.

14 ▷ The natural stone, glass, steel and fabric which give the entrance area its identity are combined to create a composition of flowing forms.

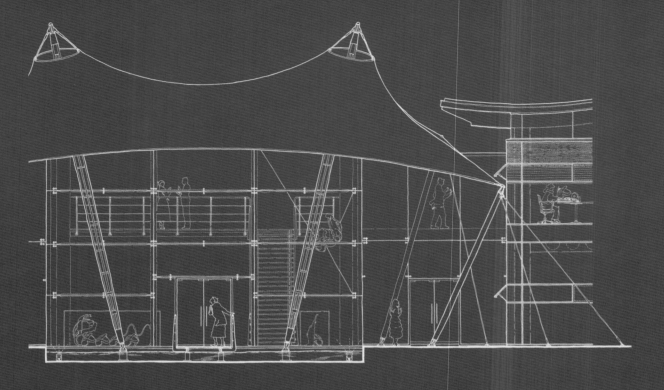

15 ▷ A lightweight membrane structure provides both a visual marker and a canopy for the entrance.

16 ◁ The canopy's double curvature relates to the waves of the main roof.

17 ▽ The interior of the entrance acts as a reception space and as a display area for the Dyson product range. Clear links to the rest of the building are also visible from this point, giving an immediate sense of place and a reference for orientation.

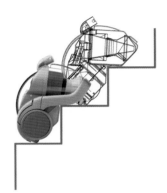

The designers and engineers aim to design everything flawlessly. This is apparent in the working environment as much as in the product. Wilkinson Eyre's new building is as humanely efficient as the vacuum cleaners made inside.
Tom Dyckhoff –
Design - Journal of the Design Council / Autumn / 98

18▷The same structure and materials are used throughout the main building, for all types of space from production to office. The wave form of the roof gives the building a strong visual identity. The decking is adapted for each interior space as appropriate.

Runs for main services are supported on specially designed ladders attached to the structural beams, feeding off as required to specific locations.

19▽Translucent smoke vents along the 'crest'of the waves introduce daylight into the deep plan spaces.

20▷Office areas have chilled beams recessed into the roof deck to provide comfort cooling – with 100 per cent fresh air.

21▷The fully glazed north facade admits daylight to the offices and meeting rooms.

22 △ A series of landscaped courtyards between the buildings provides break-out space for the users.

23 △ Once the planting has matured, Peter Burke's sculptures will inhabit the landscaped courtyards.

24 ▷ Access to the courtyards is under a glazed bridge, which links the buildings and allows the traffic of goods, fork-lift trucks and staff.

22
23

24

25△ The exterior skin of the building comprises three main components: the roof, wall cladding and glazing. A single-ply membrane covers the wave form of the roof.

26▷ The north elevation is fully glazed, not only providing the building with a.dramatic public front but also ensuring well-lit work spaces behind.

27▷ All other elevations are clad with profiled-steel sheeting. A continuous glazed clerestory beneath the roof plane visually separates the roof from the wall cladding and also provides the interior spaces with daylight.

Painted in lilac, the structure complements the silver PVF2 paint finish of the roof deck and wall cladding.

28▷ To minimize any bulkiness of appearance, the profiled steel sheeting is divided into modular bays.

Wilkinson Eyre have engineered a flexible space, their 'supershed', with which Dyson can do what he wishes … it functions as a slick machine creating a creative and contented workforce.
Tom Dyckhoff –
Design - Journal of the Design Council / Autumn / 98

James Dyson regards his new headquarters building as an asset on many levels. Not only does the building work extremely well; it also helps to 'sell' the company to potential employees. 'We are competing for the very best engineering and computer science graduates,' says Dyson. 'The image of the building undoubtedly helps.'
Kenneth Powell – Architects' Journal / 3 -10 / December / 98

Location:	Malmesbury, Wiltshire UK
Commission date:	1996
Completion date:	August 1999
Site area:	Refurbishment 10,000m²/ New building 22,500m²
Client:	Dyson Appliances Limited
Structural engineer:	Anthony Hunt Associates
Quantity surveyor:	Leeson Associates
Main contractor:	Kier Western
Commissioned artist:	Diana Edmunds
Awards:	Civic Trust Award Commendation 1999
	Royal Fine Art Commission Trust /
	BSB Building of the Year Award Commendation 1999

02

Bridges

South Quay Footbridge

At last, Docklands gets some
well-designed infrastructure.
Time Out / 22 - 29 / July / 98

South Quay Footbridge was the first of a series
of bridge projects undertaken by Wilkinson Eyre
Architects.

The bridge forms part of a programme of
infrastructure development undertaken by the
London Docklands Development Corporation
to improve pedestrian connections in the
Docks. Comprising nine bridge projects
procured through design competitions, the
series marked the beginnings of a renaissance
of popular interest in bridge design in the UK
and a resurgence in the widespread
involvement of architects.

The South Quay bridge is the most visible of
these projects, spanning the wide stretch of
water between South Quay and Heron Quays
and Canary Wharf beyond.

01△With the rapid rate of change taking place in the area, a complex brief required the bridge to be built in temporary form, in order that it could be shortened and relocated later to an adjacent location.

The dock was to be narrowed by reclaiming land and the revised bridge was then to be incorporated into the Canary Wharf master plan by placing it axially to the centrepiece building. A further requirement dictated that the bridge must open to allow boats to pass through the dock.

A single idea addresses and turns to advantage the complex demands of the brief. The bridge takes the form of an S-shaped deck with canted masts and stay cables. It has two identical curved sections: onepart is fixed; the other can swing to allow boats to pass.

02▷Formally, the solution arises from a geometric reaction to the constraints of the brief: the bridge is set diagonally across the dock, starting at the temporary northern landing and ending near the intended final southern landing. The southern half, operational as a swing-opening bridge, can slew into its new position orthogonal to the dock without the need for constructional relocation. Careful positioning of the pivot point allows the bridge geometry to satisfy the new dock width whilst maintaining the bridge as two equal halves. The northern half can be removed and relocated elsewhere as necessary in the final configuration.

03△Development of the plan form into an S-shape allowed the construction of two identical bridge sections, joined to form one sinuous composition, shown here in the competition model. The curve of each section allows for a cantilevered deck, supported from a central raking mast by stay cables.

04◁Hogarth's *Analysis of Beauty* of 1753 compares and analyses the form of a variety of curves; the one deemed by the artist to be the most beautiful corresponds closely to the geometry of the South Quay bridge.

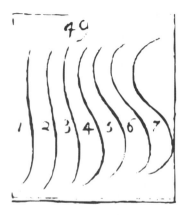

01

04

03

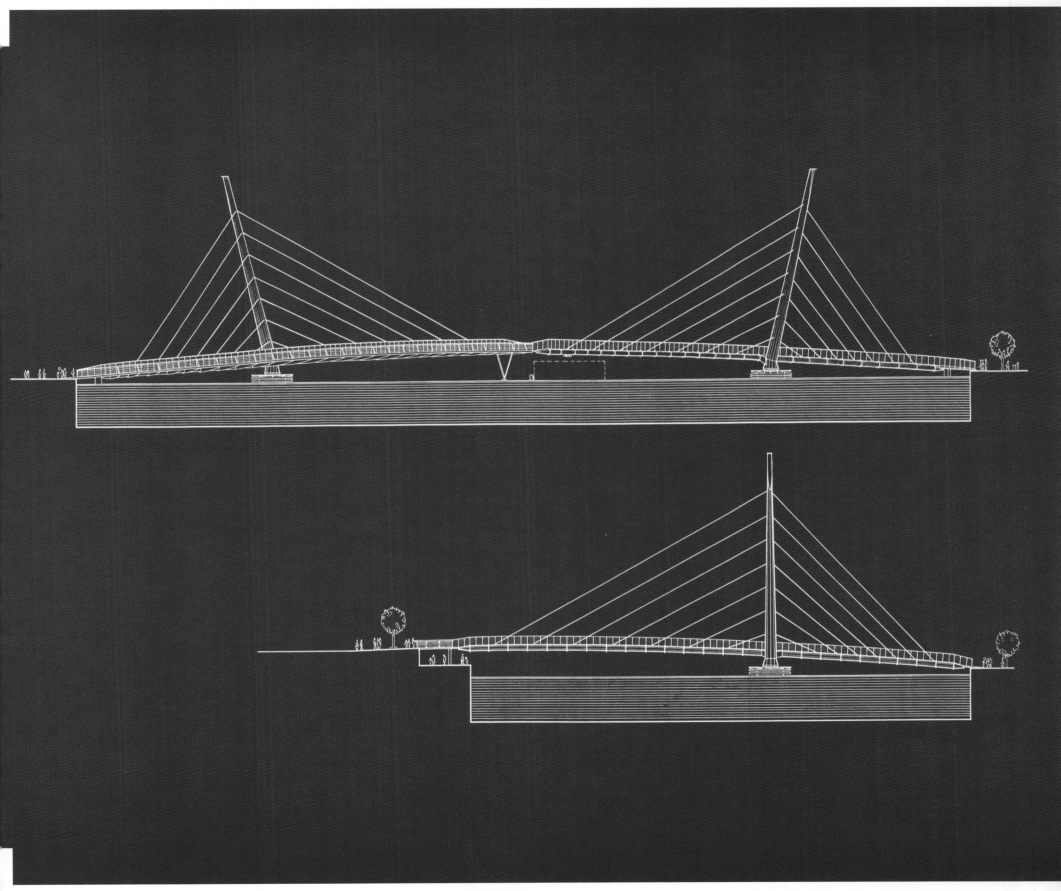

Its sinuous twists seem to invite you to follow dreams...
Evening Standard / 25 / January / 99

05 ◁ The plan shows the bridge in the short term (black), the long term (red) and open (blue).

06 ▽ The curve and countercurve of the bridge distinguishes it, both as a form and as an experience, from the rigidity of the urban grid, its sinuous shape and raking masts providing a visual contrast to the mass of the surrounding architecture.

07 ▷ People call the bridge 'the yellow brick road' because it has an appealing way of drawing pedestrians along it. Not being able to see one end from the other builds up a sense of mystery and emphasizes this magnetic attraction.

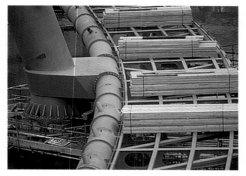

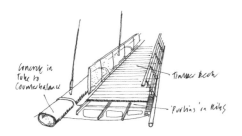

08◁The deck is clad in European oak, a material familiar in the English maritime environment. As the timber matures, its soft honey tone turns to a silver hue, which is entirely in keeping with the neutral scheme of the structure. Combining grand gesture and an attention to detail on a human scale, the bridge celebrates the act of crossing, while the deck provides an environment that invites lingering as much as movement.

09△The planks are fixed so that they lie parallel to the dock: a constant, albeit subconscious, reminder for the pedestrian of the bridge deck's geometric relationship with the urban grid.

10△The deck cantilevers from a cable-supported torsion beam via a series of tapering ribs. The composition implies a directional focus to the cross section which is reinforced by the provision of differing parapet conditions on either side of the deck

11▷The pedestrian is protected from prevailing winds by a man-made hedge. The perforated metal screen is designed to mimic the way a natural hedge breaks down and distributes heavy gusts.

12◁Shaped in a form which bows towards the deck, the high – and at acute angles, opaque – screen lends a sense of enclosure to the environment and increases the pull-across effect of the deck geometry.

13▽At obtuse angles the screen appears much more transparent than its 50 per cent open perforation would suggest, relinquishing the views that were hidden and giving impetus for halts in the journey across.

14△An extruded, elliptical aluminium rail contains continuous concealed lighting provision for the deck so that at night, while the mast and cables are lit up from the spine beam below, the deck is lit without revealing the source of its illumination. The size of the rail makes it a lean-rail, rather than a handrail, encouraging the pedestrian to break the journey.

15◁A low, raking balustrade on the outer edge of the deck gives open views to the dock and provides a counterbalance to the closed aesthetic of the screen. Its form and relative lightness combine to emphasize its position on the cantilevered edge of the structure.

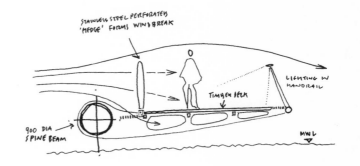

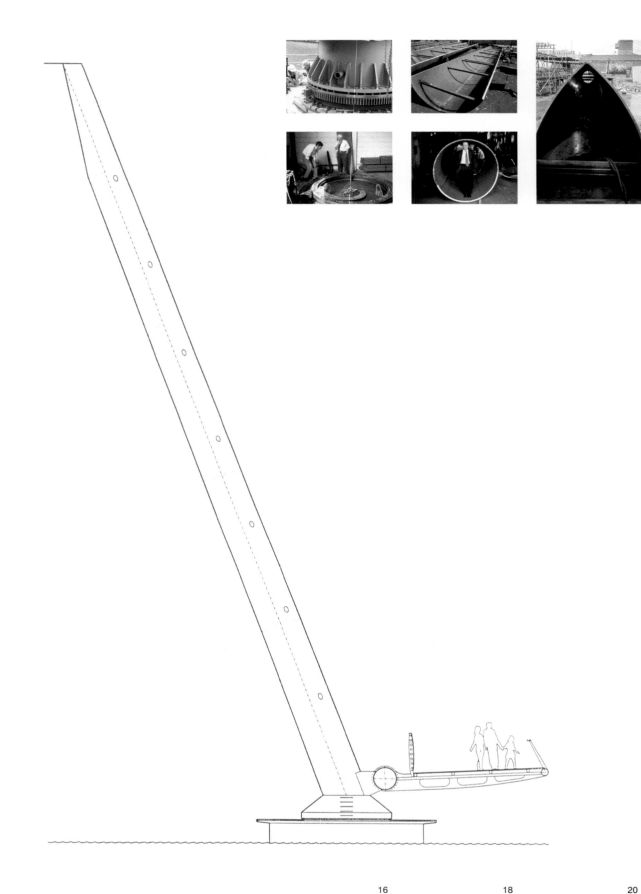

16▷The structural system depends on the interaction of the bridge's curves with the raking of the mast to achieve a perfect balance, putting the centre of gravity over the bearing about which the bridge rotates.

Each mast marks a crescendo in the journey – one at the structure's geometric focus and the other where the deck is widest. The mast of the opening bridge is also the pivot point, around which the whole assembly simply rotates.

17◁The bridge swings around a machined slewing bearing at the mast's base, powered by a low-inertia electric motor.

18◁Finding the exact centre of gravity was crucial.

19◁The tapering profile and apparently complex shape of the mast is actually a simple geometric design which can be constructed quite economically. The 30-metre hollow structure evolves from a circular base into an acute leaf-shaped section at the top.

20◁A cylinder is rolled to the base dimension and a long tapering cut is taken out of each side before the two halves are laid out for reconnection. The two halves are rejoined and the welded seam ground flush. John Cutlack, the engineer, stands in the pre-cut section, which measures 1.8 metres in diameter.

21◁A slice taken from the top of the mast shows the leaf section reduced to the form of a gothic arch. Towards the top of the arch the circular section of the base is visible 30 metres away in the background.

22▷Not really a lightweight structure, the mast – and the bridge as a whole – acquires an apparent lightness by standing in stark contrast to the scale and geometric rigour of its surroundings.

23▷Due to the pace of development in the area, the existence of the bridge in full form was short-lived; the northern half of the dock began to be reclaimed less than two years after its opening.

Location:	London UK
Commission date:	1994
Completion date:	March 1997
Bridge span:	180m
Client:	London Docklands Development Corporation
Structural engineer:	Jan Bobrowski & Partners
Main contractor:	Christiani & Nielsen
Steelwork subcontractor:	Kent Structural Marine
Awards:	Institute of Structural Engineers Special Award 1998
	Design Council Millennium 'Product' Award 1998
	Structural Steel Design Award Commendation 1998
	Civic Trust Award Commendation 1998
	British Construction Industry Award for
	'Outstanding Fusion of Architecture & Engineering' 1997
	American Institute of Architects
	Excellence in Design Award 1997

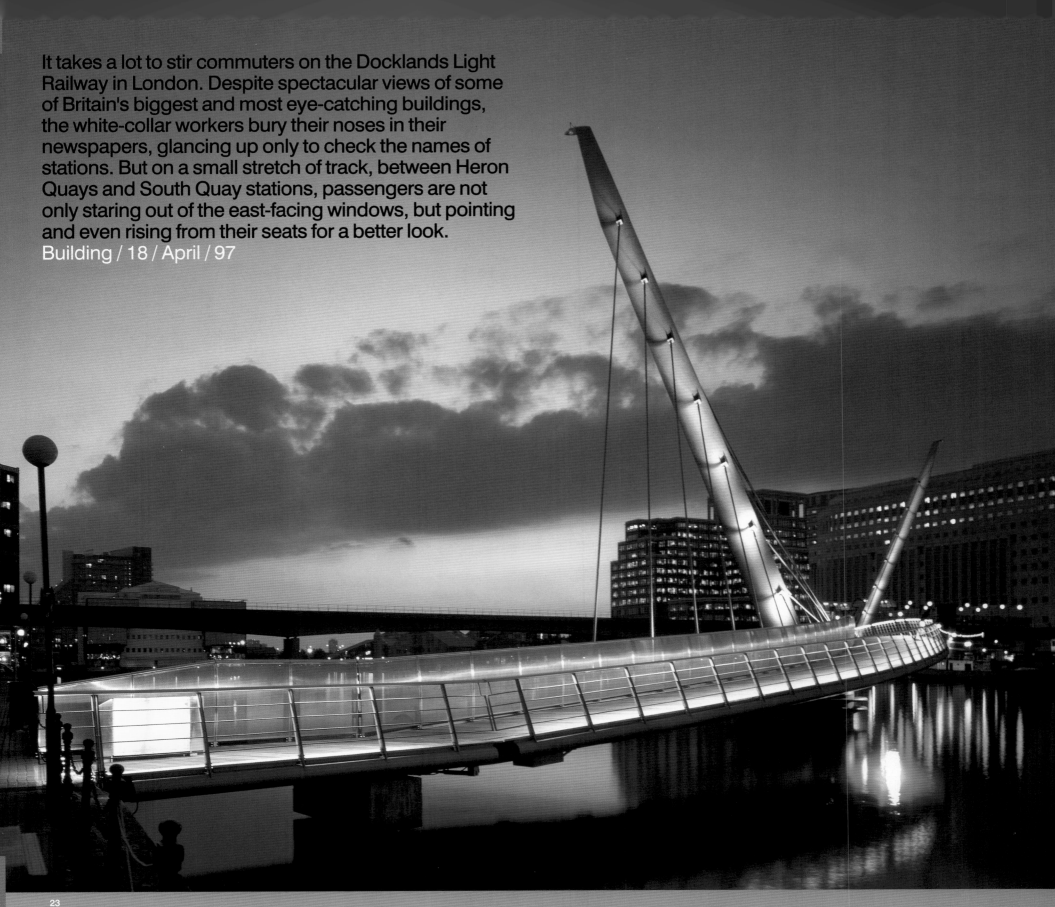

It takes a lot to stir commuters on the Docklands Light Railway in London. Despite spectacular views of some of Britain's biggest and most eye-catching buildings, the white-collar workers bury their noses in their newspapers, glancing up only to check the names of stations. But on a small stretch of track, between Heron Quays and South Quay stations, passengers are not only staring out of the east-facing windows, but pointing and even rising from their seats for a better look.
Building / 18 / April / 97

Hulme Arch

An elegant, single arch which spans the Princess road diagonally, tapering in opposite directions in plan and elevation. Pamela Buxton – Building Design / 28 / July / 95

Hulme Regeneration Limited held an international competition in 1996: to design a bridge that would become the flagship for its urban regeneration programme.

The Hulme district was physically divided in half in the 1960s by a new dual carriageway cutting (Princess Road). The design brief in 1996 called for a new bridge that would act as both a landmark on the Princess Road approach to Manchester and as a gateway effective from two directions – to tie together the two halves of Hulme by giving continuity to the Stretford Road above.

Known locally as 'Hulme Arch', the winning design was Wilkinson Eyre's second bridge project. A single arch, built on a diagonal, spans both Princess Road and Stretford Road. Users of both roads pass under the arch, and it is possible to read its iconic form from all four approaches.

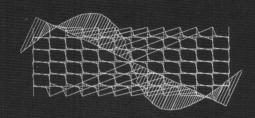

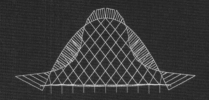

01 ▽ The arch supports the deck below with an array of cables, which fan out to each side of the deck, forming an overlapping arrangement. This helps to unite the two halves of Hulme visually.

02 △ The asymmetric form and the twisting action of the cables cause uneven loads on the arch. Structural analysis was carried out at competition stage by Arup and it was demonstrated that a negligible increase in the arch's weight would counter this effect. The site-specific design solution was justified.

03 ▷ The crown of the arch is wider and shallower than its base, in order to deal with the twisting action. In cross section the arch is constantly changing, its blade-like quality created by its trapezoidal form.

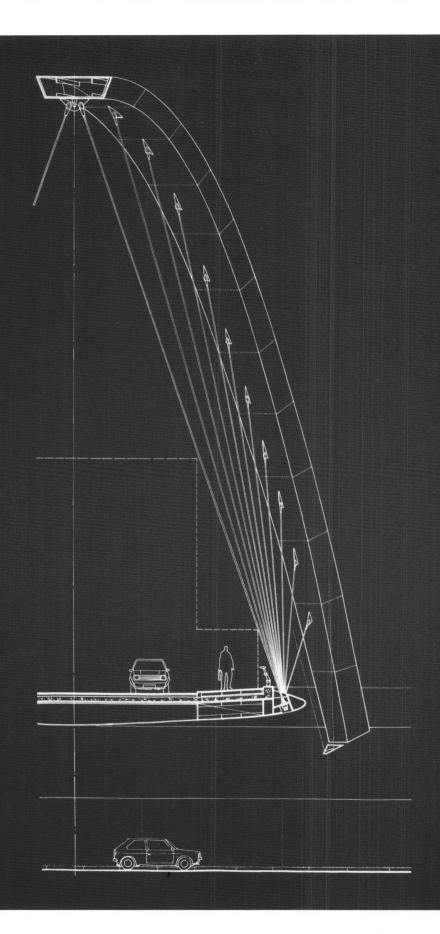

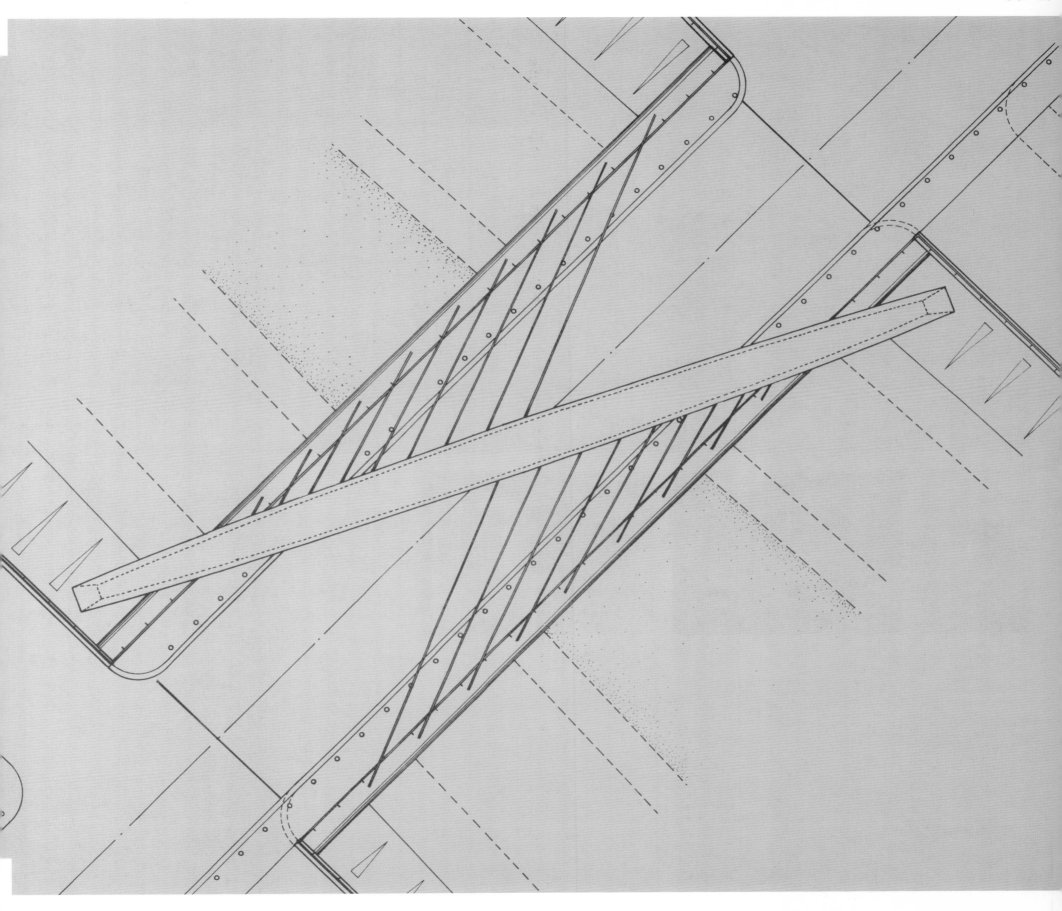

04 △ Completed in May 1997, construction of the bridge had taken sixty weeks. Here a plated assembly awaits the attachment of the cable anchor at the edge of the deck. A circular tube sits in front of the anchors to brace the edge of the deck and to act as a 'nose cone'.

05 △ The structure supporting the deck is of plated construction. Welded studs are lined up ready for keying into the deck of reinforced concrete, which will be laid on top.

06 △ The base of the arch lies on its side in the steelworkers' yard. The slimmer but wider crown profile is seen in the background.

07 ▷ Looking up at the centre of the arch before the cables are attached, the connection plates and eyes that punctuate the curved plane are visible.

08▷From Stretford Road the arch appears very tall. The twisting array of cables only becomes obvious at relatively close quarters.

08

09◁From Princess Road the arch and
deck present a strong form symbolizing the
gateway to Manchester – an icon for Hulme.

10▷The interplay of arch and cables creates a
powerful visual dynamic from many viewpoints.

Location:	Hulme, Manchester UK
Commission date:	1995
Completion date:	May 1997
Bridge span:	60m
Client:	Hulme Regeneration Corporation & Manchester City Council
Structural engineer:	Ove Arup & Partners
Main contractor:	Henry Boot Limited
Steelwork subcontractor:	Watson Steel
Awards:	Design Council Millennium 'Product' Award

Design Council Millennium 'Product' Award	1999
RIBA Award for Architecture	1998
Structural Steel Design Award Commendation	1998
Civic Trust Award Commendation	1998
Institute of Civil Engineers Merit Award	1998

Butterfly Bridge

The simple lines are evocative
of leaf forms or insects, such as
the butterfly.
Jim Eyre

The Butterfly Bridge was the winning design out of 79 entries in an open competition held in November 1995. The bridge spans 28 metres over the River Ouse in Bedford, in a park subject to occasional flooding .

'Embankment Renaissance Footbridge', the title of the competition, inferred the design brief. The function of the bridge was to connect Russell Park with the amenities on the west bank of the river and to improve facilities and communications for the annual river festival.

The design concept comprises a twin-arched structure and suspended deck which opens out to engage with the space around it.

Webster's 1888 Suspension Bridge provides a memorable landmark which epitomizes Bedford at the end of the nineteenth century. The aim is to build a bridge which similarly marks the end of the twentieth century and the beginning of the twenty-first. Bedford Borough Council competition brief

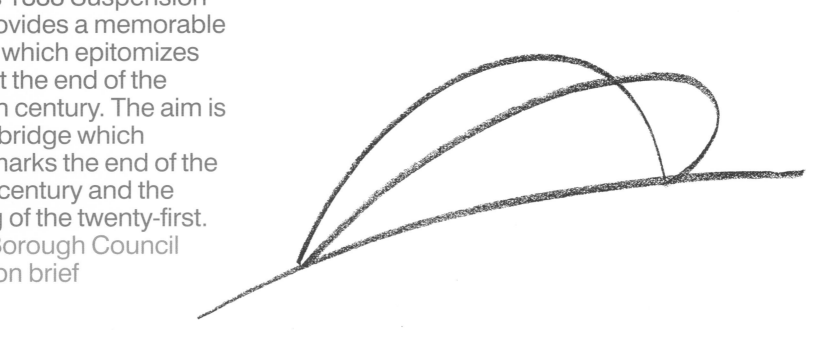

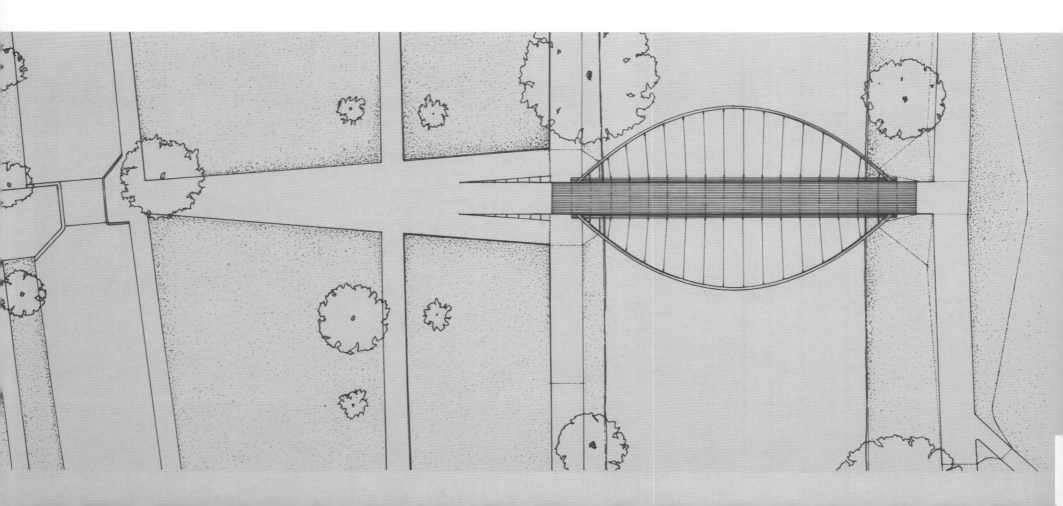

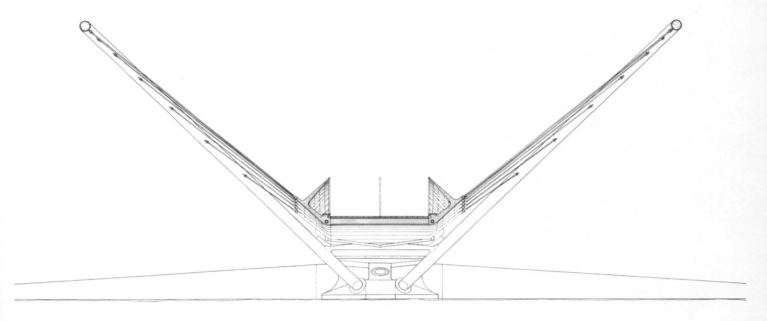

01 ◁ Nearby there is a footbridge designed by J.J. Webster in 1888. With twin arches and a suspended deck, it is very elegant and serviceable, but this early bridge does not provide step-free access to modern standards. It does, however, provide inspiration for the new structure.

02 △ Splaying the arches of the Butterfly Bridge produces a feeling of containment on the deck, and yet simultaneously offers an openness to the sky.

03 ▷ A pair of cranes hoisted the parabolic arches (circular hollow tubes 323.9 millimetres in diameter) into position with the cables already attached. The deck, comprising edge tubes and cross-member plates, complete with baluster/hanger profiles, was added later.

04 ▷ At each end both the steel arches are grounded in a single concrete abutment; it is sculpted to form an articulated tongue which connects to the deck.

05△ The balustrades combine with a steel footplate, covering longitudinal deck lighting, to encourage people to use the bridge as a viewing platform to watch oarsmen passing underneath. During the river festival the bridge is temporarily formalized as a 'grandstand'.

Location:	Bedford UK
Commission date:	1995
Completion date:	May 1997
Bridge span:	32m
Client:	Bedford Borough Council
Structural engineer:	Jan Bobrowski & Partners
Main contractor:	Littlehampton Welding Limited

Lockmeadow Footbridge

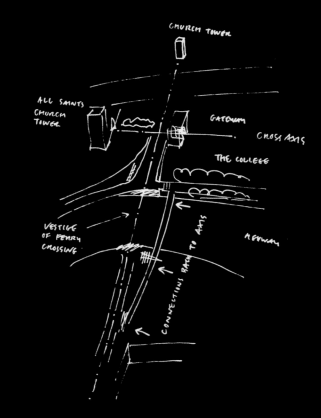

01 △ Lockmeadow Bridge is located at the historic core of Maidstone, at the site of a medieval ferry crossing of the River Medway, adjacent to the Archbishop's Palace. The 1997 competition brief called for a design that was sensitive both to the location and to the modern idiom.

There is a strong east–west axis running down to the Medway on the town side, flanked by All Saints Church and The College. On the southern bank, the bridge needed to span the river's flood plain, to minimize obstruction to flood waters.

Springing from a high point off-axis on the town side, the footbridge curves gently back to connect with the axis on the south bank. From the town side the bridge comes gradually into view on the far side without impeding the historic aspect.

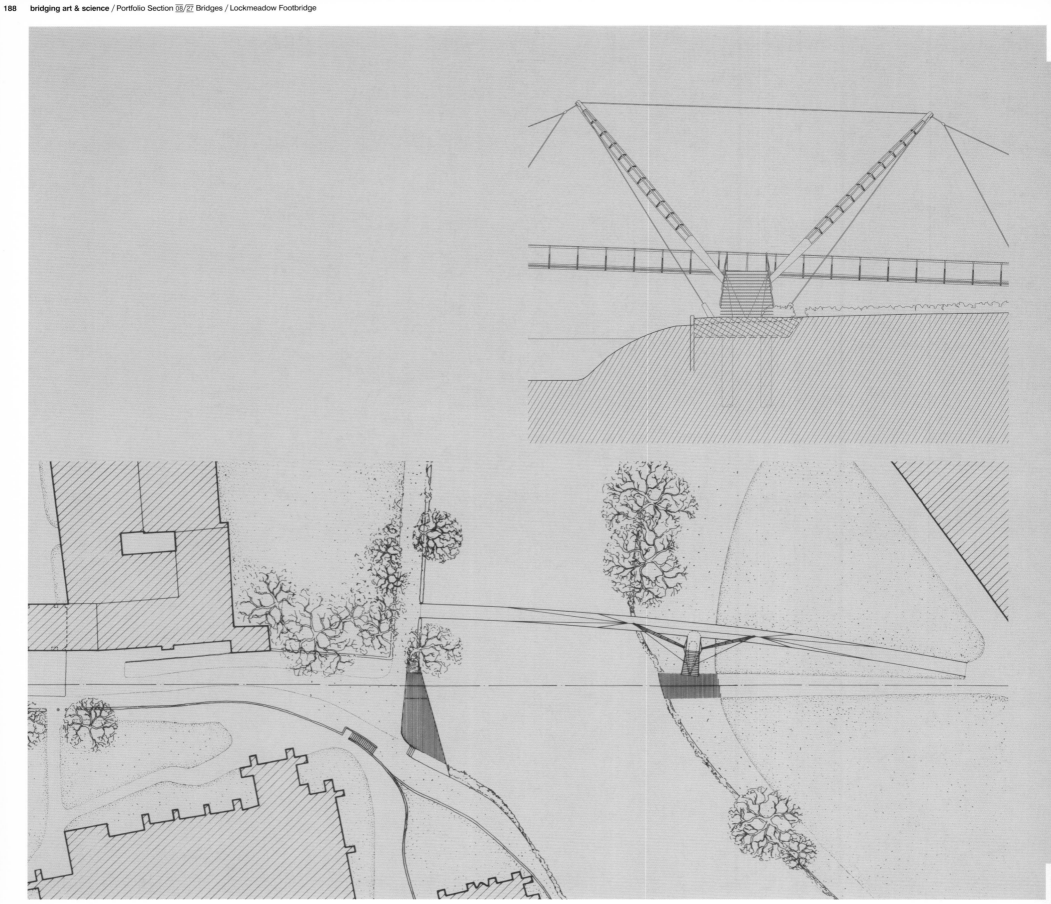

02◁A central foundation on the south bank provides a compositional fulcrum for the bridge.

03▷The central 'cutwater' construction refers to a traditional form which facilitates the passage of water around the bridge pier. The cutwater incorporates steps from the bridge deck to the river's edge, reconnecting the pedestrian and the historic axes.

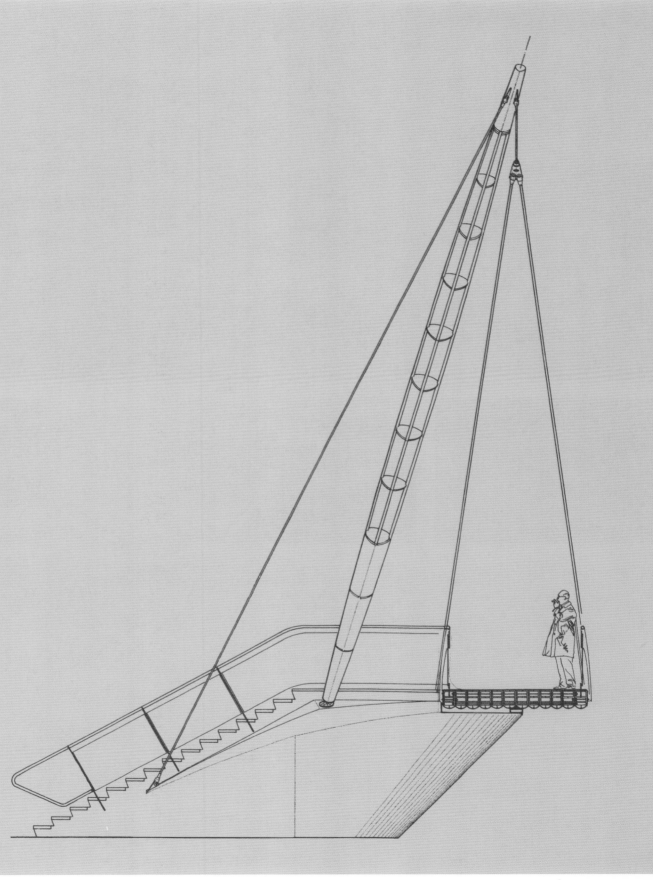

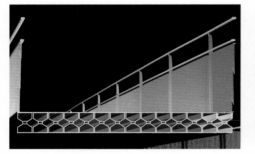

04 △ One of the key objectives of the design was to reduce the visual impact of the river span, which was achieved, and is expressed, by reducing the structure to a minimal profile.

05 ▷ Structure and surfacing are combined in a single assembly for the deck of the bridge. Through an economic use of material an extremely thin profile is achieved at the outer edge.

06 △ A standardized aluminium extrusion is profiled in such a way that it can be clamped in series, to form an interlocking deck assembly. The top surface of the extrusion is ribbed and serrated to provide a safe surface for traffic.

07 ◁ Clamping rods perpendicular to the deck are used to post-tension the system and to allow for the curvature in plan.

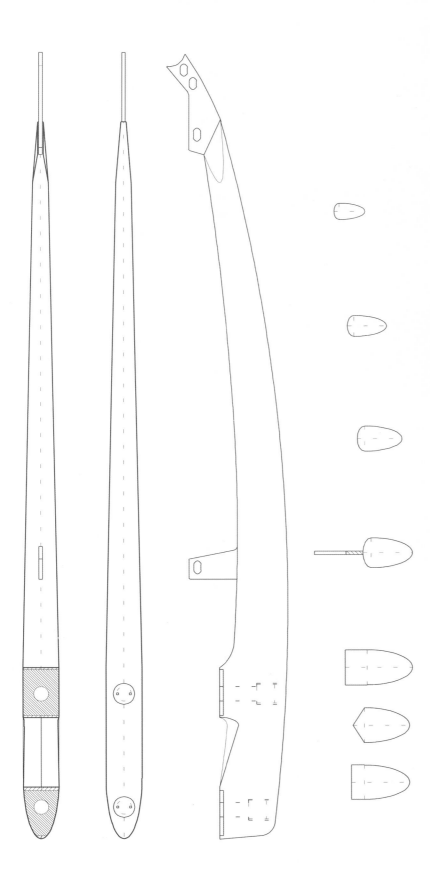

08◁Parapet posts are resin-filled carbon-fibre forms. Their F1 manufacturing technology allows a complexity of shape which complements the formality of the system's other components.

09▷Panels of stainless-steel 'wedge wire' form the parapet infill; they vary in transparency, depending on the viewpoint.

10 ◁ Deck, parapet and cables combine to form a lightweight composition that stands in contrast to the mass of the medieval buildings.

11 △ A cast arrangement at the masthead picks up the stay-cable, back-stay and tie-cable sockets.

12 ▷ The skeletal masts are disguised within the random form of the surrounding trees. When seen in its entirety and in context, the bridge makes only a modest incursion into the surrounding historic area, its strong identity countered by the understated design.

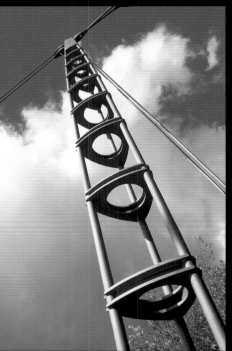

Location:	Maidstone, Kent UK	
Commission date:	1997	
Completion date:	October 1999	
Bridge span:	80m	
Client:	Maidstone Borough Council, Technical Services	
Structural engineer:	Flint & Neill Partnership	
Main contractor:	Christiani & Nielsen Limited	
Steelwork subcontractor:	D&B Darke Limited	
Awards:	Structural Achievement Award	2000
	Institute of Civil Engineers Merit Award	2000
	Design Council Millennium 'Product' Award	1999

Metsovitikos Bridge

Location: Metsovo, Greece
Commission date: 1998
Completion date: 2003
Bridge span: 560m
Client: Egnatia Odos AE
Structural engineer: Ove Arup & Partners

01 △ Won by Wilkinson Eyre in an international competition run by Egnatia Odos AE, this project is the jewel in the crown of a major new highway that will stretch across the whole of northern Greece, and is designed to act as an east-west link across the peninsula.

The commission was for a 500-metre-span, rock-anchored suspension bridge, a rare if not unique form of structure on this scale, which was to occupy an extraordinarily beautiful setting close to the town of Metsovo in the Pindos mountains of Epiros in north-west Greece.

02 ▷ The concept is one of minimal but graceful expression, comprising simply a bridge deck, supporting cables and catenaries.

03 ▷ Long tunnels have been blasted through the mountains on either side to allow the motorist to emerge, high in the landscape, into a valley of cables which echoes the form of the river valley below. The customary towers are absent from this design; the supporting catenary cables sail far beyond the tunnel portals into the mountainside above.

04 ▷ The design of the portals has been coordinated with the bridge. Elliptical cones are penetrated by the bridge deck at the mountain face.

05 ◁ The binocular tunnels at either end thereby translate into single openings, which give onto views of the surrounding countryside.

Canary Wharf Bridges

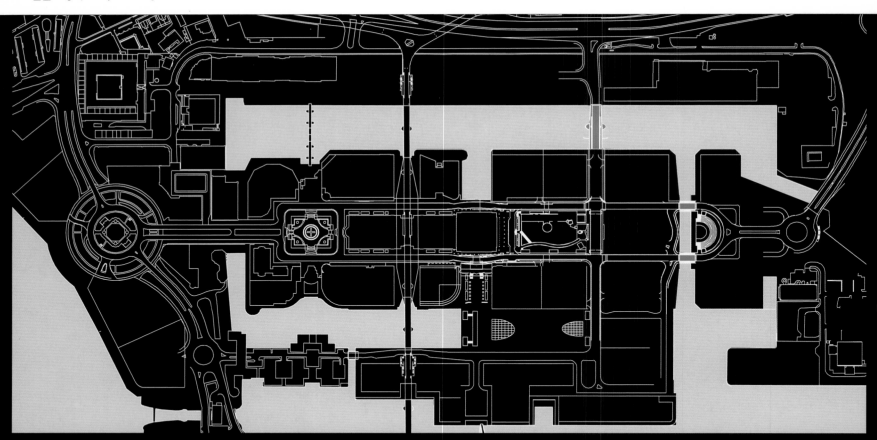

01 △ In 1998 a group of three opening bridges was commissioned to facilitate the second phase of urban development at Canary Wharf in London's Docklands.

Two identical bridges span the Bellmouth Passage Canal, linking the development with the east; while the third bridge, at Great Wharf Road, links the development with the north.

Both the bridge designs are unusual variants of commonly used bascule types. They all offer clearance for boats to pass through – 15 x 15.5 metres when open and 15 x 4.5 metres when closed – as required by the brief.

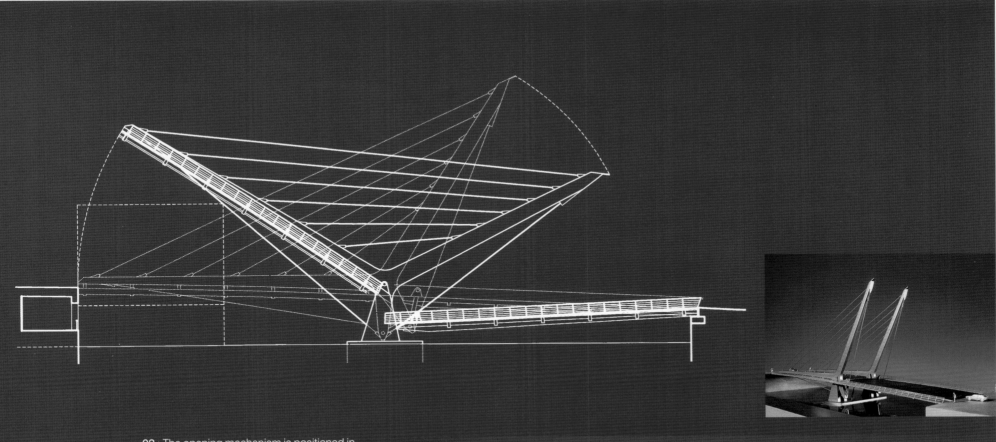

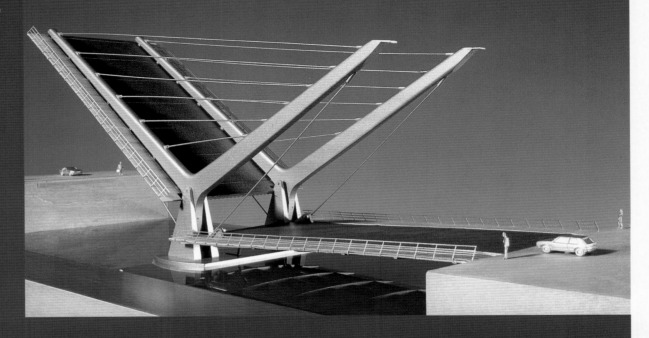

02 △ The opening mechanism is positioned in the middle of the 60-metre-wide dock, giving the bridge on the Great Wharf Road a strong central presence, whether the bridge is open or closed. Unusually for a bascule bridge, it is masted with cable stays.

03 ◁ In the closed position the bridge adopts the appearance of a fairly simple cable-stayed structure, which belies its capacity to open. In fact, the back span is linked to the opening span and acts as a counterbalance in the opening system.

04 ▷ When the bridge opens the whole composition is engaged in, and celebrates the spectacle of, opening: the masts lean back to poise the bascule section in the centre of the dock while the back span section dips towards the water.

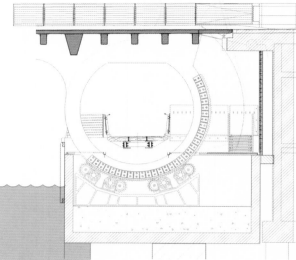

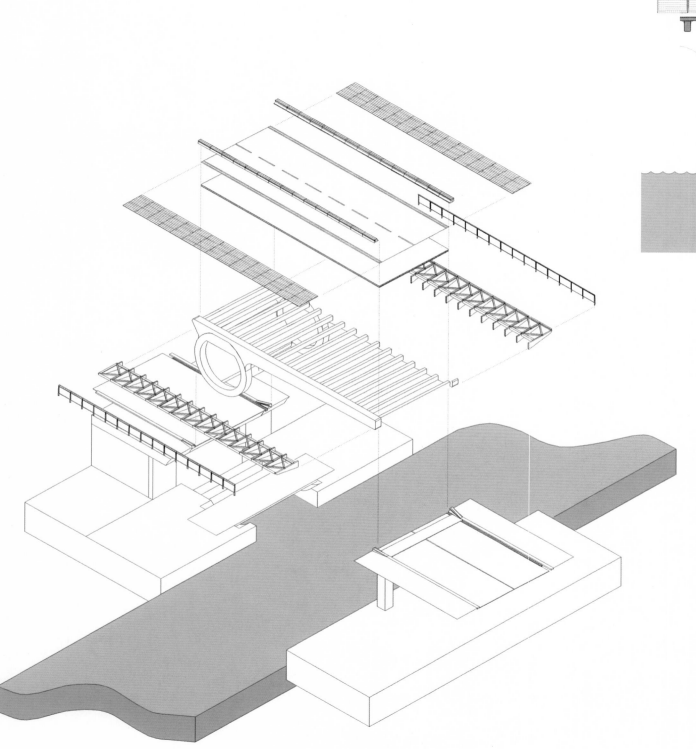

05◁ The pair of bridges spanning Bellmouth Passage are a variant on the 'rolling bascule', indigenous to London's Docklands. The brief dictated that the bridges should be modest, with no structure above deck level. The design relies on the dramatic potential of the bridge's opening function, therefore, as the outlet for architectural expression.

A conventional bascule bridge would comprise a cantilevered deck and a short counterbalancing back span, with the whole assembly pivoting around a pair of trunnion bearings, but low-level quayside walkways exist on either side of the bridges which restrict the space available. Accordingly, their presence informs the design concept.

06△ Wilkinson Eyre has enlarged the bearing assembly – introducing a pair of hoops running on cogs – and has allowed the quayside walk to run right through the bearing's centre of rotation. Not only does this reduce the bridge span, the walkway also remains available during the opening sequence.

07◁ The bridge's opening capability is expressed in its form, and is clearly seen from the low-level quayside walk.

08▷ Ultimately, the bridges are discreet compositions in which the opening feature is experienced most dramatically from within the rotating device.

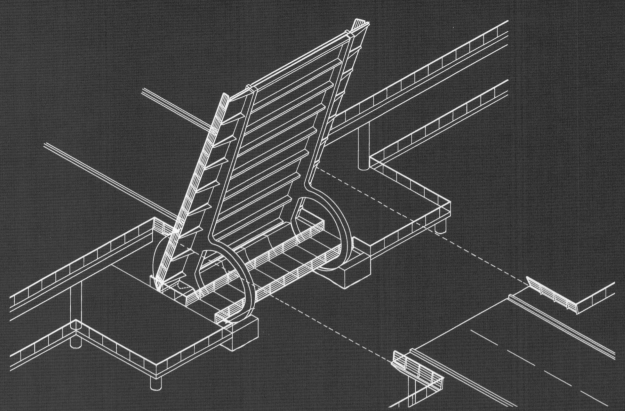

Location:	London UK
Commission date:	1998
Completion date:	2001
Client:	Canary Wharf Limited
Structural engineer:	Jan Bobrowski & Partners
Main contractor:	Cleveland Bridge

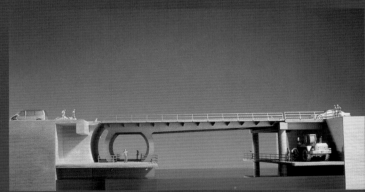

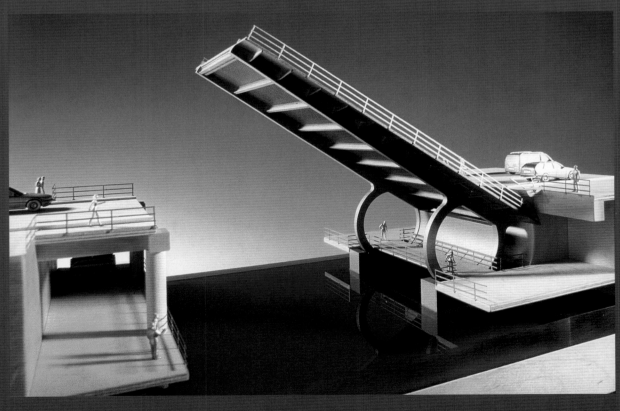

Lyckoben Bridge

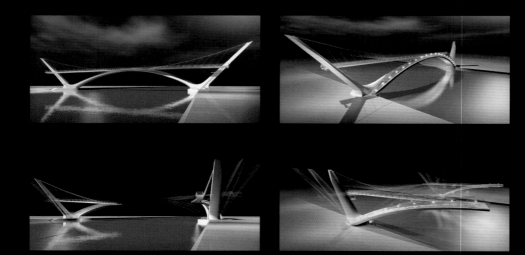

01◁ Wilkinson Eyre won the commission to design an opening bridge at Hammarby Sjostad in an international design competition in 1997. The bridge was intended to ease connections between islands in the Stockholm archipelago.

The bridge will span a major shipping route (80 metres wide), and will require clearance of 18 metres when the bridge is closed to allow frequent traffic to pass through. The primary elements of the bridge make reference to Stockholm's vernacular bridge typology although with adaptations – to facilitate 'opening'. Approach ramps, in answer to the need for a high bridge deck, would have been incredibly long, and obtrusive on the landscaped spaces to either side. The decision was made, therefore, to contain the vertical circulation within the environs of the bridge.

02▷ The arched form allows the integration of a stairway into the primary structural member, which provides the most direct quay-to-quay access. The stairs are augmented by a lift, which runs at an angle along the counter-balancing mast. The deck is connected back to the masts at high level and supported by a self-anchored suspension arrangement. People requiring step-free access will be able to use the lifts and from the deck, which spans the full width of the bridge, they will be able to enjoy the views, including those back into the city.

03▷ The plan arrangement is slightly curved, which helps to articulate movement around the structure and to assist in balancing each half of the bridge on the centre of rotation at the landing points.

The speed at which the bridge opens is sufficiently slow to allow people to step on and off the bridge while it is moving; thus safety gates are only required at the centre of the span.

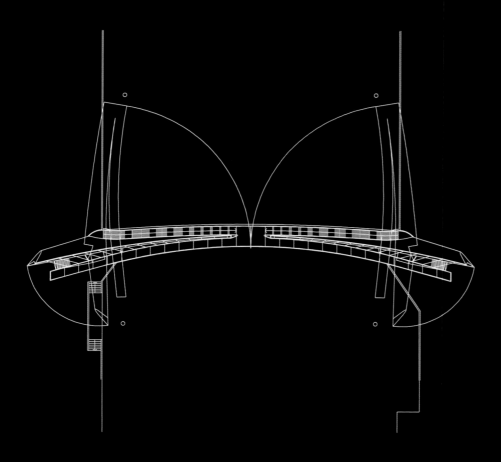

04▷ The dynamic, iconic solution contains an element of surprise and drama in its opening operation. The mast and arch base are sculpted from concrete and the remainder is in steel. Materials are not only deployed functionally but are also exploited to create the flowing forms that give the bridge its sense of unity.

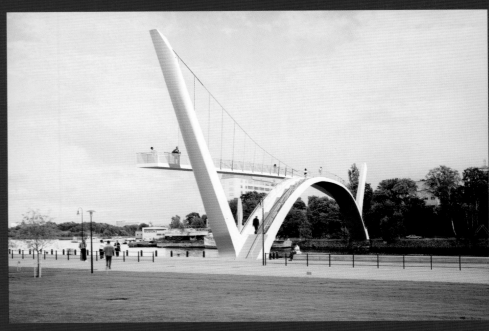

Location:	Stockholm, Sweden
Design proposal:	1997
Bridge span:	80m
Client:	Stockholm Stad Gatu-och fastighetskontoret
Structural engineer:	Flint & Neill Partnership

Bay Bridge East Span

Location:	San Francisco Bay, USA
Design proposal:	1997
Client:	Caltrans
Structural engineer:	Mott MacDonald /
	Parsons Brinkerhoff /
	HNTB

01△San Francisco and Oakland are today connected by a double-deck carriageway, part of which collapsed during the earthquake in1989. The existing west spans, which lead to Yerba Buena Island, comprise a pair of back-to-back 1930s suspension bridges. From here, after a short tunnel, a steel-truss viaduct structure continues for a further 5 kilometres (3 miles) to Oakland. It was this viaduct that suffered the partial collapse. The proposals are for a replacement for the east spans (Yerba Buena–Oakland); they were commissioned by the engineering consortium vying for the job.

Two suspension designs were considered: one a self-anchored suspension bridge with a clear span of 303 metres, linked to a skyway structure of short repetitive spans; the other a set of twelve back-to-back self-anchored cable-stayed suspension bridges spanning the full 5-kilometre (3-mile) width of the crossing.

02▽The self-anchored span option was complicated by the need to accommodate a slight curve in the alignment (to avoid a fault in the base rock) and to unravel the existing piggy-back deck configuration when the carriageways emerge from the tunnel on Yerba Buena island.

03◁These constraints informed the design and added to the potential drama, with the possibility of stepped decks curving around to give a grandstand view back to San Francisco.

04▷The alternative multi-span arrangement, however, was felt to be more compatible with the existing west spans. Here a rhythm is set up by the structure, providing the opportunity for a 'signature' bridge, not just a span. The constructional concept is based on the premise that whole spans can be jacked up into position complete with their above deck masts and stay cables, after which suspension elements can be added to accommodate live loads.

05◁Both solutions perform well seismically but the second design has the advantage of needing fewer piers - expensive to construct in the shallow waters over immensely deep mud (resulting from gold rush activities) above the base rock.

Passerelle Bercy-Tolbiac

Location:	Paris, France
Design proposal:	1999
Bridge span:	250m
Client:	Ville de Paris
Structural engineer:	Ove Arup & Partners with RFR

01 △ In 1998 Wilkinson Eyre was invited to submit a design proposal for a new footbridge across the River Seine, linking the Parc de Bercy with the new national library on the Left Bank.

02 ▷ The proposal is for a defiantly slender ribbon bridge across the full 250-metre span. The deck is split into two to conform to the multiple destination choices enjoyed by users of the bridge. On each side of the bridge there are three potential departure points with three corresponding destinations on the opposite bank. The main connection is at high level – between the library and the park – but there is a link also between the footpaths adjoining the arterial roads at low level – on the river banks.

03 ▷ The two decks stabilize each other, but the upper deck carries most of the load, being highly stressed across the span. Loads are taken back into the ground by armatures spanning the roads on either side. The top deck is wider (12 metres) and includes small kiosks for selling books, while the lower deck rises up in the middle of the bridge – within the confines of the upper deck – to allow for interconnection of the routes. The proposal is technically challenging, but essentially feasible and within the bounds of known technology, and will result in a centre span of unprecedented slenderness for the given width of the crossing.

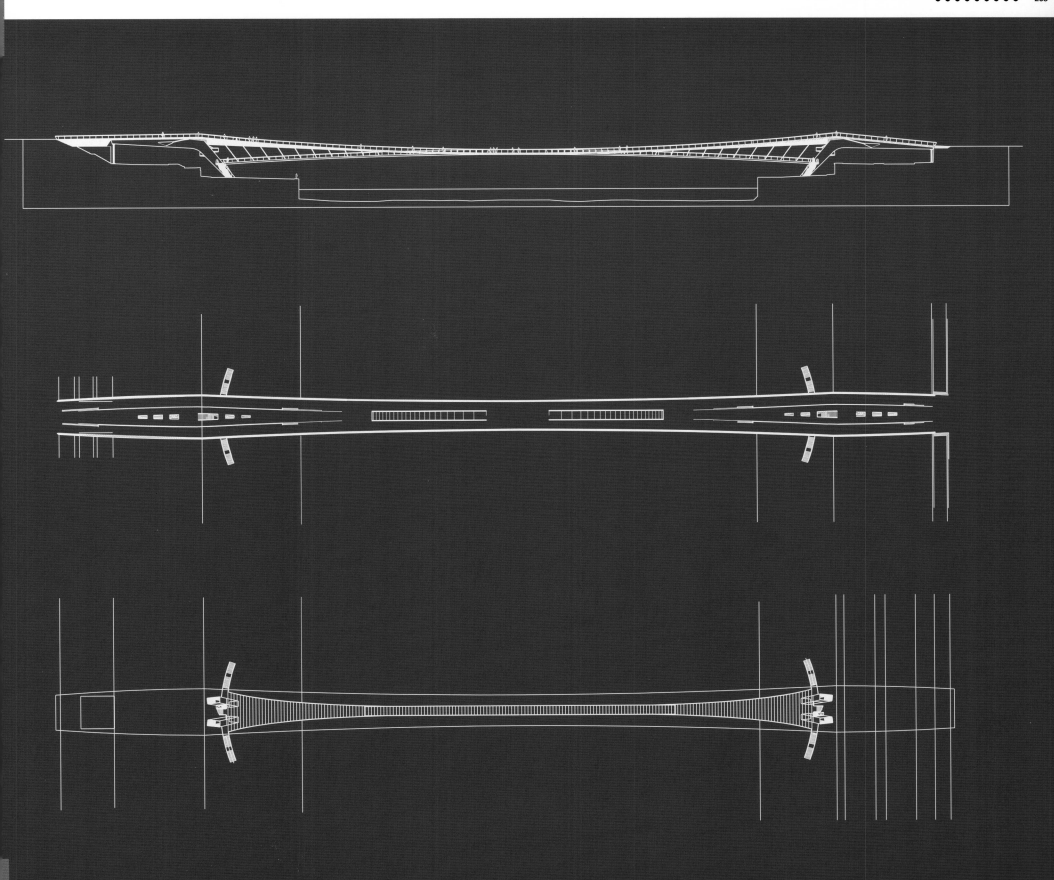

Gateshead Millennium Bridge

We already have one of the world's best collections of bridges on the Tyne, which has been built up over the past two centuries. The Gateshead Millennium Bridge will be the first new bridge of the next century and the next millennium, as well as the first opening bridge of its kind anywhere in the world.
George Gill –
Gateshead Council Leader / 98

The design was the winning entry in a competition held in 1997 for a major new crossing over the River Tyne. The bridge links the newly developed Newcastle Quayside with the ambitious redevelopment of East Gateshead, including the Baltic Centre for Contemporary Art and the Northern Regional Music Centre. It is a key ingredient in the regeneration of the surrounding area.

While recognizing the contextual importance of the Tyne's existing bridges, the brief required a clear channel for shipping and a low-level crossing for pedestrians and cyclists. The design echoes the arch of the famous 'Tyne Bridge', which is visible behind the new bridge to the west.

[EAST]

BALTIC F. MILL
CONNECTS

"CONTAINED"

CITY

CITY

QUAYSIDE LOOP

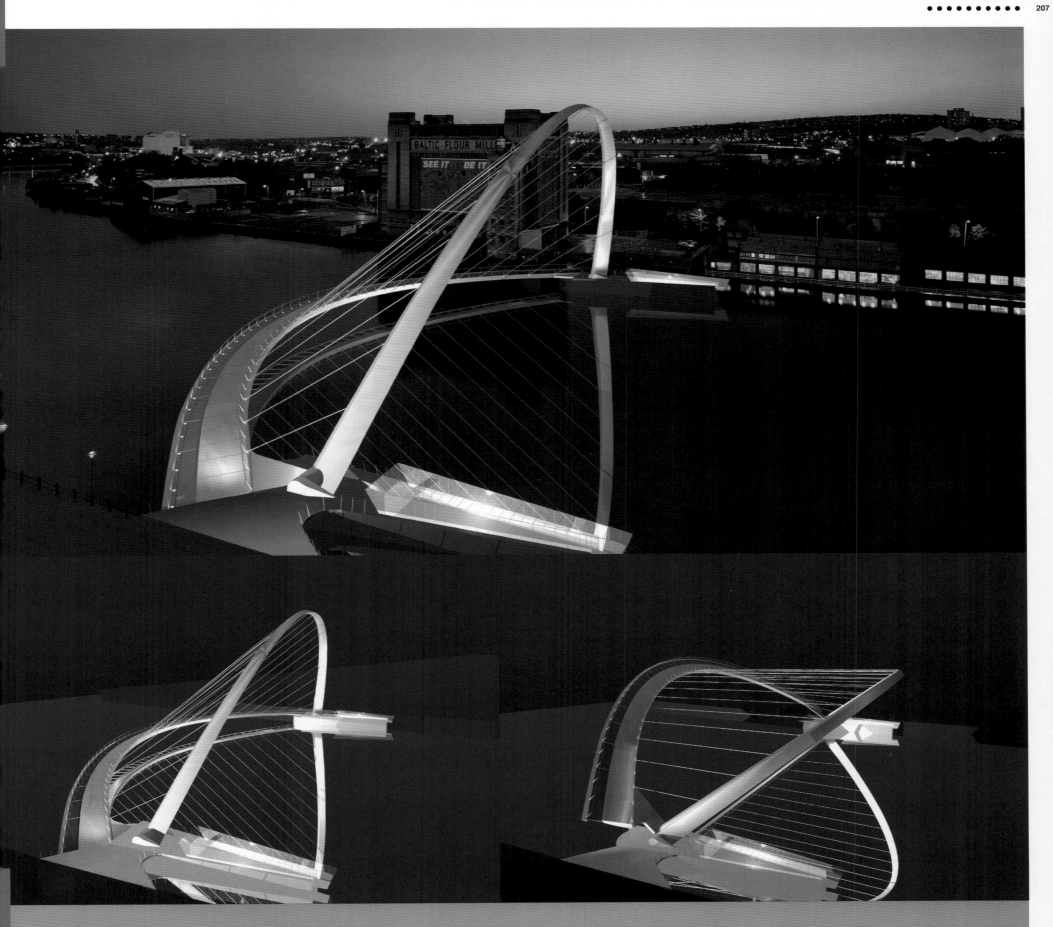

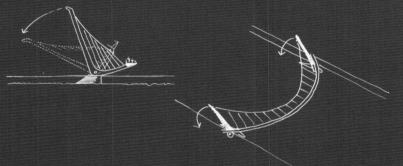

01◁Initial design concepts focused on the idea of a curved, suspended deck which would be pivoted to 'open' the bridge. Permissible gradients for pedestrians disallowed a straight crossing but an elongated curved deck produced sufficient length and also satisfied clearance requirements. The curvature adds a sense of theatre to the journey.

02▽The final design is a simple idea: a pair of arches (one forming the deck, the other supporting it), which pivot around their common springing point to allow shipping to pass beneath. The proposed movement is similar to that of a slowly opening eyelid. The profile of the arch changes dramatically between the closed and open positions.

03▷The bridge spans the river between two new 'islands' that run parallel to the quaysides. Public access to these areas – a glazed hall providing amenities in a highly dramatic location, with incredible views of the structure and the Tyne – adds another dimension to the exciting functions of the bridge itself.

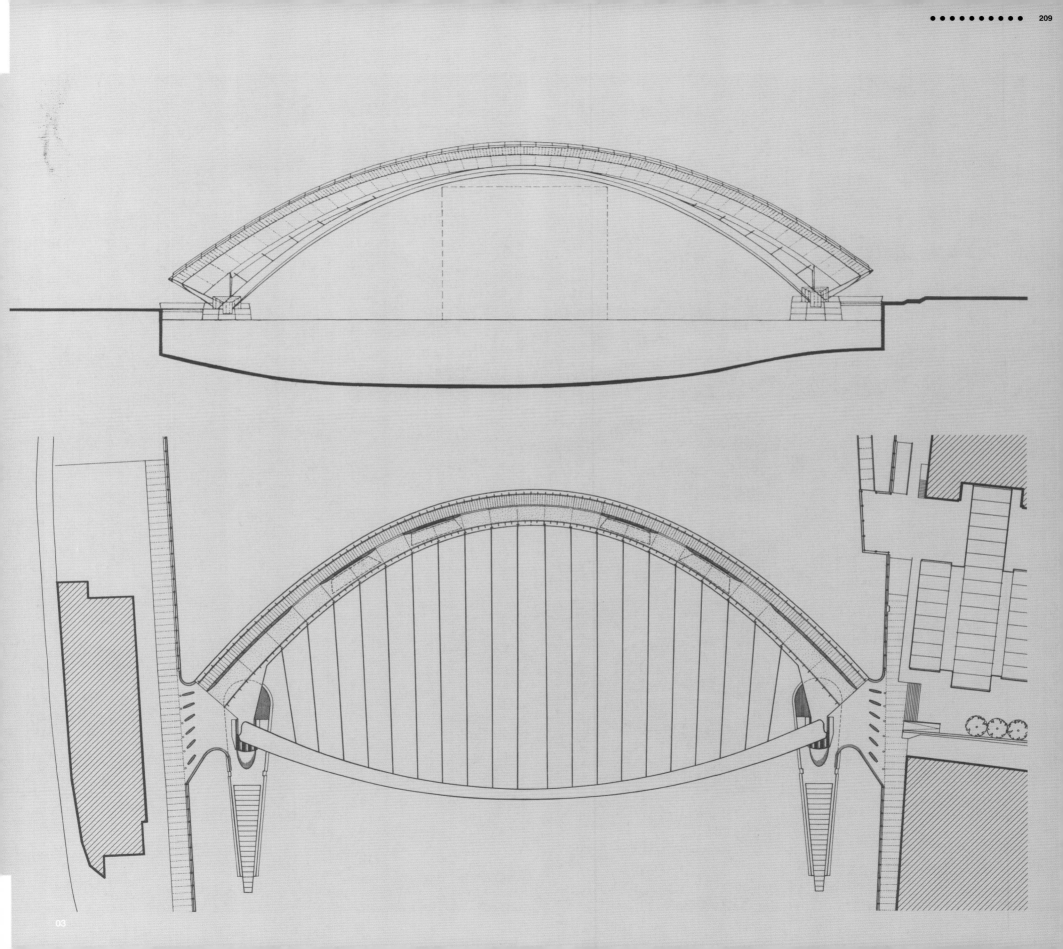

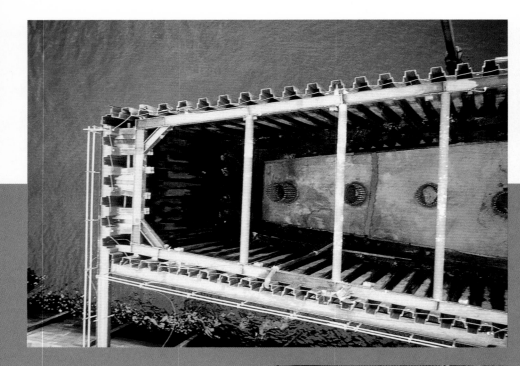

04△Coffer dams give the first impression of the footprint of the structure. The two vast encasements house the end supports of the bridge.

05▷Four trunnion-bearing pedestals support the spindle around which the bridge rotates.

06▷The proposed rotation of 38.62 degrees is sufficient to offer clearance for shipping of 25 x 30 metres at high tide.

07▷A scale model of the bridge (1:50) was tested for stability in various simulated wind conditions at the Boundary Layer Wind Test Laboratory in Canada.

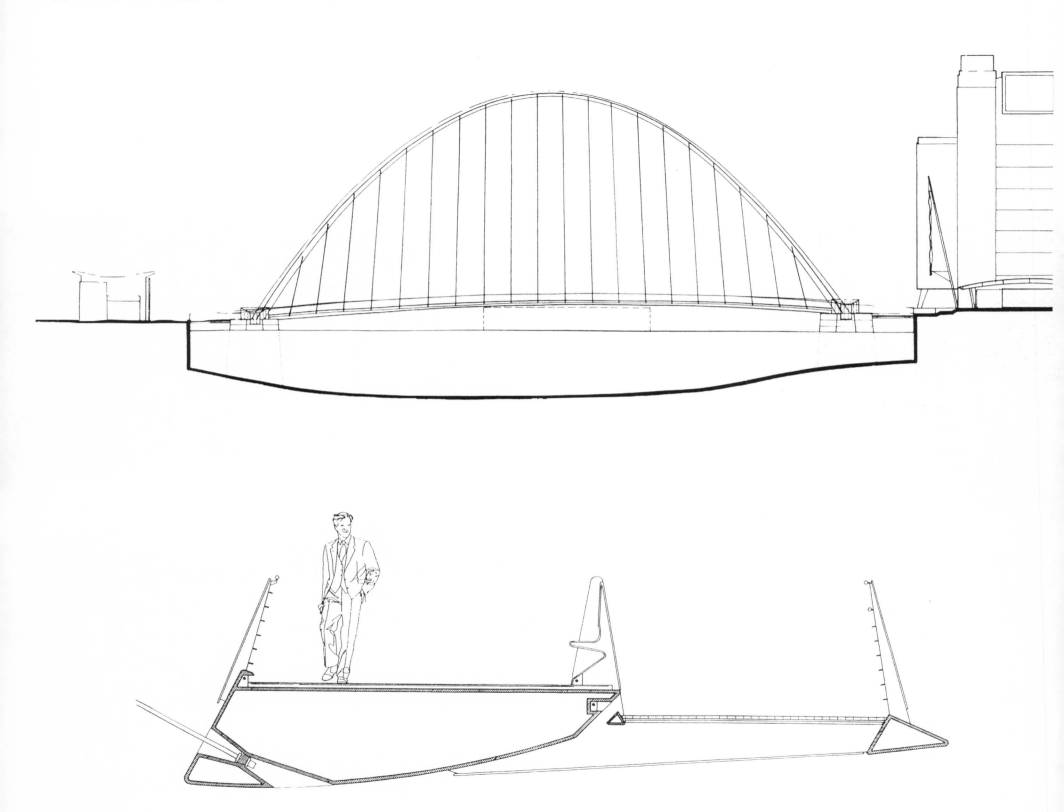

08◁When the bridge is closed the lower deck provides two traffic routes: one for pedestrians and one for bicycles.

09▷Cantilevered steel beams, extending from a coated-steel box on which pedestrians cross, provide support for a surfaced aluminium decking for cyclists – the two decks sit side by side.

10△ The pedestrian deck during fabrication at Watson Steel.

11△ The arch seen during fabrication in segments, Spring 2000.

12△ The pointed segment joins onto the barrel through which the trunnion bearing passes.

13◁The project is conceived in the great tradition of engineering in Tyneside. The design is, above all, an engineering structure, one that will stand proudly among the engineering feats of previous generations on the Tyne.

14▷The project, funded by the Millennium Commission, was selected by the Royal Mail to be featured on the first-class stamp of the Millennium People and Places series in June 2000.

Location:	Gateshead Quays UK
Commission date:	1997
Completion date:	2001
Bridge span:	105m
Client:	Gateshead Metropolitan Borough Council
Structural engineer:	Gifford & Partners
Main contractor:	Harbour & General Works
Steelwork subcontractor:	Watson Steel
Awards:	Royal Academy AJ/Bovis Grand Award 1997

Stand on the bank of the Tyne River sometime
early next millennium and you may have the good
luck to witness a coup of architectural theatre: 700
tons of steel, poised just above the water, will swing
up to form a momentary arch against the sky.
Adam Goodheart –
Civilisation / Feb - March / 98

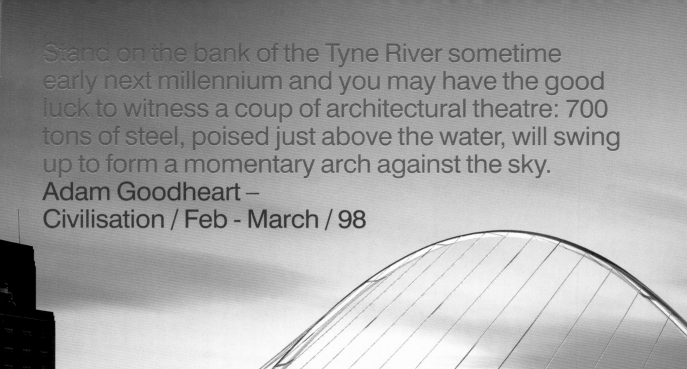

Small Projects & Products

Park Hall Road

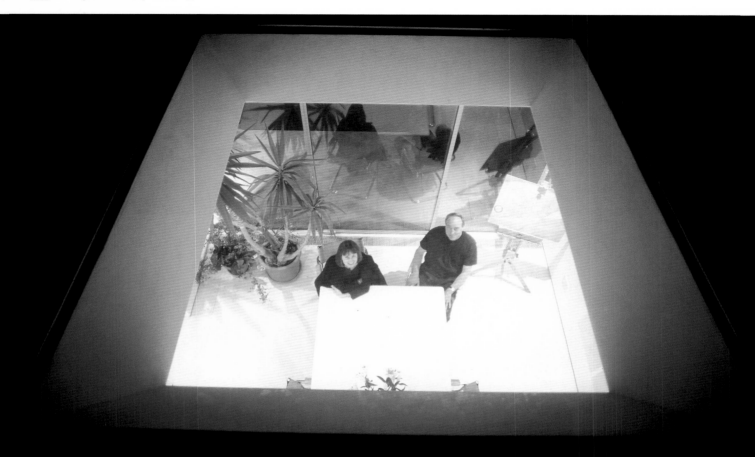

01◁The small dining room extension at Park Hall Road in Dulwich embodies the same design approach as the practice's larger projects, addressing the spatial relationship between the inside and the outside in an innovative way.

The brief was to replace a dilapidated conservatory, creating a 'garden room' within a volume of 4 x 4 x 3 metres facing south onto a small urban garden, and to improve circulation within the family home.

Solid and transparent planes create and blur the boundaries between internal and external space.

02◁Drawing inspiration from James Turrell's Meeting House installation, a central skylight with chamfered reveals punctures the ceiling and challenges conventional perceptions of depth of field.

The skylight frames an ever-changing skyscape, providing a constant reminder of the external environment.

Location:	Dulwich, London UK
Commission date:	1994
Completion date:	September 1996
Building area:	16m²
Client:	Diana Edmunds and Chris Wilkinson
Structural engineer:	Whitby Bird & Partners
Awards:	RIBA Regional Award 1997

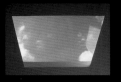

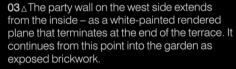

03 △ The party wall on the west side extends from the inside – as a white-painted rendered plane that terminates at the end of the terrace. It continues from this point into the garden as exposed brickwork.

04 ◁ The limestone floor also extends through from the inside to the outside forming a small terrace into which is set a long, thin rectangular pool. Diana Edmunds's light reeds reflect sparkling light back into the space.

A carefully detailed glazing system gives a high level of visual transparency on the south side between the interior space and the garden. Horizontal framing is recessed into the ceiling and floor planes, as are the channels of the sliding-door gear and the glazed return. The only structure that remains visible is the minimal framing of the sliding glazed door.

05 ▷ The flat roof above the dining room, accessed by french doors from an upper-level room, is used as a sun terrace. Finished with hardwood decking laid flush with the glazing to the skylight, it creates an exciting outside space, with views to the room below.

It is much more than just another room, it is more like an inhabited light and space installation which can be tuned to suit one's mood.
Chris Wilkinson

Princes Club Ski-Tow Pavilion

The Ski-Tow Pavilion was commissioned by the Princes Club, a water sports and fitness club at Bedfont Lakes, following the submission of a number of design studies and a master plan for the whole site.

The brief called for an elegant, low-cost, waterside pavilion. This simple building of 72 square metres was built for less than £60,000.

The ski tow is a boatless skiing system, which makes the sport very accessible. It comprises a moving high-level cable, edging the lake, and supported at each corner by a tall raking mast. Skiers are pulled around the lake by ropes trailing at intervals from the tow cable.

The pavilion incorporates the tow plant, operator and launch jetties, as well as providing viewing, ticketing and storage facilities.

01 ▷ The simple steel frame comprises three structural bays: two are glazed and the third is clad in timber. Four steel angles abutted back to back with separating plates create a cruciform, which forms a column. The column is tapered to a point at the base and at its head an articulated joint connects it with the perimeter roof channel. The size of the steel member was minimized so that the roof would appear as slim as possible.

02 ◁ A separate roof canopy of tensile fabric cantilevers over the water to provide shelter for the operator and to mark the launch point.

03 △ The materials of construction are minimal: steel, glass, timber and fabric. The floor is made of hardwood decking and the solid-wall enclosure is constructed out of plywood panels with a lacquered finish. The glazing is also extremely simple: full-height sheets are fixed into recessed channels at the top and bottom. Rainwater is collected in one corner of the roof from where it drops down a chain into the water below.

Location:	Bedfont Lakes UK
Commission date:	1995
Completion date:	April 1996
Building area:	192m²
Client:	The Princes Club
Structural engineer:	Buro Happold
Awards:	RIBA Award for Architecture
	(Stephen Lawrence Prize Shortlist) 1998
	Architects Journal/Robin Ellis Small Projects Award 1997

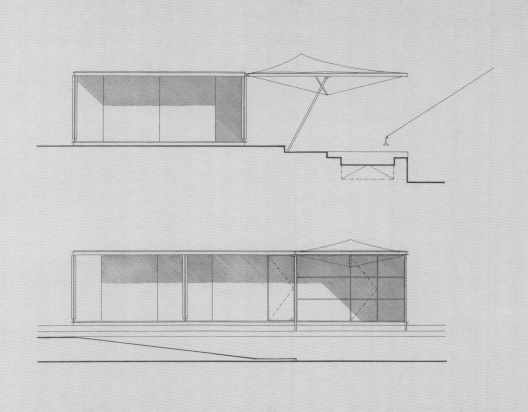

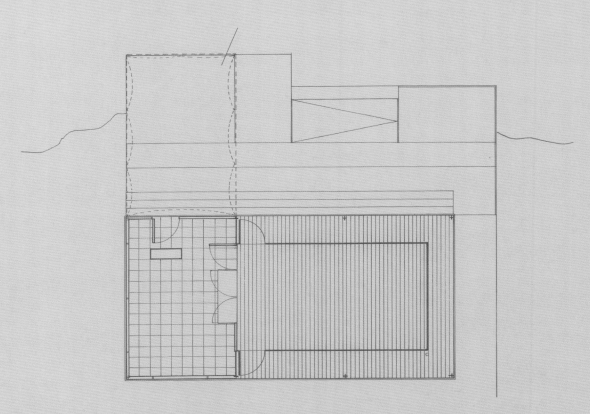

Half plywood enclosure and half glass box set back within a steel frame, it is an elegant addition to the modernist pavilion tradition.
Jessica Cargill Thompson – Building Magazine / 27 / February / 98

Retail Warehouse

01△ The retail warehouse provides an interesting vehicle for exploring the design of double-curvature forms. The brief, which called for a landmark gateway building for the Merryhill Shopping Centre, is fulfilled through the use of a strong geometric form. It is both sympathetic to and contrasts with the existing rectilinear buildings.

02◁ Drawing inspiration from shell forms such as the sea urchin, possible shapes were explored through computer and physical modelling.

03▷ The design is derived from an ellipse in section and is circular in plan. A curved chord is cut away from the shell form to give a front facade to the building.

This squashed spherical form with radial ribs provides an economic structure. Laminated timber ribs are clad with a stressed skin of plywood.

A central boss connecting the structural ribs keeps the curved timber within the permitted bending radius for the material.

04▷ Cladding doubly curved forms can be expensive, but in this design a rain screen of lightweight woven stainless-steel mesh, stretched over a single-skin welded membrane, provides a low-cost alternative.

This concept involves strands of stainless-steel wire being woven in a diamond pattern and shaped in segments that can be clamped together to achieve the required form. The mesh is then supported off the membrane on cast-glass spacers. The overall construction for the enclosure is relatively simple, and easy to fabricate on site.

05◁ Drawings and models demonstrate how the spectacular interior space fulfils the required functions.

The project illustrates the potential of shell structures to create flexible space and dynamic form.

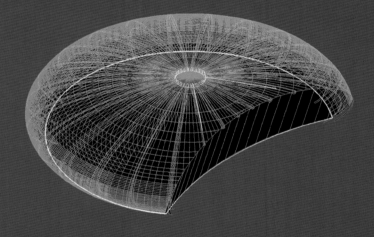

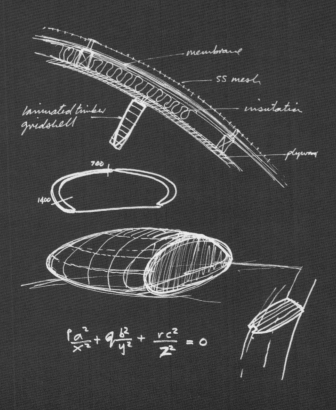

Location: Merry Hill UK
Design proposal: 1997
Client: Chelsfield Plc
Structural engineer: Ove Arup & Partners

$$p\frac{a^2}{x^2} + q\frac{b^2}{y^2} + r\frac{c^2}{z^2} = 0$$

WC Pod

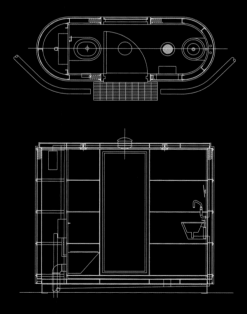

During 1999 the Design Council awarded just over 1,000 products 'Millennium Product' status. Six Wilkinson Eyre projects received this accolade: Stratford Station, South Quay Footbridge, the Challenge of Materials 'active' bridge, Lockmeadow Footbridge, Hulme Arch and the WC Pods at Stratford Market Depot. Only one or two multimillion-pound companies with large research budgets exceeded this number of awards.

01 △ The WC Pods are one of several special components purpose-designed for Stratford Market Depot. The scale of the main train shed means that distances to the central cloakrooms are too great for convenience. Five pods were needed within the building and a design was developed accordingly. Characterized by robust finishes, the pods are manufactured from stainless steel. They make a welcome and more contemporary alternative to commercially available pods typically used in public places.

02△ Internal finishes, with stainless-steel wall panels and sanitary fittings, complement those outside.

03▷ Seen against the translucent cladding of the south wall of the Stratford Market Depot, the WC pods provide a reference to human scale in this vast industrial building.

Location:	London UK
Commission date:	1991
Completion date:	April 1996
Client:	London Underground Limited
Structural engineer:	Hyder Consulting Limited
Manufactured by:	AME-EURO
Awards:	Design Council Millennium 'Product' Award 1999

02

03

Camera Arm

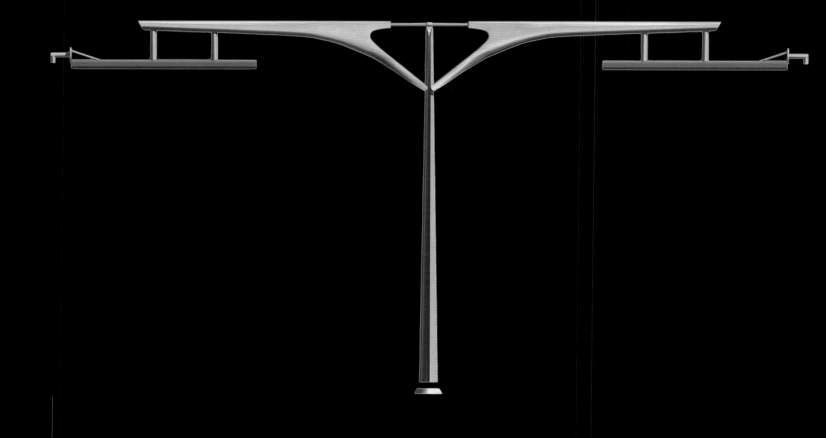

The London Underground system includes a large number of architecturally interesting stations, many of which have listed or protected status. These are referred to as 'heritage' stations, and all new work here must be of a high design quality and is subject to the scrutiny of English Heritage.

01 △ The design for the camera support arm and post is for use at a number of stations on the Piccadilly Line. Although London Underground Limited have a basic standard post and arm, they were not considered appropriate to these stations.

02 ◁ In the new design there are 32 assemblies installed in varying configurations. The posts are either set back at a minimum distance from the platform edge, or centred on an island platform. They support a standard CCTV camera on a system-wide 'Videmech' bracket, which positions the camera at a specific height and clearance in relation to the trains. The cameras provide live coverage of platform activity for train drivers on monitors sited at the ends of the platforms.

03 ▷ The support arms come in three different lengths to suit varying conditions but are derived from the same geometry. The form is sculpted in a hollow bone-like arrangement, which works visually, either singly or in pairs. The void makes it possible to incorporate a mass damper to iron out vibrations (from wind gusts) which would otherwise impair camera performance. The standard vertical hangers supporting the camera bracket are held by a spigot fixing.

The project, and the arm in particular, demonstrates the dichotomy between machine and craft-based fabrication. The double curvature form is complex and would have been difficult to manufacture using machine processes. The use of more traditional metalwork skills proved a more economic way to produce the desired result.

Location:	London UK
Commission date:	1996
Completion date:	December 1996
Client:	London Underground Limited
Structural engineer:	Whitby Bird & Partners
Main contractor:	Crane & Rowbury Architectural Metalworkers

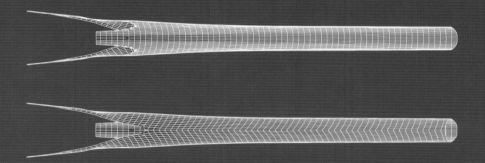

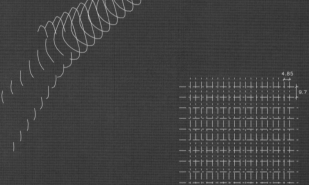

4.85

9.7

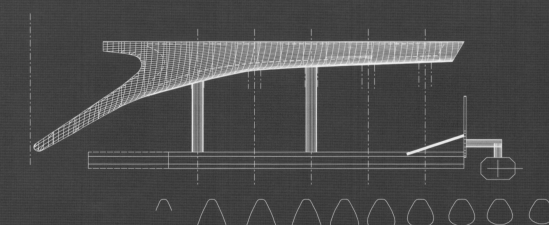

04

Commercial & Leisure

Merry Hill Multiplex

The spiral concept represents a totally new approach to the design of multiplex cinemas which is both functional and exciting.
Chris Wilkinson

01◁ Merry Hill is an extremely successful regional shopping centre which is likely to achieve the status of a town. In 1998 Wilkinson Eyre Architects were invited to advise on the master plan to add leisure facilities – including a new multiplex cinema – to the area on the north side of the shopping centre alongside the refurbished and straightened Dudley Canal.

The site is located on a newly formed plateau 12 metres higher than the shopping centre to the south of the canal. North of the canal the land continues to rise towards Brierly Hill High Street. These changes in level presented a challenge when integrating the scheme with the shopping centre.

The ring road provides access to Merry Hill Shopping Centre, running at a low level around the south of the site. A new light transit system is planned, with a station on the site. Running along the canal at a high level, it will connect with Sandwell. The master plan also provides easy connections across the site and uses the canalside for leisure and public amenities.

02◁ The 20-screen multiplex cinema provides the focus for other retail and leisure activities within the master plan.

03◁ The design for the multiplex cinema, with seating for 4,100 people, is unique. In order to provide 19 auditoria of various sizes and a 294-seat 3-D Imax within a restricted site, multi-level stacking was required. The resulting form resembles a nautilus shell.

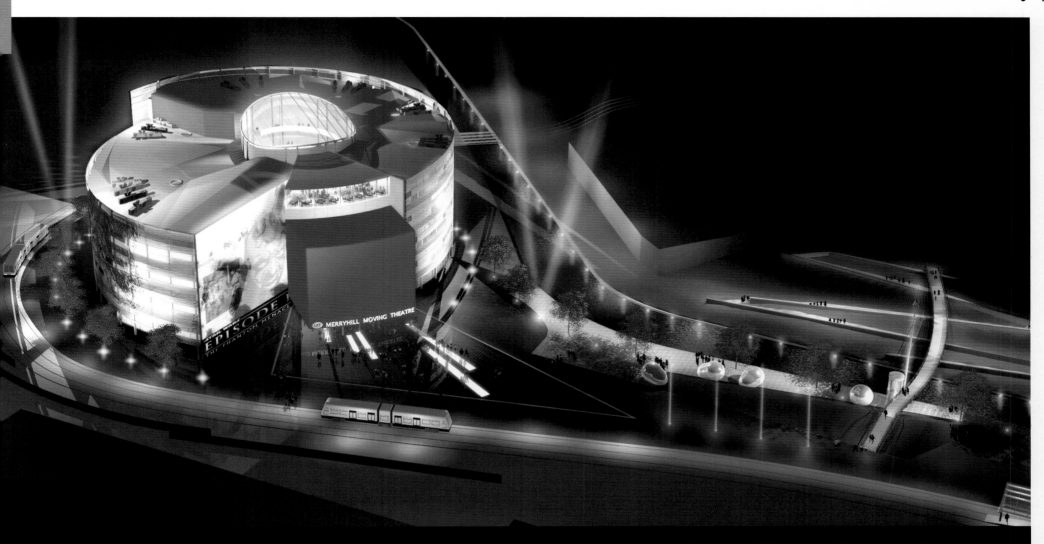

01

02

04◁ The auditoria, accessed by a spiral ramp,
are placed around a central circular space,
stacked in twos and threes according to size.

05▷ The vertical arrangement of each
stack of auditoria is defined by the ramp levels.
Flexibility for the point of access, however, is
provided by racked seating, which makes it
possible to achieve an even gradient of 1:15
with 1:20 breaks for the circular ramps.

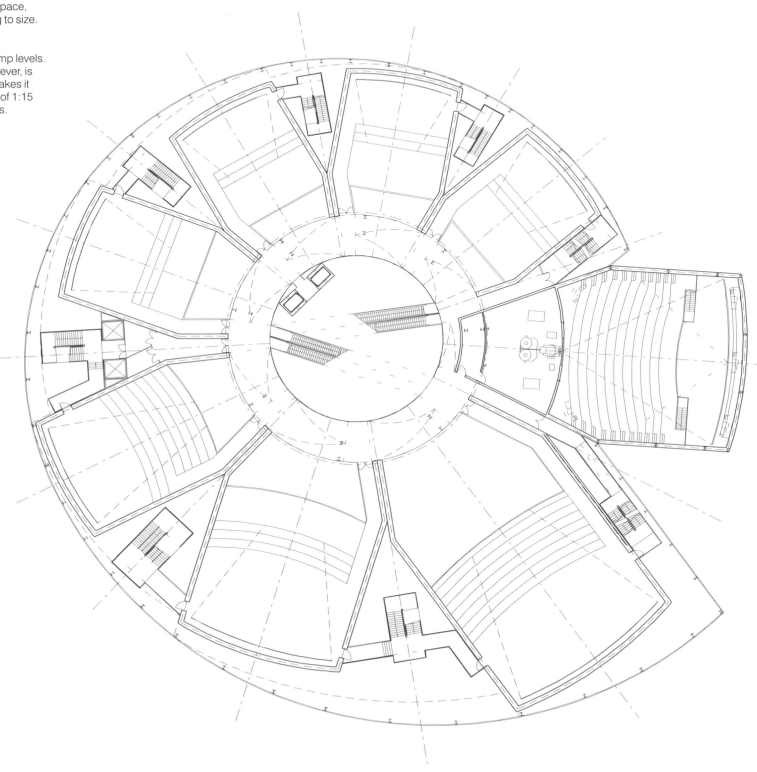

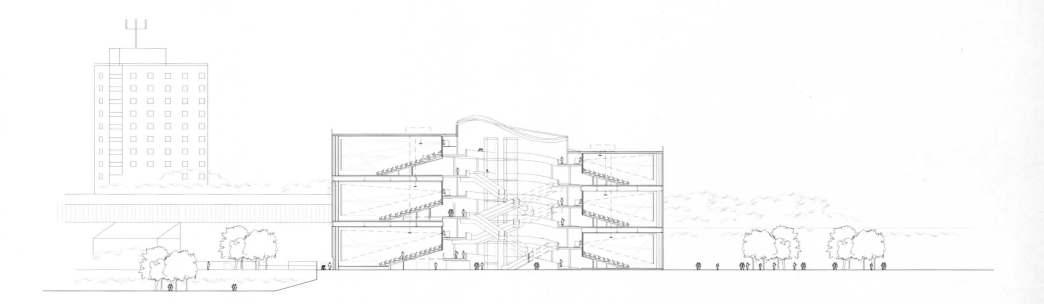

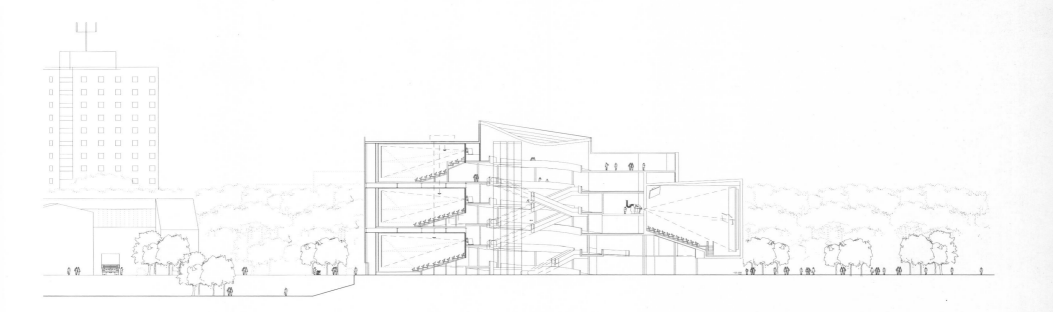

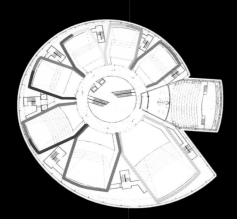

Location:	Merry Hill UK
Commission date:	1998
Completion date:	September 2001
Site area:	15,000m²
Client:	Chelsfield PLC
Structural engineer:	Allott and Lomax
Quantity surveyor:	Davis Langdon & Everest
Services engineer:	John Packer Associates
Fire engineer:	Buro Happold FEDRA
Acoustic engineer:	Cole Jarman Associates

06△ The animated central space provides a focus for the building while the transparent fabric cushion roof creates a well-lit protected environment. Food and retail activities are housed at ground level. Speedy access to the upper levels is supplied by escalators, which crisscross the space, and lifts. There is a direct route to the Imax, located above the entrance, where a waiting area and upper-level bar offer views over the canal. The projection booths to each auditorium connect, extending over the ramps, so that the outer skin, which houses a back-projection screen, can be seen from the central space.

07▷ The stacks of auditoria open out on the outer perimeter, creating wedge-shaped spaces which are used for fire escapes and the distribution of services. Visible through the transparent enclosing skin, these are painted in a series of bright colours following the order of the spectrum.

08▷ The cladding, which follows the structure's spiral form, is characterized by six different levels of transparency. This affects the intensity of colour seen from the outside so that the otherwise blank facade becomes a lively and exciting elevation which changes as the lighting varies.

Teesside Millennium Building

01 △ The Teesside Millennium Building is an exciting fast-track design project with a number of sports and leisure facilities under one huge roof on the north bank of the River Tees.

02 ▷ Wilkinson Eyre developed the idea of a 'supershed' in order to create one of Europe's biggest buildings and one that would become an important landmark structure.

03 ▷ The design proposes a shell form measuring 840 x 160 metres, to house: a 10,000-seat arena, an ice pad, an indoor competition-rowing water-course, sports club, a rackets centre, a biomedical sciences research centre, an environmental research centre and residential accommodation for the university. The final internal footprint covers over 13 hectares.

A lightweight roof constructed of titanium panels with glazed rooflights is supported on a steel structure with few internal columns. The facade facing the river incorporates intelligent glass systems to maximize environmental performance.
The internal watercourse uses recycled water from the river and follows the curved line of the building's north elevation. The curved shape, moulded into the landscape on the north side, reduces the appearance of visual mass and helps to minimize obstruction to the wind.

The use of a widespan roof enclosure results in a single iconic identity, despite the multiple functions enclosed.

Location:	Teesside UK
Design proposal:	1995
Site area:	50 acres
Client:	Teesside Development Group
Structural & services engineer:	Ove Arup & Partners

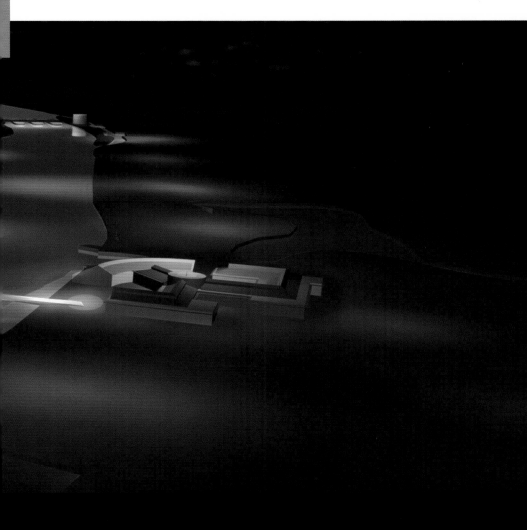

It will combine building technologies in a way never before attempted. It will set new standards in materials, computer modelling, architectural design and energy efficiency.
Duncan Hall –
chief executive of the Teesside Development Corporation

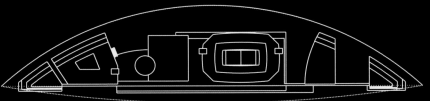

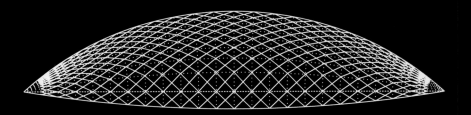

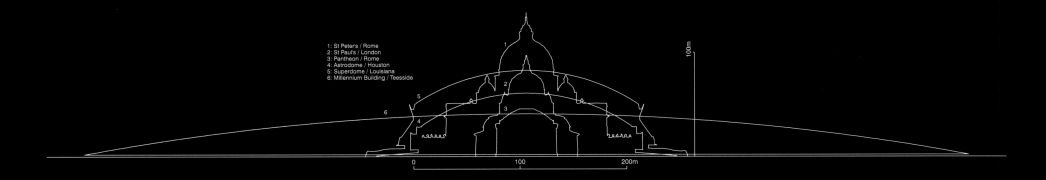

1: St Peter's / Rome
2: St Paul's / London
3: Pantheon / Rome
4: Astrodome / Houston
5: Superdome / Louisiana
6: Millennium Building / Teesside

0   100   200m   100m

City Tower

Commissioned in 2000, City Tower is Wilkinson Eyre's first skyscraper project. The design addresses the demand in the City of London for large, single-occupancy, modern office space by replacing a relatively small-scale development on the site with one that offers 57,000 square metres of lettable space, comprising office and retail areas.

01▷The site is one of very few that could accommodate a tower remaining in the core City area, situated on the junction between Gracechurch Street and Fenchurch Street and reaching back to Lime Street.

02△ The City of London context means that there are planning issues to consider. The debate about whether or not to allow tall buildings in the City focuses on how such buildings are positioned in relation to existing clusters of buildings, with particular reference to the dominance of Tower 42 (formerly the Natwest Tower). So the relationship of City Tower, both with key London views in general and the nearby dome of St Paul's Cathedral in particular, is of prime importance. This project provides an interesting opportunity, therefore, to explore the design of a skyscraper constrained by height restrictions and a limited footprint area.

03▷The tower is composed of two shell-like forms of differing heights which seem to have slipped apart. Despite its modest height, the design achieves a feeling of verticality and slenderness more characteristic of taller skyscrapers in North America.

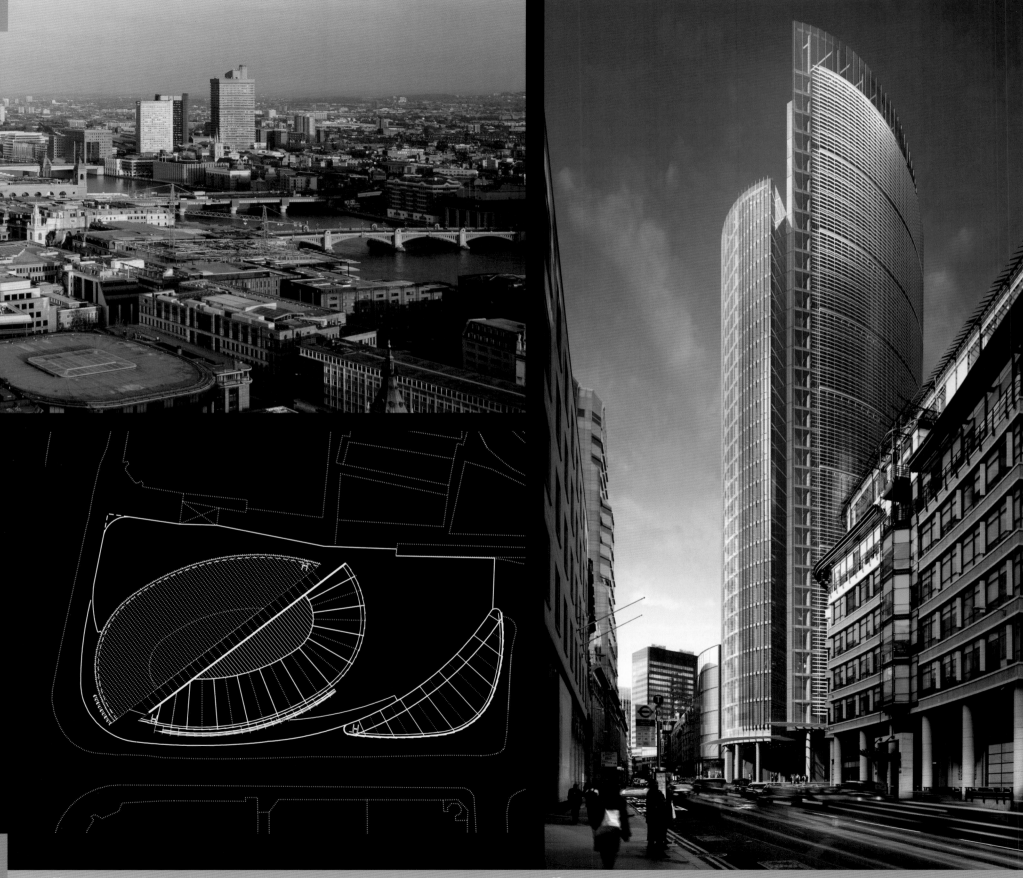

04 ▷ The tower's vertical emphasis is most marked at the important junction of Gracechurch Street and Fenchurch Street. A six-storey podium structure fills the site at street level, but the dynamic form of the tower emerges from the side of this structure; set back from the two main traffic routes, it is given space to express its dynamism. Optimum public space is provided at street level; retail space and three deep-plan dealer floors utilize the lower floors, while there is office space above, arranged around a central core containing all the lifts, escape stairs and toilets.

05 ▷ At the head of the tower one side drops away. The extruded forms are cut at opposing angles, which lightens the overall impact and provides visual interest, as well as reducing overshadowing. The tower is predominantly glazed, the degree of transparency of the glass varying according to orientation. Bands of louvres reduce the cooling loads of the building and help to reduce energy consumption. Horizontal louvres on the south elevation also serve to minimize glare, while a vertical band of louvres on the west elevation specifically shields the building from lower-angle direct sunlight.

06 △ The context of the building has been considered very carefully. The panorama of the City of London that opens up from Waterloo Bridge is particularly important. From here there is a clear view of St Paul's Cathedral, Tower 42, the Commercial Union building, the Lloyds building, Wilkinson Eyre's City Tower scheme and the Kleinwort Benson Tower, with DS7 at Canary Wharf in the distance.

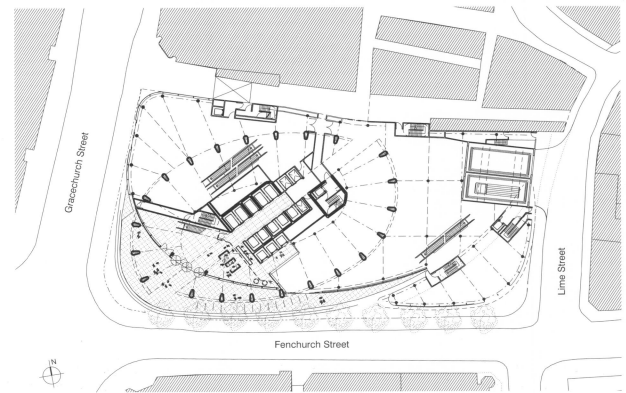

Gracechurch Street

Lime Street

Fenchurch Street

N

04

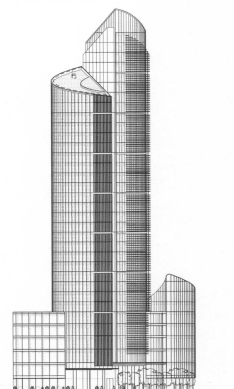

05

06

07 △ Views from the east are more restricted but the tower's gentle, non-rectilinear forms are designed to sit easily within the varied cityscape.

08 ◁ An increasingly lively destination since its recent rejuvenation, the South Bank is today attracting significantly greater numbers of visitors than it used to. This view of the City has therefore become more important too.

Location: City of London UK
Commission date: 2000
Building area: 57,000m²
Client: Churchill Securities Limited
Structural &
services engineer: WSP Group
Environmental engineer: WSP Group

05

Cultural

Challenge of Materials Gallery

They rose to the challenge and
made the walkway of glass, giving it a
phosphorescent sheen by fibre optics.
Crossing it is like walking on water.
Nonie Niesewand –
Independent / 9 / April / 98

01 ◁ The Challenge of Materials Gallery at the
Science Museum, which opened to the public
in May 1997, was Wilkinson Eyre's first museum
project. Working in collaboration with the
Exhibition Designer Jasper Jacobs Associates,
the firm won the commission in a design
competition in 1995.

Challenge of Materials demonstrates the
diversity of materials and the limits to which they
can be manipulated. Both the actual exhibits
and the form and construction of the
architecture of the gallery are dictated by
the theme.

02 ▷ An innovative glass-and-steel bridge
provides a focus for the gallery and an icon for
the scheme.

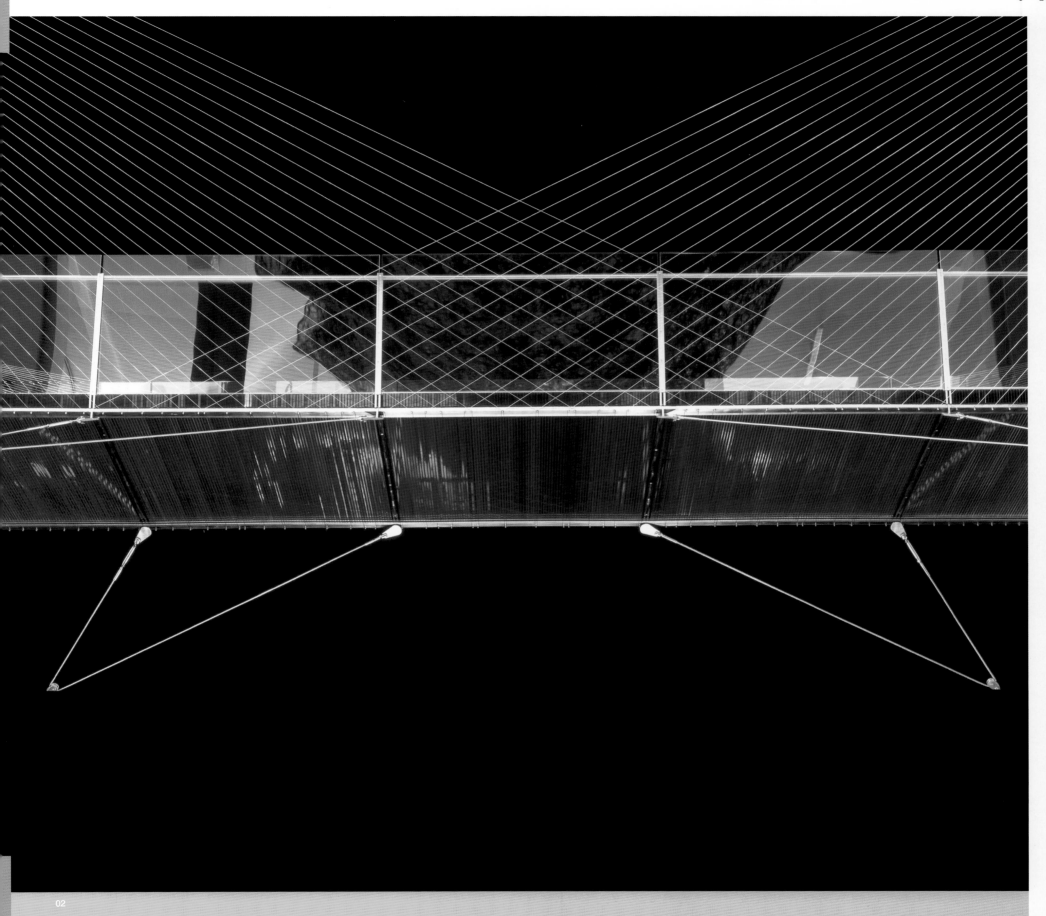

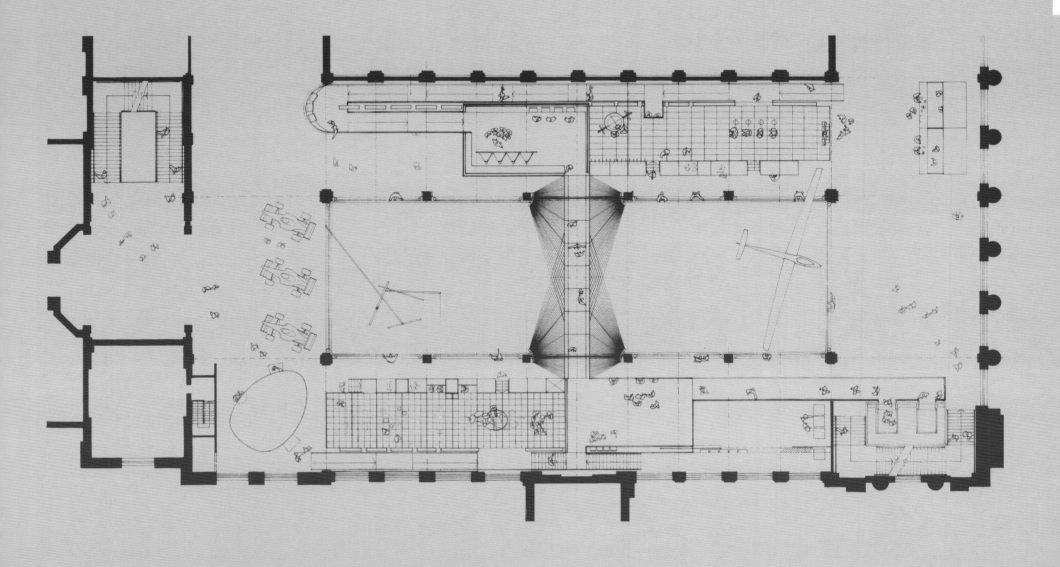

03 △ Located on the first-floor gallery around the Science Museum's atrium, the gallery comprises a series of varied architectural interventions – creating a thematic framework for the visitor. The various accretions of past exhibitions have been stripped back in order to reveal the original fabric and to allow natural light to re-enter the space.

04 ▷ The existing windows benefit the gallery with natural daylight, while a translucent skin in front of the glazing prevents both the harmful effects of direct sunlight and heat gain on the south wall.

05 ◁ The dynamic relationship between the open gallery and its internal sub-spaces, which house a series of interactive and audio-visual displays, provides pace for the visitor. Features include walk-through glass showcases and vast information plates of steel and glass, cantilevered vertically from the floor.

06 △ A steel mezzanine at one end of the glass-and-steel bridge is a good place to gain a view right across the gallery.

07 ▷ Access to the mezzanine from ground level is provided by a special reproduction of the extruded aluminium stairway designed by Richard Rogers & Partners for the Lloyds building.

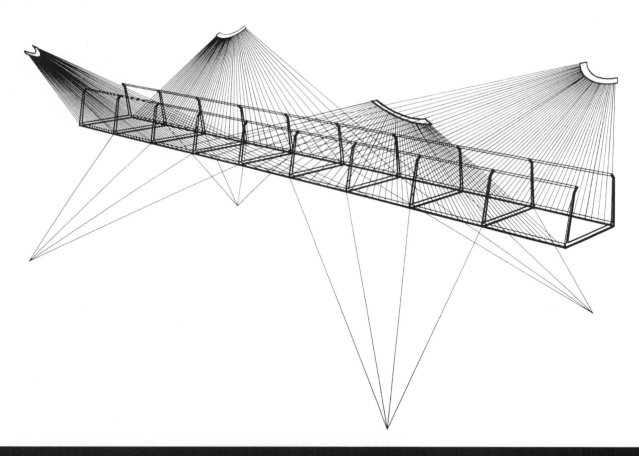

08◁The steel cladding of the audio-visual enclosure (built on two levels) is in itself a display of all the different steel panels produced by British Steel.

09▷At the heart of the gallery the dramatic Challenge of Materials Bridge spans the atrium. Having been designed to the limits of technical feasibility, the bridge acts as a legible demonstration of material capability. Challenging visitors to cross, it becomes an interactive exhibit.

10△Computer modelling was used to explore the minimal design concept of the bridge. The glass deck is held in position by a vast number of ultra-fine stainless-steel wires.

08   10   09

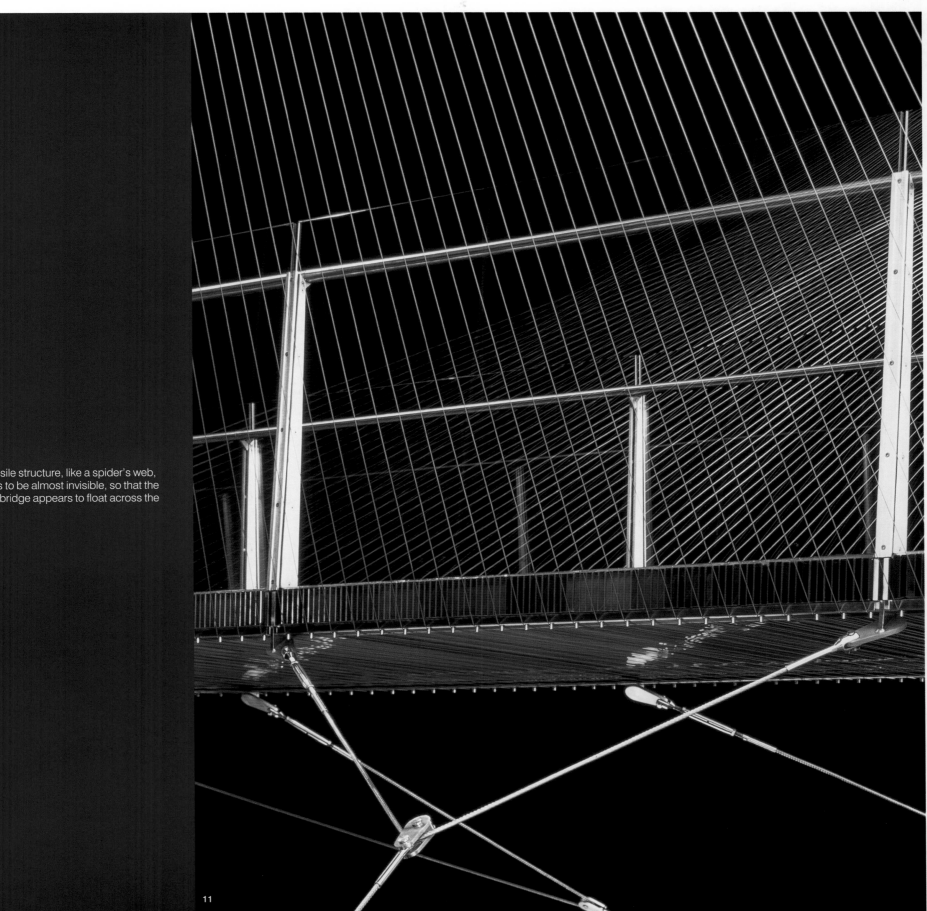

11 ▷ The tensile structure, like a spider's web, is so light as to be almost invisible, so that the deck of the bridge appears to float across the space.

12◁Laminated glass planks laid vertically onto a stainless-steel channel (25 millimetres deep) form the deck of the bridge. Running from the main fabric of the building, the supporting wires (1.5 millimetres in diameter) wrap around a protruding peg, pass under the deck and connect back to the architectural framework.

13◁The wires are attached to a crescent-shaped stainless-steel plate which is then fixed to the building structure by a larger, angled steel plate. Purpose-designed bronze piano pegs secure the wires and provide the means to tension the structure. Load cells in the fixtures are linked to a computer.

14▷This computer makes the bridge a unique musical instrument. While the wires hum when amplified, the computer relays the compositions of sound artist Ron Geesin, triggering sounds related to the loads imposed by visitors crossing the bridge when sensors on the underside of the bridge pick up variations in movement.

The successful integration of architecture and exhibition design at the Challenge of Materials Gallery has informed the firm's subsequent museum projects.

Location:	London UK	
Commission date:	1995	
Completion date:	May 1997	
Client:	Science Museum, London	
Exhibition design		
& lead consultant:	Jasper Jacob Associates	
Structural engineer:	Whitby, Bird & Partners	
Sound & light artist (bridge):	Ron Geesin	
Services engineer:	Atelier Ten	
Awards:	RIBA Award for Architecture	1998
	Design Week Award for Exhibition Design	1998
	Challenge of Materials Footbridge:	
	Design Council Millennium 'Product' Award	1998

Making the Modern World Gallery

The objects' past life gives resonance.
They aren't just interpreting what
happened, they are what happened.
They are witnesses to history and actors
in it. ... You are allowed to explore the
various layers of meaning within this
room for yourself.
Deyan Sudjic –
Observer / 25 / June / 2000

01▷A major new gallery for the Science Museum, Making the Modern World opened to the public in July 2000. Here, for the first time in a single mixed-media gallery, the most important and iconic artefacts of the museum's collections are exhibited.

Wilkinson Eyre's involvement in the project dates from 1997 when, as a result of a design competition, the firm was appointed Lead Designer, responsible for all aspects of the exhibition design.

02▷Forming a long vista through the gallery, a dramatic sequence of iconic objects charts a cultural history of the rise of the modern industrial world – arranged chronologically from 1750 to the present day. Exhibits include Stephenson's locomotive 'Rocket'; Nick Ut's Leica camera, which was used to take the adjacent famous picture of Kim Phuc running down a road in Vietnam following a napalm attack in 1972; Crick and Watson's DNA spiral model; and the Apollo 10 command module, which orbited the moon in 1968.

The scale and proportions of the gallery are similar to those of a cathedral. Working with the existing architecture, removing some elements entirely and enhancing others, the structure of the exhibition design has transformed the interior to create a light, bright space. A Pietra Serena limestone floor, crisp glass cases and barriers and white concrete plinths for major objects are some of the additions that reinforce the feeling of contemporary monumentalism.

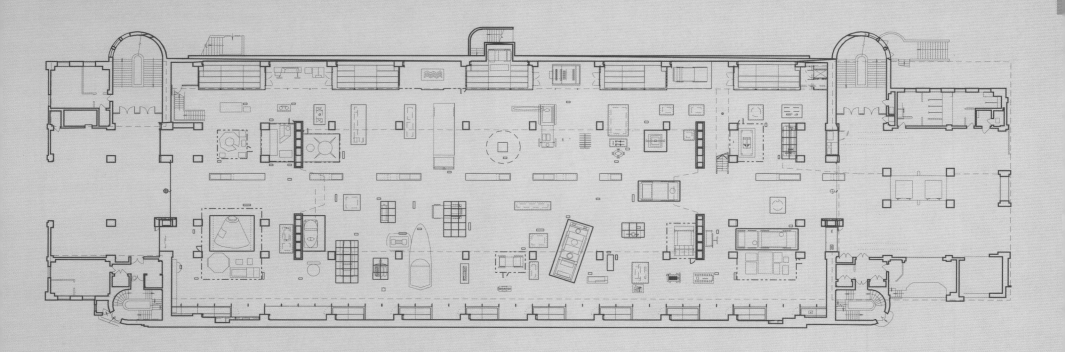

03△ While the principal exhibits occupy the central space, parallel displays run up both sides.

04◁ To the north a long case 5.5metres high stretches the whole length of the gallery, rather like the glass facade of a building – and detailed accordingly. At the lower level it displays a vast range of objects referred to as 'Technology in Everyday Life', and at the upper level there are a range of models covering the same period. Not only has the latter rejuvenated a mezzanine walkway, it also allows direct comparisons to be made between the historic iconic objects and the contemporary technology of each period, without the use of extensive explanatory graphic panels.

05△ A smaller-scale linear gallery on the south side comprises nine bays, each exploring a theme pertinent to a particular historical period: the Age of the Engineer, Defiant Modernism and Design Diversity, to name but a few. In order to facilitate the display of smaller objects and art works, the design had to be flexible enough to accommodate changes in scale, material and lighting levels; the series of glass fins that define the bays also support a canopy, which appears to reduce the scale of the gallery itself.

06▷ The objective of the design was to create a space that felt – and looked – like an art or sculpture gallery. Interpretive material is generally confined to simple captions, only a few special monoliths offering discrete active displays. As well as providing the visitor with an opportunity to sit and contemplate the exhibits, a central line of benches – which incorporate cases – emphasizes the linear chronology of the gallery.

Location:	London UK
Commission date:	1997
Completion date:	June 2000
Building area:	2,000m²
Client:	Science Museum, London
Structural engineer:	b-Consultants
Services engineer:	SVM
Lighting consultant:	Richard Aldridge
Graphic designer:	Farrow Design
Main contractor:	Mansell

Wellcome Wing

Opened by the Queen in June 2000, the Wellcome Wing at the Science Museum has been well received – by the museum profession and scientists as well as by the general public. Wilkinson Eyre were appointed Masterplanners and Exhibition Designers for the main ground-floor gallery of the new building (designed by MacCormac Jamieson and Prichard) as a result of a design competition held in 1997. The project represents for the firm both a new venture in cutting-edge interactive exhibition design and a continuation of a strong working relationship established between Wilkinson Eyre and the Science Museum.

01◁In order to make computer monitors and digital displays easily legible, the Wellcome Wing has been designed to be dark. A blue glass wall on the west elevation combines with side walls lit by blue lighting to create an intensely blue space. The entrance, meanwhile, is framed by a glowing orange zone – to create maximum contrast between the new wing and the naturally lit Making the Modern World Gallery next to it.

02▷In the entrance area, with lifts and stairs to the left, visitor information to the right and a restaurant straight ahead, there are extensive views of the Wellcome Wing's multi-level 'Theatre of Science'. Displays in this space include several 'Talking Points': a Maclaren Formula One racing car which crashed at 200mph; and a sculpture by Marc Quinn of a vase of flowers frozen in liquid silicone.

03◁A kinetic light sculpture by Peter Sedgeley provides a visual and physical link between the entrance area and the rest of the Wellcome Wing. His beacon, revolving slowly like a gyroscope, moves diagonally through the space along a cable. Constructed of polycarbonate rings and dichroic light chambers, it emits an array of coloured reflections.

04 ◁ The main activities of the gallery are defined by clear circulation routes. Lighting plays a significant role: large backlit signage panels in each zone provide easy identification, while all exhibits glow with coloured light and ambient lighting has been kept to a minimum.

In the restaurant the row of glowing, glass-topped tables – standing beneath a line of neon tube lights (suspended by virtually invisible cables) – underlines the strong linear form.

05 ▽ Adjacent to the restaurant, Antenna was conceived as a regularly updated display of Science and Technology news. The central glowing benches house touch-screen computer monitors, updated daily, which offer the opportunity to explore the very latest science news.

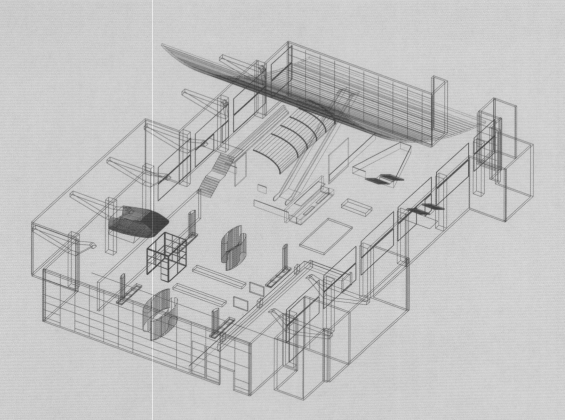

06 ▽ Temporary exhibitions, changed every week, utilize the areas at the sides of the space. The backlit display panels (4 metres high), constructed from purpose-made aluminium extrusions and curved polycarbonate panels, have extended plinths so that a variety of exhibition display systems – including computer monitors – may be added as and when necessary.

07 ▷ Pairs of curved and perforated stainless-steel foil screens (3 metres high) form the (very flexible) Features display; interlocked, they create a single display unit, while opened up, they provide a contained exhibition space. A curved lightweight open-web structure – similar to that of an aircraft wing – forms the steel framework. Neon lighting fixed to this structure glows through the external skin.

08 △ The Pattern Pod zone, designed for children under eight years old, is a contained space, a curved steel structure covered by a stretched membrane – scaled down to fit children. It houses interactive displays and games which explore the theme of patterns, providing opportunities to learn about science through play. Children can even generate their own patterns which are then projected onto the fabric screens and the main end wall of the building.

Location:	London UK
Commission date:	1997
Completion date:	June 2000
Building Area:	2,000m²
Client:	Science Museum, London
Structural engineer:	b-Consultants
Building design:	MacCormac Jamieson & Prichard
Services engineer:	SVM
Lighting consultant:	DHA Design Services
Graphic designer:	Johnson Banks
Main contractor:	Mansell

Explore @ Bristol

Explore at-Bristol re-uses its pioneering reinforced concrete structure and innovative new glazing to blur the distinction between building and exhibition.
Jeremy Melvin –
RIBA Journal / January / 2000

Explore at-Bristol science centre was the first major cultural building project won by the practice, following the Challenge of Materials project at the Science Museum. It presented an opportunity to develop further the idea of responsive buildings.

The brief called for the conversion of a listed Great Western Railways train shed – with new additions. It was to be the first of the next generation of science centres, based on the ideas of Frank Oppenheimer and Richard Gregory, the team which founded the Exploratorium in San Francisco and had set up the Exploratory (Explore's precursor) in Bristol. The main requirement of the brief was the provision of a flexible space to house a wide range of 'plores' (hands-on science exhibits) within a low-energy, environmentally friendly building. Building costs had to be within the budget fixed by the Millennium Commission.

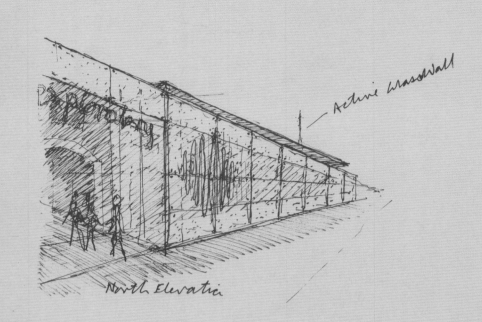

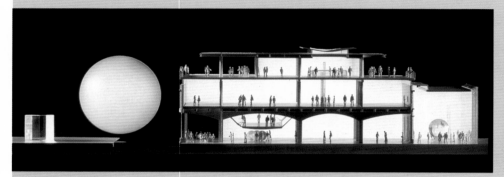

01 ▽ Explore at-Bristol is located on the Bristol waterfront and forms part of an ambitious scheme for the regeneration of the area.

02 △ The dilapidated state of the existing building presented a formidable challenge for reuse and restoration. The 1903 Hennebique reinforced concrete structure and enclosing walls were rough and grimy. The proportions of the ground floor space were grand and serviceable. However, the low floor-to-ceiling height of the first-floor space and close column spacing were not so adaptable.

03 △ Wilkinson Eyre's design concept makes maximum use of the existing building. Three simple interventions realise flexible exhibition space: a double height gallery to the north, a covered arcade and planetarium to the south, and a new roof addition covering approximately half of the floor area. The final design is essentially a refinement of the competition-winning scheme.

Traditional museums can appear rather elitist with closed imposing exteriors that deter people from entering. The scheme for Explore aims to engage the public by opening up the exterior of the building.

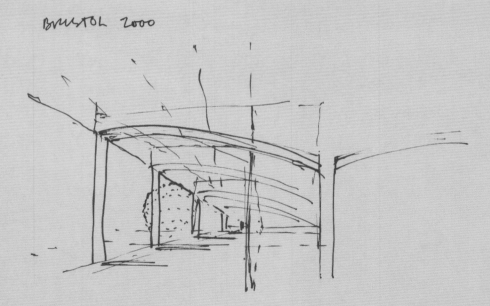

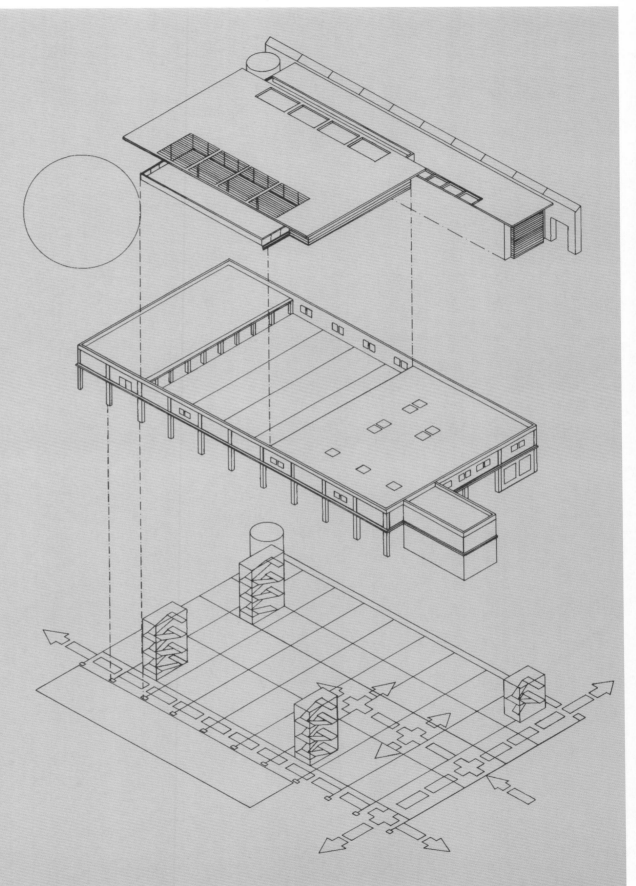

04▽ The double-height gallery to the north has a 90m long glass facade facing Bristol Cathedral, which creates an expansive gallery/shop window. The entrance leads through to an arcade around the perimeter of the building.

05◁ The covered pedestrian arcade on the south side faces Anchor Square and Millennium Square and encourages people to walk close to the building and look inside.

06▷ A rectangular hole has been punched through the existing roof and a two-storey steel box dropped in to create greater height and flexibility inside.

07▷The glazing to Anchor Road is conceived as an active glass wall, which is animated, and constantly changes to give life and interest. The concept draws inspiration from a chameleon.

08▷There are multiple light sources connected to a sophisticated computerized control system, which can change completely the appearance of the building. Computer visualizations show how different surfaces can be lit with a range of different colours. These can be programmed or controlled by environment changes such as temperature or wind speed. Alternatively, the palette of colours could be 'played' by visiting artists.

09▽The glazing is a purpose-designed, suspended glass wall with glass fins. A strip of constantly changing applied film is fitted on the inside, along the length of the façade. It incorporates still images of differing opacity in prismatic, holographic, dichroic and thermographic sections. It is responsive to movement and variations in light from inside and out. Surface applied films include lenticular images, which are like holograms, and prismatic films, which break up the light in different ways.

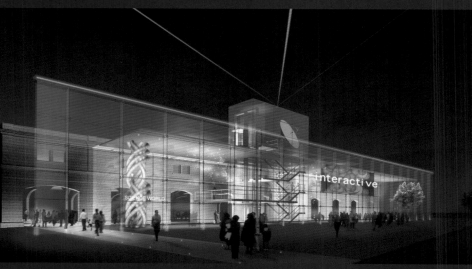

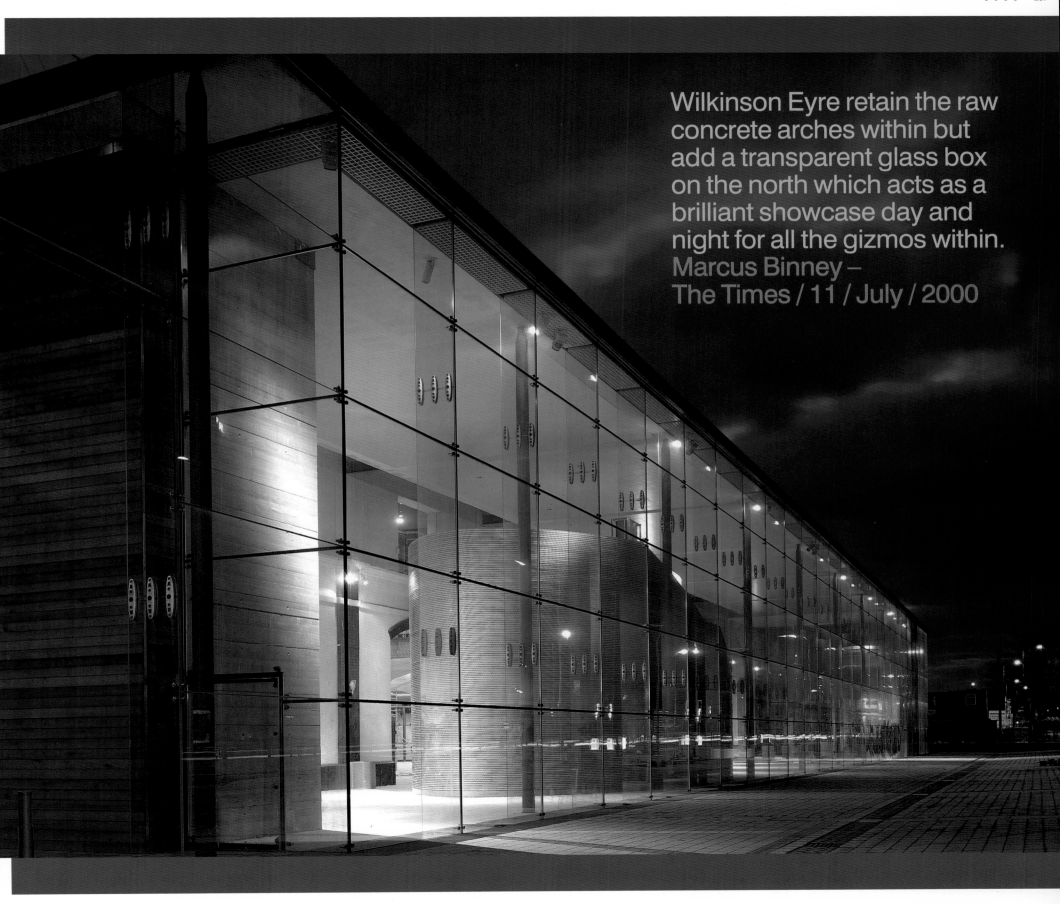

Wilkinson Eyre retain the raw concrete arches within but add a transparent glass box on the north which acts as a brilliant showcase day and night for all the gizmos within.
Marcus Binney –
The Times / 11 / July / 2000

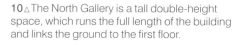

10△ The North Gallery is a tall double-height space, which runs the full length of the building and links the ground to the first floor.

11◁ The full-height glazing on one side provides clear views through to the street and the cathedral beyond.

12◁ A timber-clad pod at the east end houses the main ground-floor lavatories and a stair, which rises up on one side to a mezzanine space from which you can look down on the exhibits. From here, the stair continues up to join the first- floor exhibition space.

13◁ At the other end of the space, a large clear acrylic tank, 7m high and 3m in diameter, filled with pink balls, provides the energy bank for the building's air-conditioning.

14▷ There are 65,000 balls of 100mm diameter, filled with eutectic salts, which change state at 27˚c. The latent energy is converted to warm or cool air, by heatpumps within the building, as required. This is backed up by a system of displacement ventilation, which uses two large thermal wheels located in the rooftop plant rooms.

13

14

15▷ The space inside varies to suit the different requirements of the exhibitions. A café on the southside, which spills onto the piazza, and a shop on the northside flank the main entrance foyer with a shopfront onto the arcade. Access through to the main ground-floor exhibition space is through a restricted entrance, which opens up to reveal the vaulted concrete spaces of the refurbished train shed, filled with interactive exhibits.

16▽ The Hennibique arched structure is clearly visible in the exhibition space.

17◁ Curtain walling along the back of the arcade emits natural daylight.

18◁ The vertical circulation to the floors above is by cores of stairs and lifts on the east and west ends of the space.

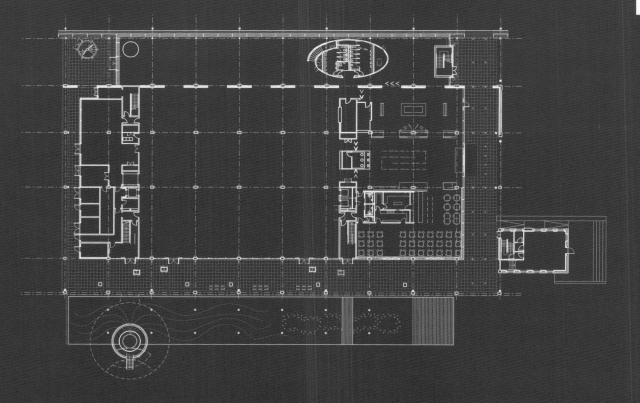

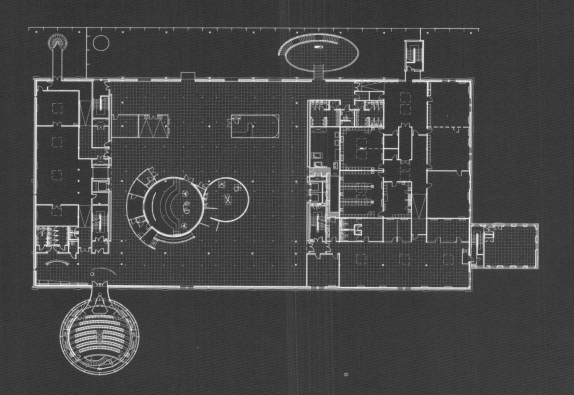

16

19▷The second-floor extension is designed as a flexible display space, which can be used for temporary exhibitions or corporate entertaining.

20◁The expansive timber-decked terraces take maximum advantage of the panoramic views of the harbourside to the south and the cathedral to the north. A canopy of angled aluminium louvres provides solar shading to the south terrace.

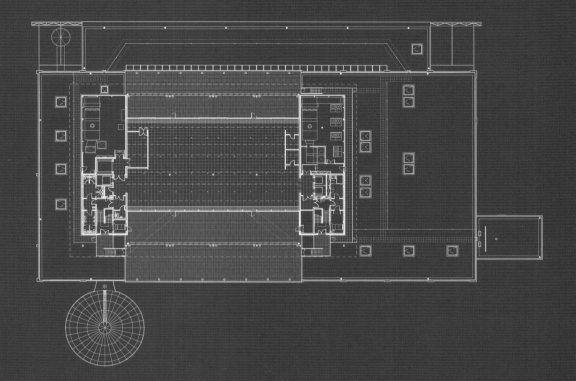

17

19
20

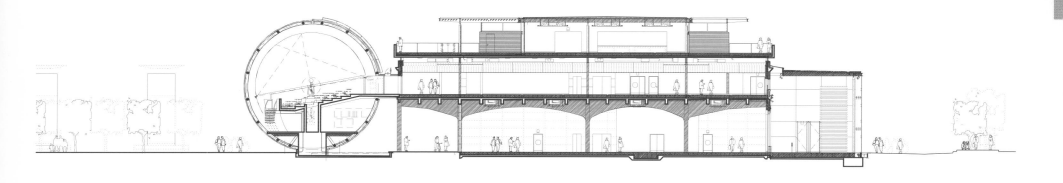

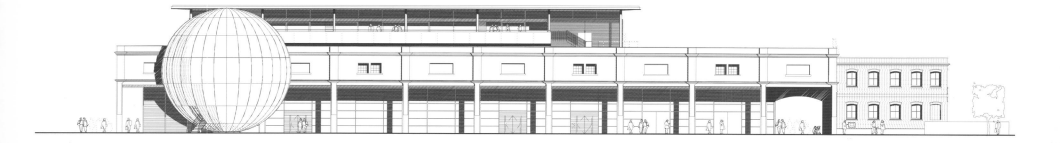

21 △ On the south elevation the arcade faces onto a shallow reflective rectangular pool, which reflects light onto the soffit above. The building enclosure is set back 6m and is constructed from a glazed aluminium walling system with solid panels of cedar cladding.

A planetarium is housed in a stainless steel sphere, 15m in diameter, which is seated on a small plinth half on land and half in water. It is accessed by bridge at first-floor level, which means the complete sphere is visible above ground level. At the base of the sphere, the shiny surface reflects the water and special equipment creates a cloud of 'mist' below the planetarium, which adds to the sense of mystery and excitement in the early evenings.

22 ▷ Cladding to the sphere is curved in one direction and arranged in vertical segments like an orange.

23 ▷ The existing GWR building has been thoroughly cleaned, repaired and painted with a translucent weatherproof paint, which maintains the essence of the concrete behind. The upper level accommodation appears as a horizontal band on tall columns, which are enhanced by the recess of the arcade. The new roof addition is separated from the existing building by a band of new in situ concrete above a line of clerestory glazing.

The Explore building has its own clear identity but it also plays an important part in the regeneration of the harbourside area. Together with Wildscreen at-Bristol (a complex which celebrates the natural world, comprising exhibition galleries, a tropical botanical house and an IMAX) and the new public spaces, it provides a new cultural centre for the City of Bristol.

Location:	Bristol UK
Commission date:	1995
Building completion date:	August 1999
Fit-out completion date:	April 2000
Building area:	8,200m²
Client:	at-Bristol
Structural engineer:	Ove Arup & Partners
Quantity surveyor:	Davis Langdon & Everest
Construction manager:	Woolf Limited

Attached to the back of
the building is a gleaming,
15m-diameter stainless-
steel sphere containing a
bijou planetarium.
Marcus Fairs –
Building Magazine /
7 / July / 2000

Magna

Magna brings new life to an industrial dinosaur and helps to regenerate Rotherham.
Chris Wilkinson

In 1998 Wilkinson Eyre were appointed as architects for the Magna Project, a scheme funded by the Millennium Commission, to be housed in the redundant Templeborough Steel Reprocessing Works.

With the story of steel as its main focus, the exhibition will explore the elements of earth, fire, air and water – all essential to the steel-making process – as subsidiary themes.

The brief called for the retention of the existing buildings and processing plant, whilst limited funds made it necessary to restrict the extent of the renovation works and to contain the area occupied by the exhibition.

01 ▷ The Templeborough Steel Reprocessing Works is a vast industrial building with three aisles, each 400m long and 35m high. The Wilkinson Eyre concept places four pavilions, connected by new steel bridges and walkways, within the existing space, each housing one of the element-themed exhibitions.

02 △ Each pavilion is designed to relate to its theme in a poetic way. The earth pavilion is constructed of solid steel plates reminiscent of tectonic plates; it is located in the basement below the ground slab. The air pavilion, meanwhile, is conceived as a dirigible airship enclosed in translucent cushion fabric and is hung high off the ground within the roof space. The water pavilion is a stainless-steel vessel sitting on the ground slab, and the fire pavilion, at the end of the space, is a black box suspended from the main structure.

Although the existing building and the processing plant had to be retained, resulting in a very large working space, these expressive forms successfully combine to create a coherent and self-contained composition within it.

03 ▷ Clad in profiled pale green sheeting characteristic of the 1970s, the sheds appeared massive on the skyline before work started. Huge pieces of plant and ductwork emerged from and re-entered the walls of the structure in places, and occasionally wrapped over the roof.

04 ◁ However there was nothing on the outside to suggest the dramatically huge impression presented by the interior space. Photographs taken on site with work in progress show how the Wilkinson Eyre scheme uses the interior in such a way that this awe-inspiring sense of scale will be retained.

05 ▷ Dramatically dark and mysterious, the space is of a monumental scale which exceeds that of even the great Gothic cathedrals. The acoustics are similar, with only gentle, echoing sounds breaking the quiet. The silence here is uneasy, however, accentuated by an awareness of the noise that once must have been generated by the machinery and the huge plant; there is a disquieting tension emanating from its redundancy.

06 ▷ Huge shapes emerge from the gloom while, framed by the massive steel structure, the great halls are punctuated by piercing shafts of light – from pinholes in the roof. Gigantic hooks hang on massive chains from overhead cranes that lie still in their tracks, and the sculptural forms of process plant interlink with service gantries still laden with pipes and cables. Everything appears to be the same colour: the tone of steelwork covered with a patina of rust and scorched by excessive heat.

07 ◁ The Magna experience starts at the gates: the route leading to the entrance is landscaped. Parking is located alongside the building and within the retained skeleton structure of what had been the third aisle of the building before it was removed. Elements of discarded processing plant stand like sculptures, triggering memories of the time when the industrial process was active, and giving hints of the experiences to be gained inside the building.

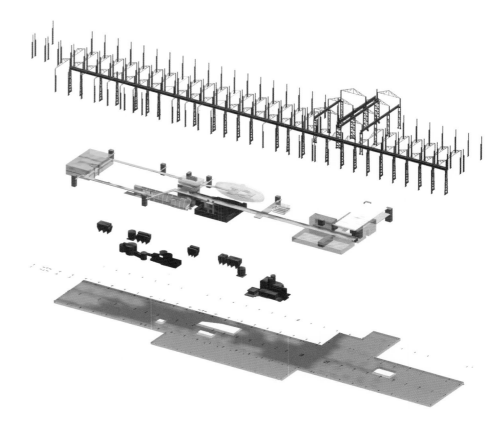

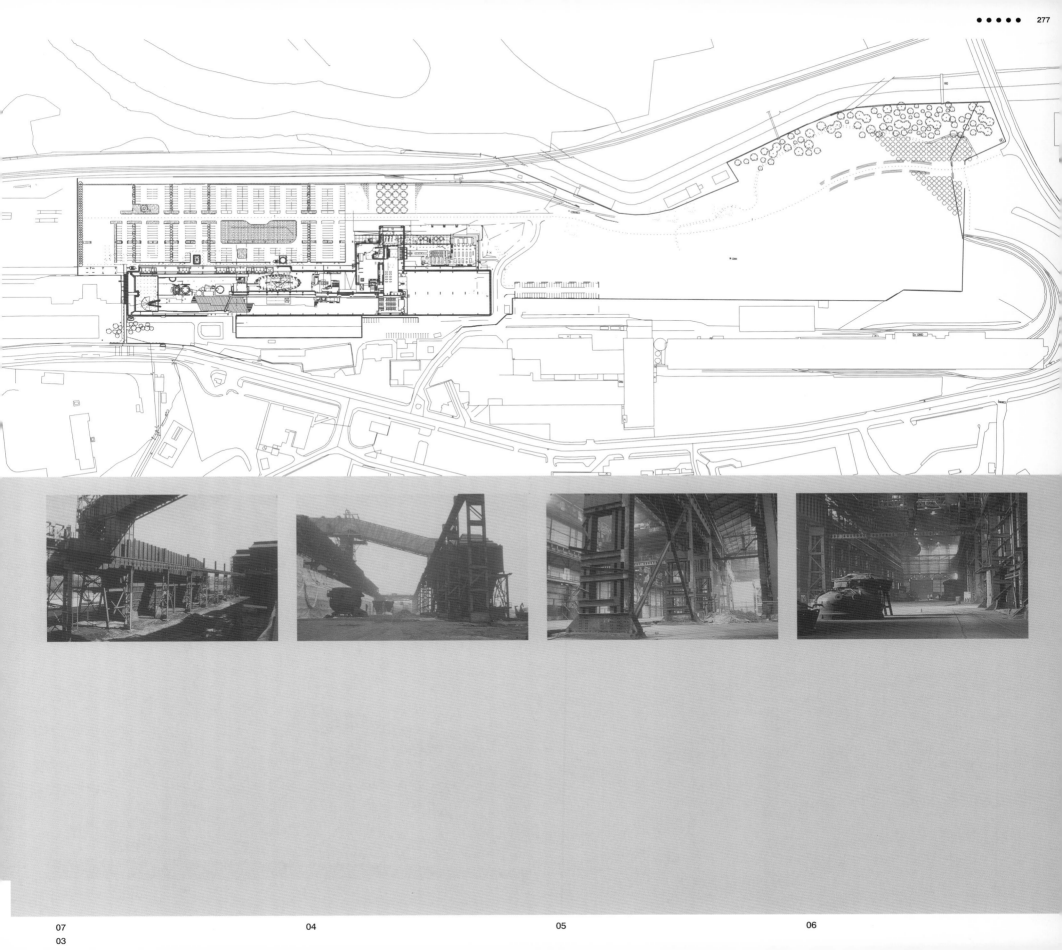

04

05

06

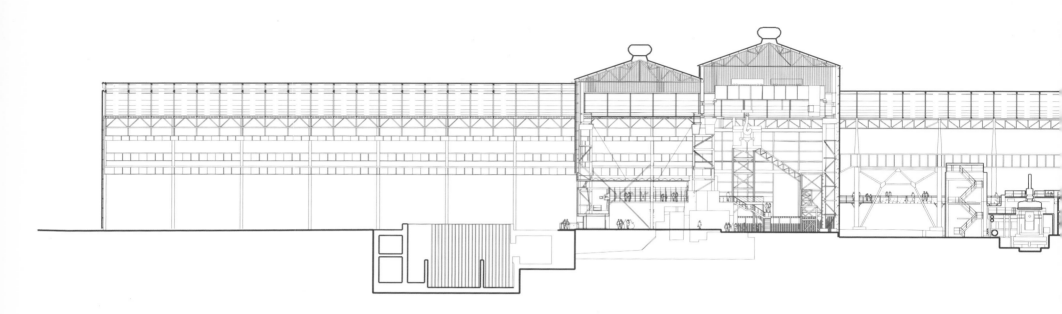

08△ The building has been repainted; it is now black, as it would have been when it was first built. The lighting is red and there is a band of new red translucent cladding on the north elevation.

With black-painted cladding, the entrance is housed in a gigantic transverse aisle. The lower levels are cut back to create an enormous porte-cochére. As the visitor approaches a crimson soffit is revealed, together with an entrance experience which includes fire and water – with a layer of mist to add mystery.

09△ The reception area inside, with daylight and modern finishes, acts as a transition zone. The story really begins when the visitor goes through a massive concrete chamber (originally part of the concasting process) and enters the Great Hall.

The Great Hall is a dark empty space over seven storeys high; it is animated only by the first exhibition display – at one end. This comprises an audio-visual homage to those who lived and worked at the Templeborough Steelworks: 'the human experience'. Once within the exhibition zone, visitors ascend to an upper-level mezzanine by either lift or stair.

Visitors arrive from 'the human experience' on the high-level walkway, which leads them into the main body of the building. It is only at this stage that the scale of the space becomes apparent. At approximately 8m above the level of the ground slab, the crisply detailed steel walkways run from one original steel stanchion to the next, offering security, protection and clear overhead views of the entire processing plant. In conjunction with the audio-visual displays, this original plant helps to tell the story of steel.

10▷ While all the four main pavilions are visible, the visitor has to proceed to the old transformer house, in the centre of the space, which has been converted into the main vertical circulation core. New stairs and lifts here provide access to the Air Pavilion in the roof zone, to the Fire Pavilion at main walkway level, to the Water Pavilion at ground level, and to the Earth Pavilion still further down in the basement.

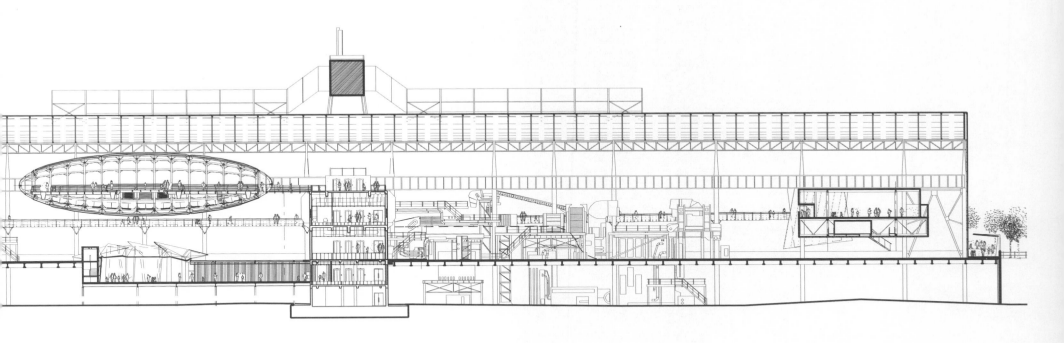

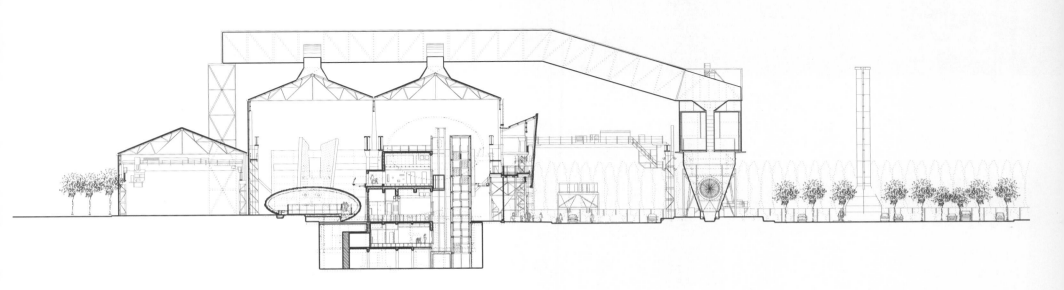

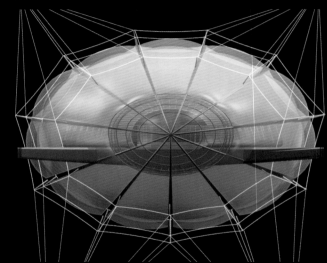

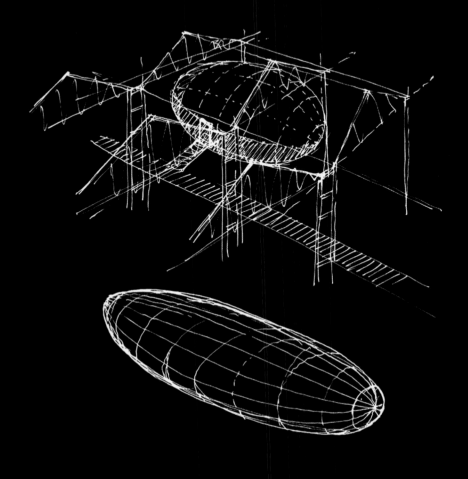

AIR

EGG in fabric like a Dirigible

11◁ The Air Pavilion is a lightweight structure, shaped like an airship and clad in translucent cushion fabric. Although it appears to hang in the roof space, the interior deck structure is, in fact, supported on four cigar-shaped steel beams which are bolted to the main structure of the building.

12◁ A light steel bridge leads to what looks like the circular opening of a jet engine lined with a transparent strip curtain; having passed through the curtain, visitors arrive in the wonderfully light space of the 'airship'. Three layers of translucent ETFE fabric form the enclosure; they are fitted between horizontal aluminium extrusions that are supported by a net structure of external cables fixed to the main building.

This tension structure was chosen in preference to compression rings because of its lightness and economy.

As regards the story of steel, the Air Pavilion helps to express the potential lightness of steel. Because the steel deck only covers part of the area of the pavilion, it is possible to experience the whole space – its curved organic form extending above and below. Moreover, through the voids in the deck, the roof of the Earth Pavilion below is visible and the structure of the Magna building itself is evident through the translucent skin, reinforcing this notion of airiness.

The exhibition, designed by Event, has taken the theme of air and used this unique space to create an exciting visitor experience.

13▽ With a large propeller-type fan at one end, this pavilion – like the others – uses forced natural ventilation.

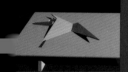   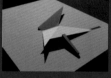 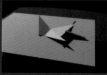 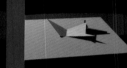

14 △ The Earth Pavilion is located below the Air Pavilion in the basement of the original building. Stairs and lifts in the transformer house provide access to this pavilion's arrival zone, where the walls are made of slag from the steel-making process. This leads into the large rectangular pavilion. Freestanding irregular walls of steel, shaped like 'tectonic plates', form the structure here, supporting a steel roof composed of similar forms.

15 △ The steel plates of the roof are raised above the slab level of the main building and are expressed as a raised platform sitting on a strip of clerestory glazing. The roof appears to buckle up into angular forms in the central zone, suggesting fractal plates disturbed by seismic activity.

The design of the exhibition inside the pavilion also takes the earth and its minerals as its theme – with interactive, graphic and audio-visual displays, and working equipment.

16 ▷ Returning to the transformer house, the high-level walkway proceeds right to the far end of the building, over the main steel reprocessor, before arriving at the Fire Pavilion, which is supported above the ground slab of the main building structure.

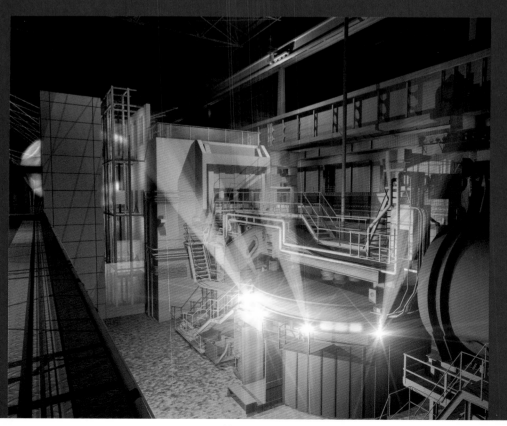

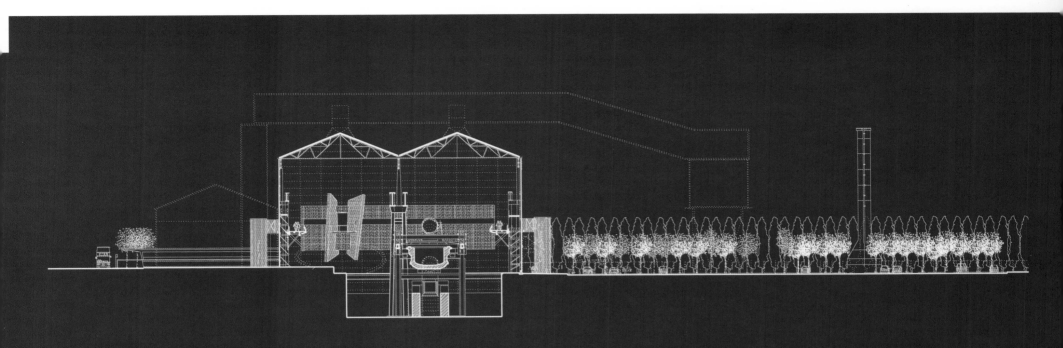

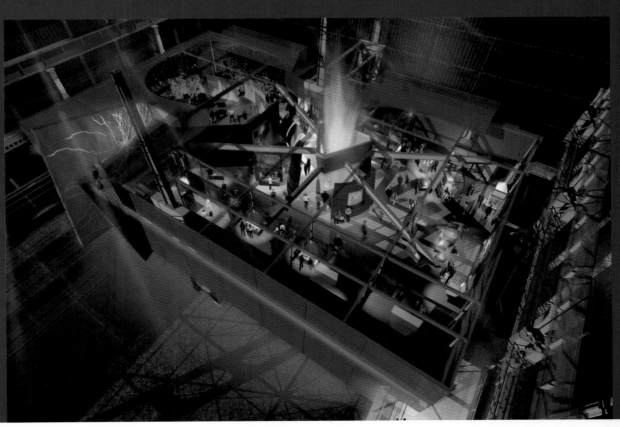

17△ This matt black rectangular structure appears mysterious and a little sinister, but its dark enclosure is suddenly highlighted by flashes of fire emanating from within.
A protected walkway in front of the pavilion leads to the entrance, which is marked by two huge angular plates of steel.

18▷ The interior of the structure is a dark space – lit by real fire. The exhibition tells the visitor about Fire and its effect on everyday life.

17

18

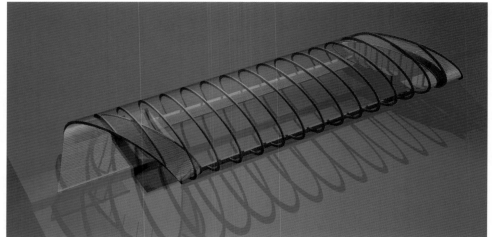

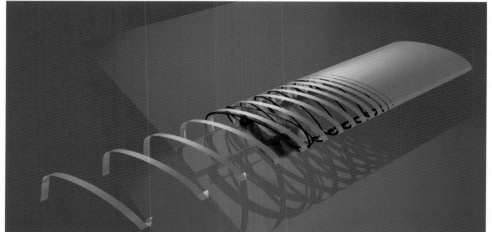

19 △ The Water Pavilion, its extruded curved form inspired by the kind of stainless-steel vessels used in the dairy and brewing industries, sits on the floor slab in the main space, with access from the transformer house feeding into one end.

20 ◁ Its unique form was developed through models, using wire mesh rolled into a tube and pulled at the ends to create an extruded spiral ellipse.

21 ◁ Computer models illustrate the geometry of the form which is composed of two ellipses extruding into a spiral. The difference in the ellipses takes account of the 1.5m step in the existing ground slab.

22 ▷ The main structural ribs are set out on an orthogonal grid for economic reasons, but the stainless-steel cladding follows the spiral form – as shown in the computer rendering. This power geometry creates its own dynamism, which is emphasized by the spiral's overhanging ends.

23 ◁ Inside the pavilion, which has water as its theme, the lighting is a cool blue. And there is an abundance of water: it runs under and over the visitors; forms part of every exhibit in the display; and provides fun for the children too.

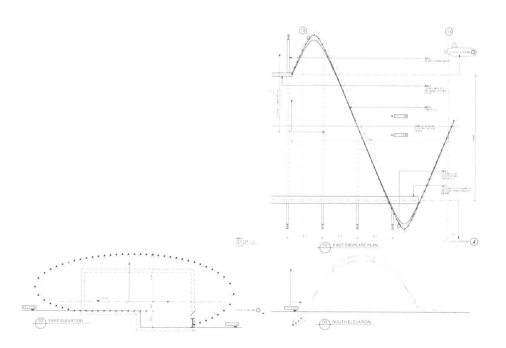

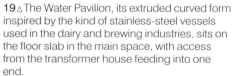

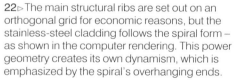

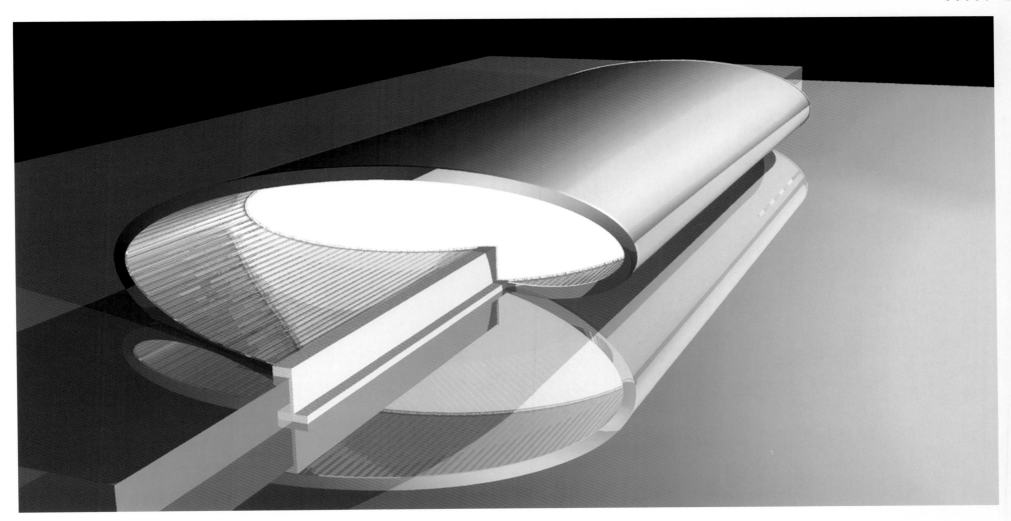

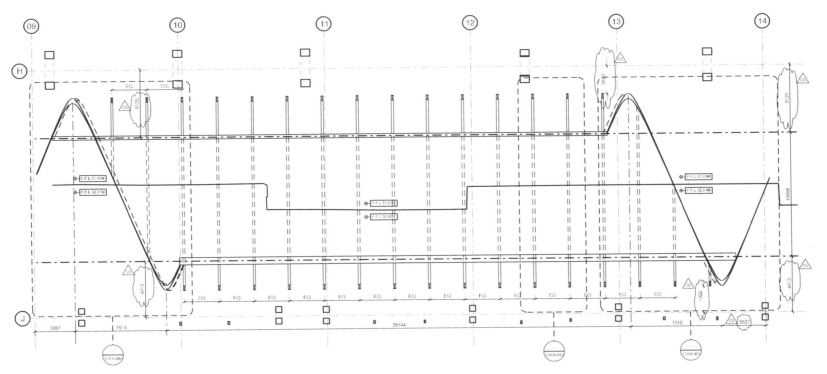

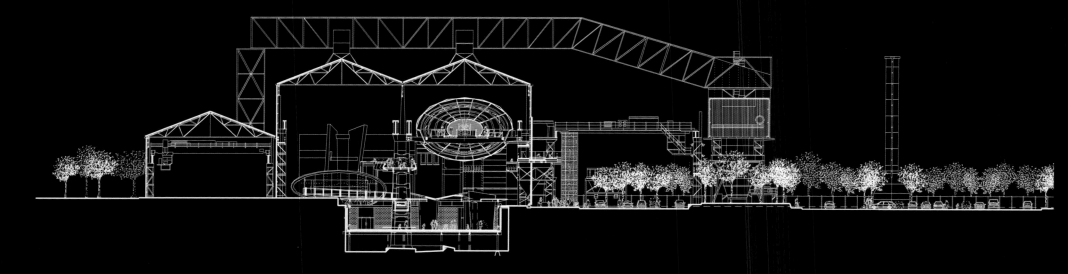

24△ The Magna experience caters for all ages and types of people: exploring this huge piece of industrial archaeology is an enjoyable and educational experience. The artworks, audio-visual and interactive displays are great fun and packed with information about the manufacture of steel and the influence steel has had – and continues to have – on everyday life. Passing along the high-level walkways and visiting the pavilions, it is impossible not to accrue knowledge of the steel-making process, developing an insight into the lives of the steelworkers who made Rotherham and Sheffield into the steel-making centre of the world.

25▷ Magna marks a new architectural approach for Wilkinson Eyre, in which the themed pavilions take on a poetic expression. However, they still bear recognizable Wilkinson Eyre characteristics: they are rigorously functional, crisply detailed and employ state-of-the-art technology. The relationship between the old and the new has also been sympathetically handled: both aspects are clearly legible in the reborn building, while the character of the original structure has been sensitively retained.

Location:	Rotherham, South Yorkshire UK
Commission date:	1998
Completion date:	April 2001
Site area:	31,500m²
Client:	The MAGNA Trust
Structural engineer:	Bingham Cotterell Mott MacDonald
M&E engineer:	Buro Happold Limited
Fire engineering:	Buro Happold FEDRA
Quantity surveyor:	Deacon & Jones
Landscape architects:	Hyland Edgar Driver
Exhibition design:	Event Communications

Chronology

IBM Travelling Technology Exhibition

Location:	London and York, UK
Commission date:	1984
Design Team:	Chris Perry, Matthew Priestman, Chris Wilkinson
Client:	IBM UK Limited
Structural Engineer:	Ove Arup & Partners
Building Architect:	Renzo Piano Building Workshop

Project managers, landscaping and design coordinators for this travelling exhibition. Design includes ramps and stairways and other add-on elements which are in keeping with the design of the exhibition building.

Body Conditioning Studio

Location:	Notting Hill, London UK
Commission date:	1984
Completion date:	1985
Design Team:	Chris Perry, Matthew Priestman, Chris Wilkinson
Client:	Dreas Reynake

Conversion of upper floor of a shop premises to provide a well-lit, spacious studio. A large glazed pyramid rooflight, fabricated out of Iroko hardwood with polished Georgian wired glass, creates a light and tranquil space.

Royal Docks Master Plan

Location:	Docklands, London UK
Design Proposal:	1984
Design Team:	Jim Eyre, Matthew Priestman, Chris Wilkinson
Client:	Rosehaugh Stanhope Developments Plc

Preparation of initial master-plan proposals and outline town planning application for regional shopping centre, commercial park, marine centre and housing on 260 acres of docklands.

Menil Foundation Special Project

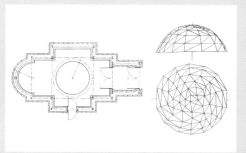

Location:	Houston Texas, USA
Design Proposal:	1985
Design Team:	Jim Eyre, Matthew Priestman, Oliver Stirling, Chris Wilkinson
Client:	Menil Foundation

Design proposal for new exhibition space to house some Byzantine frescos in a conserved chapel.

Ten Trinity Square Courtyard Enclosure

Location:	City of London UK
Design Proposal:	1986
Design Team:	Jim Eyre, Clinton Terry, Chris Wilkinson
Client:	Willis Faber
Structural Engineer:	Anthony Hunt Associates

A glazed roof supported on steel 'trees' over an open courtyard. The roof rises up at an even gradient to the centre producing a high pyramidal roof over each of the central triangular spaces. This was possibly the first proposed use of 'tree structures' and featured on the cover of the *Architectural Review*, May 1989.

Yves St Laurent Shop

Location:	Sloane Street, London UK
Commission date:	1986
Completion date:	May 1987
Design Team:	Jim Eyre, Oliver Stirling, Chris Wilkinson
Client:	Hecuba Limited

New high-fashion boutique for men and women in converted car showroom. Design developed with St Laurent's design coordinators in Paris.

Thomas Miller, International House

Location:	London UK
Commission date:	1986
Completion date:	November 1987
Design Team:	Jim Eyre, Oliver Stirling, Chris Wilkinson
Client:	Thomas Miller & Co.
Services Engineer:	JE Greatorex & Partners
Main Contractor:	John Nugent Construction Plc

Master plan and implementation of refurbishment projects for a City insurance company.

Alfie's Antique Market

Location:	London UK
Design proposal:	1987
Design Team:	Paul Baker, Marc Barron, Guy Comely, Jim Eyre, Chris Wilkinson
Client:	Alfie's Antique Market

Design proposal for refurbishment of existing antique market and additional floor of office accommodation.

Goldschmied House

Location: Putney, London UK
Commission date: 1987
Completion date: 1989
Design Team: Mark Armstrong, Guy Comely,
Matthew Priestman, Mike Stacey,
Chris Wilkinson
Client: Elinor Goldschmied
Structural Engineer: Ove Arup & Partners
Main Contractor: CJ Halvorsen

Awards: Eric Lyons Housing Award 1995

Courtyard house which provides the maximum space and
light on the restricted walled garden site.

Uplighter Design

Design date: 1987
Design Team: Jim Eyre, Chris Wilkinson
Client: Chris Wilkinson Architects

Prototype design for a 2.4-high uplighter with a stainless-steel
skeletal tension structure.

70/77 Cowcross Street

Location: Clerkenwell, London UK
Commission date: 1987
Completion date: 1989
Design Team: Jörg Burchard, Jim Eyre,
Oliver Stirling, Chris Wilkinson
Client: St George Securities
Structural Engineer: Alan Baxter Associates

Refurbishment of warehouse building to office use.

Artist's Studio

Location: Kennington, London UK
Commission date: 1988
Completion date: 1988
Design Team: Jim Eyre, Oliver Stirling,
Chris Wilkinson

Conversion of top-floor studio in Georgian terraced house.
The interior is opened up with two continuous rows of rooflights
and the ceiling raised to maximize the space. A shower room
features purpose-designed stainless-steel fittings.

La Casa piu Bella del Mondo

Location: Po Valley, Italy
Design Proposal: 1989
Design Team: Guy Comely, Jim Eyre, Chris Wilkinson

Competition design for a private house oriented to take advantage
of both the sun and the fine views across the valley. A high ashlar
wall separates the quiet living spaces, from the more public
activities such as the home office, creating a long shadow which
moves round with the sun during the day.

Four Seasons House at Liston Hall

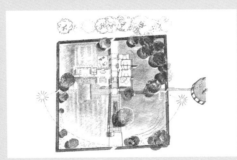

Location: Suffolk UK
Design Proposal: 1989
Design Team: Guy Comely, Jim Eyre, Oliver Stirling,
Chris Wilkinson

Exhibited at the Royal Academy Summer Exhibition 1989, design
for a special house within a listed walled garden which relates the
living accommodation to the structured garden landscape –
planned in four sections themed to the seasons.

Supersheds

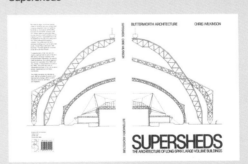

Publication date: 1991
Second edition: 1996
ISBN: 0-7506-2490-6
Japanese edition: 1995
Author: Chris Wilkinson
Publisher: Butterworth Architecture

Supersheds – The Architecture of Long-Span, Large-Volume
Buildings is the definitive text on the history of long span, large
volume buildings.

Winsor Park Housing

Location: East Beckton, London
Commission date: 1991
Completion date: 1996
Design Team: Zoë Barber, Marc Barron,
Dominic Bettison, Keith Brownlie,
Stafford Critchlow, Jim Eyre,
Stewart McGill, Chris Wilkinson
Client: Consortium of eight housing
associations
Main Contractor: Alfred McAlpine

Master plan and urban design for an estate of 550 mixed
social housing units for a consortium of eight housing
associations, carried out by Alfred McAlpine under a Design and
Build Contract.

Ten Trinity Square

Location: City of London, UK
Commission date: 1991
Completion date: April 1994
Building Area: 11,150m²
Design Team: Paul Baker, Zoë Barber, Keith Brownlie, Stafford Critchlow, Simon Dodd, James Edwards, Jim Eyre, Chris Grech, Oliver Tyler, Chris Wilkinson
Client: Willis Corroon Group
Structural Engineer: YRM Anthony Hunt Associates
Main Contractor: Trafalgar House Construction Management Limited
Services Engineer: JE Greatorex & Partners

Refurbishment and fit-out of existing offices in well-known landmark building (Grade II*-listed HQ for the Port of London Authority, designed by Sir Edwin Cooper in 1922).

Stratford Market Depot

Location: London UK
Commission date: 1991
Completion date: April 1996
Main Building Area: 19,000m²
Design Team: Paul Baker, Zoë Barber, Dominic Bettison, Keith Brownlie, Stafford Critchlow, Simon Dodd, James Edwards, Jim Eyre, Stewart McGill, Nicola Smerin, Oliver Tyler, Chris Wilkinson, Jonathan Woodroffe
Client: London Underground Limited
Structural Engineer: Hyder Consulting Limited
Services Engineer: Hurley Palmer Partnership
Environmental Concept: Loren Butt
Quantity Surveyor: Hyder Consulting Limited
Main Contractor: John Laing Limited

Competition-winning design for Jubilee Line Extension comprising 15,000m² train maintenance and repair depot with extensive additional office, amenities and ancillary buildings on a 22 acre site.

WC Pod

Location: London UK
Commission date: 1991
Completion date: April 1996
Design Team: Dominic Bettison, Simon Dodd, Jim Eyre
Client: London Underground Limited
Structural Engineer: Hyder Consulting Limited
Manufactured by: AME-EURO

An innovative, transportable toilet cubicle with an ergonomic shape – easy to use and economical in use of space.

CrossRail Liverpool Street

Location: London UK
Commission date: 1992
Building Area: 13,000m²
Design Team: Paul Baker, Zoë Barber, Marc Barron, Rowena Bates, Keith Brownlie, Stafford Critchlow, Simon Dodd, Jim Eyre, Chris Grech, Jason McColl, Stewart McGill, Chris Poulton, Robert Troup, Chris Wilkinson, Sarah Yabsley
Client: London Underground Limited and London Transport Property
Structural Engineer: WA Fairhurst Partners
Services Engineer: MPBL and Mott McDonald
Quantity Surveyor: Currie and Brown

A comprehensive redevelopment of London Underground Liverpool Street Station is proposed as part of the CrossRail project, including a 10,000m² air-rights property development over.

Dyson Headquarters I

Location: Chippenham, UK
Commission date: 1994
Building Area: 7,500m²
Design Team: Paul Baker, Zoë Barber, Marc Barron, Jim Eyre, Maurice Friel, James Parkin, Nicola Smerin, Geoffrey Turner, Oliver Tyler, Chris Wilkinson
Client: Dyson Appliances Limited
Structural Engineer: YRM Anthony Hunt Associates
Services Engineer: Atelier Ten
Quantity Surveyor: John Ashley Associates

Initial design for an assembly building for the production of Dyson Cyclone vacuum cleaners. The building has a masted structure in stepped units with overlapping roofs for construction in phases. This development was aborted in favour of the site in Malmesbury.

Park Hall Road

Location: Dulwich, London UK
Commission date: 1994
Completion date: September 1996
Building Area: 16m²
Design Team: Oliver Tyler, Chris Wilkinson
Client: Diana Edmunds and Chris Wilkinson
Structural Engineer: Whitby Bird & Partners
Main Contractor: CJ Halvorsen

Design for a dining room: a pure and simple space that responds to the occupants and the elements outside. A central rooflight has chamfered sides which control the light, reduce the visual impact of the roof depth and provide an expansive view of the sky.

Stratford Regional Station

Location: London UK
Commission date: 1994
Completion date: May 1999
Building Area: 4,000m²
Design Team: Zoë Barber, Marc Barron, Stafford Critchlow, Jim Eyre, Maurice Friel, Matt Hale, James Parkin, Vinny Patel, Chris Poulton, Robert Troup, Geoffrey Turner, Oliver Tyler, Chris Wilkinson
Client: London Underground Limited, Stratford Development Partnership Limited, London Borough of Newham
Engineering, Traffic & Landscape Consultant: Hyder Consulting Limited
Environmental Concept: Loren Butt
Civil Engineer: Ove Arup & Partners
Quantity Surveyor: Franklin & Andrews

Competition-winning design for redevelopment of Stratford Regional Station comprising 4,000m² of new concourse and subways. The new station is the terminus of the Jubilee Line Extension and an interchange with four other lines. It forms a key part of the regeneration plans for the area.

South Quay Footbridge

Location: London UK
Commission date: 1994
Completion date: March 1997
Bridge Span: 180m
Design Team: Dominic Bettison, Keith Brownlie, Jim Eyre, Chris Wilkinson
Client: London Docklands Development Corporation
Structural Engineer: Jan Bobrowski & Partners
Main Contractor: Christiani & Nielsen
Steelwork Subcontractor: Kent Structural Marine

Landmark footbridge to span the dock between South Quay and Heron Quays. The competition-winning design is an opening cable-stayed bridge featuring two raking masts and a sinuous deck curved in both plan and elevation, creating an iconic 's'-shape.

Hulme Arch

Location:	Hulme, Manchester UK
Commission date:	1995
Completion date:	May 1997
Bridge Span:	60m
Design Team:	Paul Baker, Dominic Bettison, Keith Brownlie, Jim Eyre, Chris Wilkinson
Client:	Hulme Regeneration Corporation and Manchester City Council
Structural Engineer:	Ove Arup & Partners
Main Contractor:	Henry Boot Limited
Steelwork Subcontractor:	Watson Steel

Competition-winning design for landmark bridge marking the regeneration of Hulme, Manchester. A 25m-high parabolic arch spans diagonally over the deck and acts as a gateway to drivers passing both over and under the bridge.

Princes Club Ski-Tow Pavilion

Location:	Bedfont Lakes UK
Commission date:	1995
Completion date:	April 1996
Building Area:	192m²
Design Team:	Dominic Bettison, Keith Brownlie, Jim Eyre, Chris Wilkinson
Client:	The Princes Club
Structural Engineer:	Buro Happold
Main Contractor:	The Princes Club

A small pavilion (12 x 16m) comprising glass, steel and timber for a mechanical ski-tow facility.

Challenge of Materials Gallery

Location:	Science Museum, London UK
Commission date:	1995
Completion date:	May 1997
Design Team:	Paul Baker, Dominic Balmforth, Zoë Barber, Dominic Bettison, Jim Eyre, Stewart McGill, Matthew Springett, Gareth Stapleton, Chris Wilkinson
Client:	Science Museum, London
Exhibition Design & Lead Consultant:	Jasper Jacob Associates
Structural Engineer:	Whitby, Bird & Partners
Sound & Light Artist (bridge):	Ron Geesin
Services Engineer:	Atelier Ten

Competition-winning design – with Jasper Jacobs Associates – for gallery, which includes: an innovative steel- and -glass bridge across the existing atrium; substantial building refurbishment; and new installations and exhibitions.

Explore at-Bristol

Location:	Bristol UK
Commission date:	1995
Completion date:	August 1999
Fit-out completion date:	April 2000
Building Area:	8,200m²
Design Team:	Paul Baker, Marc Barron, Chris Brown, Stafford Critchlow, Simon Davis, Jim Eyre, Bosco Lam, Natasha Le Comber, Stewart McGill, Daniel Parker, Geoff Turner, Lindsay Urquhart, Chris Wilkinson
Client:	at-Bristol
Structural Engineer:	Ove Arup & Partners
Quantity Surveyor:	Davis Langdon & Everest
Construction Manager:	Woolf Limited

Conversion and additions to a listed 1903 Hennibique concrete GWR goods shed. The competition-winning design includes a eutectic thermal storage system, and an 'active wall' – which are themselves central exhibits of the science centre.

Teesside Millennium Building

Location:	Teesside UK
Design Proposal:	1995
Site Area:	50 acres
Design Team:	Jim Eyre, Stewart McGill, Oliver Tyler, Chris Wilkinson
Client:	Teesside Development Group
Structural & Services Engineer:	Ove Arup & Partners

Design proposal and Millennium bid for one of Europe's largest enclosed buildings, set along the north bank of the River Tees to house a mixture of sports, leisure and educational uses.

Butterfly Bridge

Location:	Bedford UK
Commission date:	1995
Completion date:	May 1997
Bridge Span:	32m
Design Team:	Keith Brownlie, Jim Eyre, James Parkin, Geoffrey Turner, Chris Wilkinson
Client:	Bedford Borough Council
Structural Engineer:	Jan Bobrowski & Partners
Main Contractor:	Littlehampton Welding Limited

competition-winning-design for a double-arched cable-stayed footbridge spanning the River Great Ouse in Bedford. The bridge is related in form to the nearby 1888 bridge which it acknowledges and updates.

Age of Transfer Project

Location:	Holmer Green School, Buckinghamshire UK
Commission date:	1996
Completion date:	October 1998
Building Area:	500m²
Design Team:	Dominic Balmforth, Dominic Bettison, Simon Dodd, Jim Eyre, Natasha LeComber, Chris McKenzie, Oliver Tyler, Chris Wilkinson
Client:	Buckinghamshire County Council
Structural Engineer:	Sheperd Gilmour
Main Contractor:	Costain

The project provides additional accommodation on a restricted site, which ties together three existing teaching buildings.

Camera Support

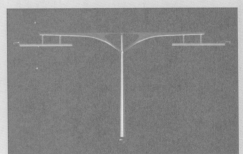

Location:	London Underground's Piccadilly Line Heritage Stations, UK
Commission date:	1996
Completion date:	December 1996
Design Team:	Dominic Bettison, Jim Eyre, Natasha Le Comber, Chris Wilkinson
Client:	London Underground Limited
Structural Engineer:	Whitby Bird & Partners
Main Contractor:	Crane & Rowbury Architectural Metalworkers

New support system for safety video cameras on London Underground's Piccadilly Line Heritage Stations. Constructed from shot-peened and brushed stainless steel for tough, durable, low-maintenance finish.

Channel Tunnel Rail Link

Location:	London/Kent UK
Commission date:	1996
Completion date:	2003
Bridge Span:	152.4m
Design Team:	Jim Eyre, Mimis Koumantanos, Clinton Terry, Chris Wilkinson
Client:	Rail Link Engineering Consortium
Engineer:	Rail Link Engineering
Main Contractor:	Miller

Design and aesthetic brief for all engineering structures on the Channel Tunnel Rail Link project, involving over 100 bridges and associated structures, including the Medway Crossing – the world's longest clear-span high-speed rail viaduct.

Dyson Headquarters

Location:	Malmesbury, Wiltshire UK
Commission date:	1996
Completion date:	August 1999
Site Area:	Refurbishment 10,000m²/ New Building 22,500m²
Design Team:	Dominic Bettison, Stafford Critchlow, Jim Eyre, Stewart McGill, James Parkin, Vinny Patel, Sebastien Ricard, Oliver Tyler, Chris Wilkinson, Sarah Williams
Client:	Dyson Appliances Limited
Structural Engineer:	Anthony Hunt Associates
Quantity Surveyor:	Leeson Associates
Main Contractor:	Kier Western
Commissioned Artist:	Diana Edmunds

Master plan and development of office, research and production facilities for the designers and manufacturers of the Dyson Cyclone vacuum cleaners. Construction in phases: 10,000m² refurbishment and extension of existing; 22,500m² new development.

Gateshead Millennium Bridge

Location:	Gateshead Quays, UK
Commission date:	1997
Completion date:	2001
Bridge Span:	105m
Design Team:	Dominic Bettison, Keith Brownlie, Jim Eyre, Martin Knight, Natasha Le Comber, Chris Wilkinson
Client:	Gateshead Metropolitan Borough Council
Structural Engineer:	Gifford & Partners
Main Contractor:	Harbour & General Works
Steelwork subcontractor:	Watson Steel

Competition-winning design for a dramatic opening foot and cycle bridge across the River Tyne, connecting Gateshead and Newcastle in sight of the river's series of historic crossings.

Lockmeadow Footbridge

Location:	Maidstone, Kent UK
Commission date:	1997
Completion date:	October 1999
Bridge Span:	80m
Design Team:	Keith Brownlie, Jim Eyre, Martin Knight, Chris Wilkinson
Client:	Maidstone Borough Council, Technical Services
Structural Engineer:	Flint & Neill Partnership
Main contractor:	Christiani & Nielsen Limited
Steelwork subcontractor:	D&B Darke Limited

Footbridge in highly sensitive site over the River Medway adjacent to collection of important ancient scheduled monuments and listed buildings. The competition-winning design is an innovative cable stayed bridge which spans the river and floodplain.

Thames Gateway Bridge

Location:	Galleons Reach, London UK
Feasibility study:	1997
Bridge Span:	240m
Design Team:	Brian Duffy, Jim Eyre, Clinton Terry, Chris Wilkinson
Client:	London Docklands Development Corporation
Structural Engineer:	Ove Arup & Partners

Feasibility design for major new road and dedicated public transportation crossing of the Thames at Galleons Reach. The design comprises an innovative multiple-span cable-stayed suspension structure.

Making the Modern World Gallery

Location:	Science Museum, London UK
Commission date:	1997
Completion date:	June 2000
Building Area:	2,000m²
Design Team:	Paul Baker, Peter Dixon, Jim Eyre, Bosco Lam, Stewart McGill, Paul Thompson, Chris Wilkinson
Client:	Science Museum, London
Structural Engineer:	b-Consultants
Services Engineer:	SVM
Lighting Consultant:	Richard Aldridge
Graphic Designer:	Farrow Design
Main Contractor:	Mansell

The competition-winning design adapts an existing large gallery space comprising a powerful display of the Science Museum's seminal objects.

Wellcome Wing Galleries

Location:	Science Museum, London UK
Commission date:	1997
Completion date:	June 2000
Floor Area:	2000m²
Design Team:	Paul Baker, Richard Cheesman, Charles Dymond, Peter Dixon, Brian Duffy, Jim Eyre, Tim McDowell, Vinny Patel, Chris Wilkinson
Building Design:	MacCormac Jamieson Prichard
Client:	Science Museum, London
Structural Engineer:	b-Consultants
Services Engineer:	SVM
Lighting Consultant:	DHA Design Services
Graphic Designer:	Johnson Banks
Main Contractor:	Mansell

Master plan and fit-out of ground-floor exhibition which explores themes in contemporary science and technology. The competition-winning design incorporates interactive exhibits, signage and lighting systems, together with a 200-seat restaurant.

Imperial War Museum North

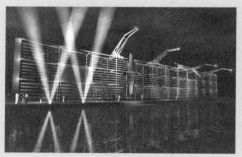

Location:	Manchester UK
Design Proposal:	1997
Design Team:	Paul Baker, Keith Brownlie, Jim Eyre, Chris Wilkinson
Client:	Imperial War Museum

Competition design for new museum on Salford Quays, which features an interactive, adaptable waterfront façade.

Bay Bridge East Span

Location:	San Francisco Bay, USA
Design Proposal:	1997
Main Span:	520m
Design Team:	Keith Brownlie, Jim Eyre, Charles Gagnon, Chris Wilkinson
Client:	Caltrans
Structural Engineer:	Mott MacDonald/Parsons Brinkerhoff/HNTB

Suspension bridge designs for replacement of the existing seismically unstable structure.

Retail Warehouse

Location:	Merry Hill UK
Design Proposal:	1997
Design Team:	Jim Eyre, Charles Gagnon, Clinton Terry, Chris Wilkinson
Client:	Chelsfield Plc
Structural Engineer:	Ove Arup & Partners

A design for a small landmark building at the entrance of a large shopping centre. The design is derived from an ellipse in section and is circular in plan.

Heritage Monolith

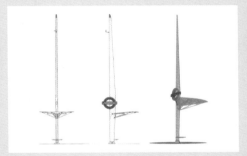

Location:	London Transport Heritage Stations UK
Commission date:	1997
Design Team:	Brian Duffy, Jim Eyre, Chris Wilkinson
Client:	London Underground Limited

Purpose-designed feature roundel support designed for the London Transport Heritage Stations incorporating seating, lighting, canopy and CCTV support.

Lyckoben Bridge

Location:	Stockholm, Sweden
Design proposal:	1997
Bridge Span:	80m
Design Team:	Keith Brownlie, Jim Eyre, Charles Gagnon, Martin Knight, Chris Wilkinson
Client:	Stockholm Stad Gatu-och fastighetskontoret
Structural Engineer:	Flint & Neill Partnership

Opening pedestrian and cycle bridge spanning high above the Hammarby Leden shipping channel and linking islands on Stockholm's inner archipelago. The competition-winning design is for an 80m-span twin-deck assisted cantilever bridge.

Westrail, Yuen Long Section

Location:	Hong Kong
Commission date:	1998
Completion date:	2002/3
Span:	8km
Design Team:	Jim Eyre, Clinton Terry, Chris Wilkinson
Client:	Kowloon Canton Railway Company
Structural Engineer:	Ove Arup & Partners

Architects to structural team responsible for 8km of elevated track, interfacing with stations; and providing a reference design for other sections at Yuen Long.

Merry Hill Multiplex Cinema

Location:	Merry Hill, UK
Commission date:	1998
Completion date:	September 2001
Site Area:	15,000m²
Design Team:	Rebecca Davies, Jim Eyre, Chris Hardie, Jonathan Head, Daniel Parker, Clinton Terry, Chris Wilkinson
Client:	Chelsfield Plc
Structural Engineer:	Allott and Lomax
Quantity Surveyor:	Davis Langdon & Everest
Services Engineer:	John Packer Associates
Fire Engineer:	Buro Happold FEDRA
Acoustic Engineer:	Cole Jarman Associates

Major leisure attraction incorporating a twenty-screen multiplex cinema, together with ancillary leisure facilities.

Magna

Location:	Rotherham, South Yorkshire UK
Commission date:	1998
Completion date:	April 2001
Site Area:	31,500m²
Design Team:	Matthew Appleton, Marc Barron, John Coop, Jim Eyre, Graham Gilmour, Bosco Lam, James Parkin, Chris Poulton, Sebastien Ricard, John Smart, Simon Tonks, Chris Wilkinson
Client:	The MAGNA Trust
Structural Engineer:	Bingham Cotterell Mott MacDonald
M&E Engineer:	Buro Happold Limited
Fire Engineering:	Buro Happold FEDRA
Quantity Surveyor:	Deacon & Jones
Landscape Architects:	Hyland Edgar Driver
Exhibition Design:	Event Communications

Major new visitor attraction exploring the theme of steel, inhabiting the vast Templeborough Steel Works. The competition-winning scheme is a Millennium-funded project.

Arachthos Viaduct

Location:	Arachthos Valley, Greece
Design Proposal:	June 1998
Bridge Span:	1,000m
Design Team:	Ben Addy, Keith Brownlie, Jim Eyre, Chris Wilkinson
Client:	Egnatia Odos AE
Structural Engineer:	Ove Arup & Partners

Design proposals for 1,000m crossing of Arachthos Valley on the Egnatia Odos project in northern Greece, featuring an undulating haunched profile derived from toroidal geometry.

Metsovitikos Bridge

Location:	Metsovo, Greece
Commission date:	1998
Completion date:	2003
Bridge Span:	560m
Design Team:	Ben Addy, Keith Brownlie, Jim Eyre, Chris Hardie, Chris Wilkinson
Client:	Egnatia Odos AE
Structural Engineer:	Ove Arup & Partners

Competition-winning design for 560m crossing of a deep mountain valley on the Egnatia Odos project in northern Greece. A rock-anchored suspension bridge solution provides a delicate landmark structure in a sensitive location.

Paragon Transport Interchange

Location:	City of Kingston-upon-Hull, UK
Commission date:	1998
Completion date:	2002
Site Area:	37,000m²
Design Team:	Ben Addy, Keith Brownlie, Simon Davis, Jim Eyre, Graham Gilmour, Martin Knight, Amin Taha, Chris Wilkinson
Client:	City of Kingston-upon-Hull / London & Amsterdam Developments

City Transport Interchange to coordinate rail and bus traffic. The project marks the fourth-generation development of the listed Paragon Station.

Bellmouth Passage Bridges

Location:	Canary Wharf, London UK
Commission date:	1998
Completion date:	2001
Design Team:	Ben Addy, Keith Brownlie, Richard Cheesman, Jim Eyre, Charles Gagnon, Martin Knight, Amin Taha, Chris Wilkinson
Client:	Canary Wharf Limited
Structural Engineer:	Jan Bobrowski & Partners
Main Contractor:	Cleveland Bridge

Competition-winning design for two new opening bridges commissioned to facilitate the second phase of urban development at Canary Wharf in London's Docklands.

Great Wharf Road Bridge

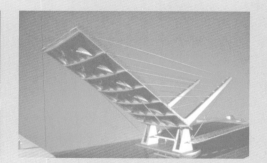

Location:	Canary Wharf, London UK
Commission date:	1998
Completion date:	2002
Design Team:	Keith Brownlie, Richard Cheesman, Jim Eyre, Charles Gagnon, Martin Knight, Vinny Patel, Amin Taha, Chris Wilkinson
Client:	Canary Wharf Limited
Structural Engineer:	Jan Bobrowski & Partners
Main Contractor:	Cleveland Bridge

Competition-winning design for a new opening landmark bridge commissioned to facilitate the second phase of urban development at Canary Wharf in London's Docklands.

Passerelle Bercy-Tolbiac

Location:	Paris, France
Design Proposal:	1999
Bridge Span:	250m
Design Team:	Keith Brownlie, Jim Eyre, Charles Gagnon, Sebastien Ricard, Chris Wilkinson
Client:	Ville de Paris
Structural Engineer:	Ove Arup & Partners with RFR

Competition design proposals commissioned for a high-profile crossing of the Seine connecting the Parc de Bercy with France's new National Library. A stressed ribbon bridge connecting at high level at each side supports a second suspended deck linking the quaysides.

Camden Town Station

Location:	Camden, London UK
Outline Scheme Design:	1999
Design Team:	Marc Barron, Charles Gagnon, Jim Eyre, Graham Gilmour, Chris Hardie, Duncan Macaulay, Robert Troup, Chris Wilkinson
Client:	London Underground Limited and London Transport Properties Civil
Structural Engineer:	Robert Benaim and Associates
Quantity Surveyor:	Franklin & Andrews
Services Engineer:	Mott Macdonald

Redevelopment of existing underground station together with above-ground development (separate contract) on site above.

Crown Place Offices

Location:	City of London UK
Design Proposal:	1999
Building Area:	35,000m²
Design Team:	Ben Addy, Paul Baker, Jim Eyre, Chris Hardie, Chris Wilkinson
Client:	Earl Estates Limited
Structural Engineer:	Buro Happold

A competition entry for a 35,000m² office development on the edge of the city.

Beadon Road Commercial Development

Location:	London UK
Commission date:	1999
Building/Site Area:	15,900m²
Design Team:	Richard Cheesman, Jim Eyre, Graham Gilmour, Chris Wilkinson
Client:	THI Plc
Architect:	Wilkinson Eyre Architects Limited with Chapman Taylor & Partners

A mixed development scheme which comprises 12,000m² offices, 2,600m² fitness club, six screen cinema and 1,300m² of associated retail accommodation.

The QMW IRC Biomaterials Network Building

Location:	London UK
Commission date:	1999
Status:	Scheme design complete; fundraising in progress
Design Team:	Stafford Critchlow, Charles Dymond, Jim Eyre, Romed Perfler, Chris Wilkinson
Client:	Queen Mary Westfield College, London University
Structural Engineer:	Allott & Lomax
Environmental Engineer:	Atelier Ten

Competition-winning design for an annexe, which provides accommodation on six floors for laboratories and research facilities. Glazed double-skin bioclimatic outer walls improve environmental sustainability for a highly serviced building.

Dyson Shop Paris

Location:	Paris, France
Commission date:	1999
Completion date:	August 2000
Building Area:	530m²
Design Team:	Dominic Bettison, Jim Eyre, Mimis Koumantanos, Richard Lee, Sebastien Ricard, Oliver Tyler, Chris Wilkinson
Client:	Dyson Appliances Limited
Structural Engineer:	Anthony Hunt Associates
Services Engineer:	Hoare Lea & Partners
Main Contractor:	Alpha International

Design for client's first major retail outlet and headquarters for operations in France. The scheme comprises 270m² of retail with an additional 260m² of administration and sales accommodation.

DERA Advanced Technology Bridge Project

Location:	Farnborough, Hampshire UK
Design Proposal:	1999
Design Team:	Ben Addy, Keith Brownlie, Jim Eyre, Martin Knight, Chris Wilkinson
Client:	Defence Evaluation Research Agency
Structural Engineer:	Flint & Neill Partnership

Competition-winning design formulated to test and showcase the use of commercial applicability of advanced manufacturing technologies in structural design.

Museum of London

Location:	London UK
Commission date:	1999
Status:	Scheme design complete; fundraising in progress
Building Area:	13,500m²
Design Team:	Paul Baker, Stafford Critchlow, Rebecca Davies, Charles Dymond, Jim Eyre, Mimis Koumantanos, Will McLardy, Chris Wilkinson
Client:	Board of Governors Museum of London
Structural & Services Engineer:	Buro Happold
Quantity Surveyor:	James Nisbet & Partners

Redevelopment of the existing Museum of London, originally built in 1976, to increase exhibition space, improve circulation and glaze in existing courtyard with a delicate catenary structure.

Peugeot Citroën Design Headquarters

Location:	Paris, France
Design Proposal:	1999
Design Team:	Simon Davis, Charles Dymond, Jim Eyre, Bosco Lam, Will McLardy, Sebastien Ricard, Simon Tonks, Oliver Tyler, Chris Wilkinson
Client:	Peugeot Citroën

Competition design proposals commissioned for a new research and development facilities for the car manufacturer at their existing car design centre site outside Paris.

Aardman Animations Headquarters

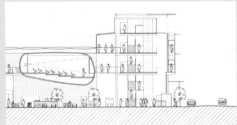

Location:	Bristol UK
Commission date:	2000
Completion date:	July 2003
Site Area:	16,000m²
Design Team:	Dominic Bettison, Jim Eyre, Richard Lee, Sebastian Ricard, Geoffrey Turner, Oliver Tyler, Chris Wilkinson
Client:	Aardman Animations
Structural Engineer:	Ove Arup & Partners
Service Engineer:	Ove Arup & Partners
Quantity Surveyor:	Gleeds

New headquarters and studio facilities for this world-renowned animations company. The competition-winning scheme brings together the client's different activities onto one site.

Wolfsburg Science Centre

Location:	Wolfsburg, Germany
Design Proposal:	2000
Design Team:	Rebecca Davies, Jim Eyre, Mimis Koumantanos, Will McLardy, Clinton Terry, Chris Wilkinson
Structural Engineer:	Buro Happold

Competition design proposal for a science centre.

Istanbul Science Centre

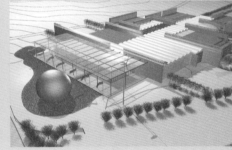

Location:	Istanbul, Turkey
Commission date:	2000
Building:	11,000m² (first phase)
Design Team:	Stafford Critchlow, Rebecca Davies, Jim Eyre, Will McLardy, Daniel Parker, Simon Tonks, Chris Wilkinson
Client:	Bilim Merkezi Bakfi (Turkish Science Foundation)
Structural/ Environmental Engineer:	Battle McCarthy
Turkish consultant:	Yapı Merkezi, Istanbul

Design for a science centre incorporating exhibition space, a 700-seat auditorium, a 300-seat restaurant, a 300-seat IMAX cinema, and a planetarium.

Anglia Polytechnic University

Location:	Chelmsford UK
Commission date:	2000
Completion date:	September 2002
Site Area:	4,500m²
Design Team:	Paul Baker, Dominic Bettison, Richard Cheesman, Jim Eyre, Richard Lee, Stewart McGill, Chris Wilkinson
Client:	Anglia Polytechnic University
Structural Engineer:	Buro Happold
Project Manager:	Mace
Services Engineer:	Atelier Ten
Quantity Surveyor:	Gardiner & Theobald

Competition-winning design for a new business and management centre for the university. The scheme comprises a rectilinear glazed building with a full-height glazed bio-climatic wall, a rooftop pavilion structure, and a titanium-clad auditorium.

Royal College of Art Extension and New Studios

Location:	London UK
Design Proposal:	2000
Design Team:	Ben Addy, Paul Baker, Stafford Critchlow, Rebecca Davies, Jim Eyre, Sebastien Ricard, Paul Thompson, Chris Wilkinson
Client:	Royal College of Art

Competition design proposal for new studios and administrative facilities on a highly sensitive site adjacent to the Albert Hall. The design incorporates an innovative glass façade.

London Bridge Station and Air-Rights

Location:	London Bridge, London UK
Commission date:	2000
Completion date:	2006
Design Team:	T P Bennett – Lead Architects with Jim Eyre, Stewart McGill, Chris Wilkinson
Client:	Railtrack Properties Limited
Structural Engineer:	Alan Baxter Associates

Design assistance to TP Bennett in redeveloping the station to provide a spectacular new pedestrian and retail concourse at street level between the existing brick viaducts and a major new air-rights office building above the platforms.

City and Islington College

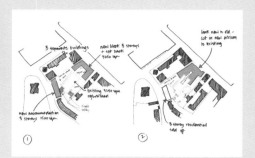

Location:	London UK
Commission Date:	2000
Completion Date:	September 2003
Design Team:	Stafford Critchlow, Jim Eyre, Tim McDowell, Chris Wilkinson
Client:	City and Islington College
Structural & Services Engineer:	Ove Arup & Partners
Quantity Surveyor:	Davis Langdon & Everest

Competition-winning design for a new sixth-form centre and public library which create a new campus for 16-19 year olds living in the London Borough of Islington.

City Tower

Location:	Fenchurch Street, City of London UK
Commission date:	2000
Building Area:	57,000m²
Design Team:	Simon Davis, Jim Eyre, Daniel Parker, Chris Wilkinson
Client:	Churchill Securities Limited
Structural & Services Engineer:	WSP Group
Environmental Engineer:	WSP Group

A thirty-storey City Tower submitted for full planning consent in July 2000. This is one of the few new tower opportunities in the City.

Audi Regional Headquarters

Location:	Glasgow, Scotland UK
Commission date:	2000
Building Area:	5,000m²
Design Team:	Dominic Bettison, Jim Eyre, Sebastien Ricard, Oliver Tyler, Chris Wilkinson
Client:	Audi International

Competition-winning design for new regional headquarters for the car manufacturer. The scheme provides: showroom facilities for both new and used cars; car maintenance workshops; an administration office; and a conference/training suite.

Halgavor Bridge

Location:	Bodmin, Cornwall UK
Commission date:	2000
Completion date:	2001
Bridge Span:	50m
Design Team:	Ben Addy, Keith Brownlie, Jim Eyre, Chris Wilkinson
Client:	The Highways Agency
Structural Engineer:	Flint & Neill Partnership
Main contractor:	Balfour Beatty

Competition-winning design for a suspension bridge with a glass reinforced polymer deck, which is strong enough to support pedestrians, cyclists and horses. The deck reduces long-term maintenance, and is cheaper than conventional materials.

Basin Developments

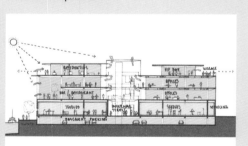

Location:	London UK
Commission date:	2000
Completion date:	2003
Building area:	10,000m²
Design Team:	Charles Dymond, Jim Eyre, Oliver Tyler, Chris Wilkinson
Client:	Basin

Purpose-built building servicing music, film, internet and new media businesses. The complex includes sound, recording and rehearsal studios, together with back-up administration and recreational facilities.

Wilkinson Eyre
Architects
London
Spring 2000

Directors
Paul Baker
Keith Brownlie
Jim Eyre
Oliver Tyler
Chris Wilkinson

Associates
Marc Barron
Stafford Critchlow

Ben Addy
Dominic Bettison
Richard Cheesman
John Coop
Isobel Cowen
Rebecca Davies
Simon Davis
Peter Dixon
Charles Dymond
Helen Eger
Charles Gagnon

Graham Gilmour
Jonathan Head
Martin Knight
Richard Lee
Bosco Lam
Ruth Lucchini
Tim McDowell
Stewart McGill
Will McLardy
Daniel Parker
James Parkin

Vinny Patel
Lucy Paterson Holt
Chris Poulton
Sebastien Ricard
John Smart
Helen Summers
Amin Taha
Paul Thompson
Simon Tonks
Adam Tucker
Geoff Turner

Other people who
have contributed over
the years include:

Mark Armstrong
Matt Appleton
Dominic Balmforth
Zoë Barber
Rowena Bate
Chris Brown
Jörg Burchard
Lauren Camberg
Becky Coffee
Guy Comely
Ben Cousins
Brian Ditchburn

Simon Dodd
Brian Duffy
James Edwards
Maurice Friel
Alexandra Gilmour
Marta Goodrich
Chris Grech
Matt Hale
Chris Hardie
Magnus Hierta
Mimis Koumantanos
Liz Lane

Natasha Le Comber
Chris Mackenzie
Stuart McColl
Rita Patel
Chris Perry
Romed Perfler
Matthew Priestman
Lucy Read
Jonathan Rose
Nicola Smerin
Matthew Springett
Mike Stacey

Gareth Stapleton
Oliver Stirling
Armelle Tardiveau
Clinton Terry
Robert Troup
Helen Tsoi
Lindsay Urquhart
Nicola Urquhart
Julia von Rohr
Sarah Williams
Jonathan Woodroffe
Sarah Yabsley

Front Cover Image:

Challenge of Materials Footbridge,
Science Museum London – James Morris

Images pages 02-14 (in order of appearance):

Stratford Market Depot – Dennis Gilbert / View
Lockmeadow Footbridge – Simon Warren
Stratford Regional Station – Morley von Sternberg
Butterfly Bridge – Jim Eyre
Lockmeadow Footbridge – Jim Eyre
Wellcome Wing Galleries – James Morris
Stratford Market Depot – Dennis Gilbert / View
Stratford Regional Station – Dennis Gilbert / View
Stratford Market Depot – Dennis Gilbert / View
Stratford Regional Station – Dennis Gilbert / View
Dyson Headquarters – Diana Edmunds
Explore at-Bristol – Lauren Camberg
Stratford Market Depot – Acer
Dyson Headquarters – Richard Davies

Photographic credits:

Art Gallery of New South Wales, Sydney: 30 (02)
John Paul Bland: 179 (bottom-left)
Bryn Bird: 30 (01)
Jim Byrne, QA Photos: 111 (01) / 116 (10)
Lauren Camberg: 91 (06) / 144 / 152 (18/20) / 155 (27)
Chris Caulfield-Dollard: 137 (top-right)
John Coop: 277 / 280 (top-left)
Daidalos Magazine 57 (15.9.95): 076 (01) / 077 (08)
Richard Davies: 88 (03) / 90 (04) / 99 (04) / 100 /
150 (16) / 151 (right) / 152 (21) / 154 (26) /
155 (top-left) / 157
Simon Davis: 36 (01)
Richard Deacon: 26 (03)
Diana Edmunds: 148 (12)
H.G.Esch: 62 (02)
Amé-Euro: 224 (01) / 225 (02)
Ian Firth: 191 (top-right) / 192 (10)
The works of Naum Gabo © Nina Williams: 36 (04)
Dennis Gilbert / View: 40 (01) / 91 (06) / 92 (02) /
99 (06) / 103 / 108 / 117 / 118 / 120-125 / 129 / 132 (10);
133 / 134 (11-12) / 135 (13-14) / 136 (15) / 139 /
225 (03) / 263 / 266 (09; bottom-right) / 267 / 268 (10) /
269 (13) / 271
Guy Hearn / Gateshead Metropolitan Borough
Council: 213
Tim James: 141 (05) / 149 (14)
Guy Jordan: 142
Susan Kay: 42 (01) / 47 (04) / 91 (07) / 137 (bottom-
right) / 138 / 165 (07) / 167 (14) / 270 (16) / 273
Peter McKinvon: 211
James Morris: 26 (01) / 37 / 51 / 83 (06) / 246-247 /
249-257 / 258 (04) / 259-261
National Gallery: 56 (02) / 58 (20)
Ove Arup & Partners: 81 (02)
Steve Place / Creative Image: 284 (19)
Positive Image: 63 / 83 (05) / 173-174 / 177 /
178 (09) / 179
Andrew Putler: 43 / 82 (03) / 114 (04) / 128 (06) /
141 (06) / 145 / 197 / 199 / 264 (03)
Julian Nieman / Country Life Picture Library: 220 (03)
Bernard O'Sullivan ABIPP /
Inside Out Photography: 172
Paul Rapson: 152 (19)
RIBA Library: 59 (03) / 77 (03/05) / 78 (01) / 82 (01)
Inga Sedgeley: 258 (03)
Timothy Soar: 143 / 153 (22b/24) / 155 (28) / 156
Morley von Sternberg: 41 / 99 (05/07) / 114 (05-06) /
115 (07-09) / 119 / 130 (07) / 134 (bottom-left) /
135 (bottom-left) / 149 (top-left) / 150 (17) / 160 / 166 /
P167 (11/13/15) / 169-171 / 218 (01) / 219 (04) / 221
Matthew Swift: 92 (01)
Oliver Tyler: 24 (02/04) / 34 (02) / 48 (01)
Simon Warren: 186 / 189 / 192 (right) / 193
Alan Williams: 38 (03) / 81 (03) / 161 / 181 /
183 (top-left; centre) / 184 (05)

Computer Visualisations:

Hayes Davidson: 47 (03) / 80 (01) / 109 /
115 (top-right) / 137 (17) / 140 / 141 (bottom-centre) /
165 (06) / 236 / 264 (01) / 266 (08)
Hayes Davidson / Nick Wood: 238-242
Melon: 83 (04) / 187 / 190 (04) / 202 (01/02) /
203 (04) / 204 / 222 (01) / 223 (05) / 231 / 235 / 275 /
281 / 282 (16) / 283 (18) / 287
Francis Vaughan: 128 (top-left)

Sketches pages 305-320 (in order of appearance):

South Quay Footbridge – Jim Eyre/305
Dyson Headquarters – Sebastien Ricard/306
Magna – Chris Wilkinson/307
Stratford Regional Station – Jim Eyre/311
Butterfly Bridge – Jim Eyre/313
Metsovitikos Bridge – Keith Brownlie/315
Dyson Headquarters – Chris Wilkinson/317
City Tower – Simon Davis/319

First published in 2001 by
Booth-Clibborn Editions Limited
12 Percy Street London W1T 1DW
www.booth-clibborn.com

Text copyright: Wilkinson Eyre Architects 2001
Design copyright: Booth-Clibborn Editions 2001

Wilkinson Eyre Architects
Transworld House 100 City Road London EC1Y 2BP
www.wilkinsoneyre.com

Chris Wilkinson and Jim Eyre have asserted their
moral right under the Copyright, Designs and Patents
Act, 1988, to be identified as authors of this work.

Design: Big Corporate Disco
Project co-ordinator & researcher: Helen Eger,
Wilkinson Eyre Architects Limited

With thanks to Paul Baker, Keith Brownlie,
Isobel Cowen, Carolyn Larkin, Richard Lee,
Ruth Lucchini, Rita Patel, Chris Poulton,
Simon Tonks, Kate Trant and Oliver Tyler.

A Cataloguing-in-Publication record for this book
is available from the Publisher.

ISBN 1 86154 153 8
Printed and bound in Hong Kong.